D1559321

MUIRHEAD LIBRARY OF PHILOSOPHY

An admirable statement of the aims of the Library of Philosophy was provided by the first editor, the late Professor J. H. Muirhead, in his description of the original programme printed in Erdmann's *History of Philosophy* under the date 1890. This was slightly modified in subsequent volumes to take the form of the following statement:

'The Muirhead Library of Philosophy was designed as a contribution to the History of Modern Philosophy under the heads: first of Different Schools of Thought—Sensationalist, Realist, Idealist, Intuitivist; secondly of different Subjects—Pyschology, Ethics, Aesthetics, Political Philosophy, Theology. While much had been done in England in tracing the course of evolution in nature, history, economics, morals and religion, little had been done in tracing the development of thought on these subjects. Yet the "evolution of opinion is part of the whole evolution".

'By the cooperation of different writers in carrying out this plan it was hoped that a thoroughness and completeness of treatment, otherwise unattainable, might be secured. It was believed also that from writers mainly British and American fuller consideration of English Philosophy than it had hitherto received might be looked for. In the earlier series of books containing, among others, Bosanquet's *History of Aesthetics*, Pfleiderer's *Rational Theology since Kant*, Albee's *History of English Utilitarianism*, Bonar's *Philosophy and Political Economy*, Brett's *History of Psychology*, Ritchie's *Natural Rights*, these objects were to a large extent effected.

'In the meantime original work of a high order was being produced both in England and America by such writers as Bradley, Stout, Bertrand Russell, Baldwin, Urban, Montague, and others, and a new interest in foreign works, German, French and Italian, which had either become classical or were attracting public attention, had developed. The scope of the Library thus became extended into something more international, and it is entering on the fifth decade of its existence in the hope that it may contribute to that mutual understanding between countries which is so pressing a need of the present time.'

The need which Professor Muirhead stressed is no less pressing today, and few will deny that philosophy has much to do with enabling us to meet it, although no one, least of all Muirhead himself, would regard that as the sole, or even the main, object of philosophy. As Professor Muirhead continues to lend the distinction of his name to the Library of Philosophy it seemed not inappropriate to allow him to recall us to these aims in his own words. The emphasis on the history of thought also seemed to me very timely: and the number of important works promised for the Library in the very near future augur well for the continued fulfilment, in this and other ways, of the expectations of the original editor.

H. D. LEWIS

MUIRHEAD LIBRARY OF PHILOSOPHY

General Editor: H. D. Lewis

Professor of History and Philosophy of Religion at the University of London

The Absolute and the Atonement by DOM ILLTYD TRETHOWAN
Absolute Value by DOM ILLTYD TRETHOWAN
The Analysis of Mind by BERTRAND RUSSELL
Ascent to the Absolute by J. N. FINDLAY
Belief by H. H. PRICE
Broad's Critical Essays in Moral Philosophy edited by DAVID
    CHENEY
Clarity is Not Enough by H. D. LEWIS
Coleridge as Philosopher by J. H. MUIRHEAD
The Commonplace Book of G. E. Moore edited by C. LEWY
The Concept of Meaning by THOMAS E. HILL
Contemporary American Philosophy edited by G. P. ADAMS and
    W. P. MONTAGUE
Contemporary British Philosophy first and second series edited by
    J. H. MUIRHEAD 2nd edition
Contemporary Indian Philosophy edited by RADHAKRISHNAN and
    J. H. MUIRHEAD 2nd edition
Contemporary Philosophy in Australia edited by ROBERT BROWN
    and C. D. ROLLINS
The Development of Bertrand Russell's Philosophy by RONALD
    JAGER
The Dilemma of Narcissus by LOUIS LAVELLE
The Discipline of the Cave by J. N. FINDLAY
Enigmas of Agency by IRVING THALBURG
Essays in Analysis by ALICE AMBROSE
Ethical Knowledge by J. J. KUPPERMAN
Ethics by NICOLAI HARTMANN translated by STANTON COIT 3 vols
Ethics and Christianity by KEITH WARD
Experimental Realism by A. H. JOHNSON
G. E. Moore: Essays in Retrospect edited by ALICE AMBROSE and
    MORRIS LAZEROWITZ
Hegael: A Re-examination by J. N. FINDLAY
A History of Aesthetic by B. BOSANQUET 2nd edition
Human Knowledge by BERTRAND RUSSELL
Hypothesis and Perception by ERROL E. HARRIS

MUIRHEAD LIBRARY OF PHILOSOPHY

EDITED BY H. D. LEWIS

PERSON
AND
OBJECT

PERSON AND OBJECT

A METAPHYSICAL STUDY

by

RODERICK M. CHISHOLM

Professor of Philosophy and Andrew W. Mellon Professor of the Humanities, Brown University

Open Court Publishing Company
La Salle, Illinois

Printed in Great Britain

Library of Congress Catalogue Card Number: 75–29952
ISBN: 0–87548–341–0

PREFACE

The three Carus Lectures constituting the nucleus of this book were presented before the Pacific Division of the American Philosophical Association in December 1967. An earlier version was presented as the Nellie Wallace Lectures at Oxford University in the winter of 1966 and 1967. Some of the material has been presented at Summer Institutes sponsored by the Council for Philosophical Studies and in courses and seminars given at Brown University, the University of Massachusetts, the University of Graz and the University of Salzburg.

I am especially indebted to Brown University: to my colleagues in the Department of Philosophy, to the members of a number of different administrations and to the many students who have attended my classes. The book would not have been completed without the epoch-making File Retrieval and Editing System developed by Professor Andries van Dam and his associates at Brown. I owe special thanks to Josiah Strandberg for introducing me to this system and for his expert and dedicated assistance. I wish also to express my thanks to my wife, to Ernest Sosa for his penetrating criticisms of an earlier version of the manuscript and to Martha Browne for her editorial assistance. Only a few of the many philosophers from whose works and criticisims I have profited are mentioned in the text; I am sorry it is not possible to mention them all.

I have incorporated portions of the following articles of mine: 'On the Observability of the Self', *Philosophy and Phenomenological Research,* xxx (1969), 7–21; 'Parts as Essential to their Wholes', *Review of Metaphysics,* xxv (1973), 581–603; 'Mereological Essentialism: Some Further Considerations', *Review of Metaphysics,* xxviii (1975), 477–84; and 'The Loose and Popular and the Strict and Philosophical Senses of Identity', in Norman S. Care and Robert H. Grimm, eds, *Perception and Personal Identity* (Cleveland: The Press of Case Western Reserve University, 1969), 82–106. I am indebted to the editors of *Philosophy and Phenomenological Research* and the *Review of Metaphysics* and to the Press of Case Western Reserve University for permitting me to include this material.

RODERICK M. CHISHOLM

31 October 1975

CONTENTS

INTRODUCTION

1 An Approach to Philosophy

Leibniz, Reid, Brentano and many other philosophers have held that, by considering certain obvious facts about ourselves, we can arrive at an understanding of the general principles of metaphysics. The present book is intended to confirm this view.

One kind of philosophical puzzlement arises when we have an apparent conflict of intuitions. If we are philosophers, we then try to show that the apparent conflict of intuitions is only an apparent conflict and not a real one. If we fail, we may have to say that what we took to be an apparent conflict of intuitions was in fact a conflict of apparent intuitions, and then we must decide which of the conflicting intuitions is only an apparent intuition. But if we succeed, then both of the intuitions will be preserved. Since there was an apparent conflict, we will have to conclude that the formulation of at least one of the intuitions was defective. And though the formulation may be imbedded in our ordinary language, we will have to say that, strictly and philosophically, a different formulation is to be preferred. But to make it clear that we are not rejecting the intuition we are reformulating, we must show systematically how to interpret the ordinary formulation into the philosophical one. The extent to which we can show this will be one mark of our success in dealing with the philosophical puzzle. Another will be the extent to which our proposed solution contributes to the solution of still other philosophical puzzles.

The present book is concerned with such puzzlement and, in particular, with philosophical questions that arise when we reflect upon ourselves. It could be said, therefore, to be an exercise in 'analytic philosophy', since it is not concerned with philosophical speculation. But it differs from the works of some contemporary analytic philosophers in presupposing that philosophy is to be taken seriously and hence that it requires, in Russell's phrase, a considerable amount of honest toil. And it differs from the works of other analytic philosophers in taking seriously certain things we have a right to believe about ourselves.

I assume that we should be guided in philosophy by those propositions we all do presuppose in our ordinary activity. In saying we have a 'right to believe' these propositions, I mean that, whether or not they are true, they are all such that they should be regarded as innocent, epistemically, until we have positive reason for thinking them guilty.

2   Philosophical Data

A list of the propositions constituting our data would be very much like the list of truisms with which G. E. Moore began his celebrated essay 'A Defence of Common Sense'.[1] And like Moore's list it would produce two very different reactions. One may say, on being confronted with the list, 'But these things are too obvious to mention. Let us get on with our philosophy'. Yet, when we do get on with our philosophy and appeal to one or another of these propositions in order to criticise a philosophical theory, *then* we will hear the objection: 'But you have no right to assume anything like *that*!' The reply is, of course, that whatever we are justified in assuming, when we are not doing philosophy, we are also justified in assuming when we *are* doing philosophy.

What is the list, then? I will set forth, but only schematically, certain things that I am justified in believing about myself. The list is schematic, for the details would be tedious. Moreover, the schematic list will be applicable to you; you may use it to fill in the details about yourself.

There are two broad subdivisions in the list and three types of fact in each.

There are, first, these three types of thing I am justified in believing about myself. '(1) I am now thinking such-and-such things. I have such-and-such beliefs, feelings, desires, attitudes. I have such-and-such experiences and such-and-such perceptions. (2) I now have a body of such-and-such a sort. And (3) I am now intentionally bringing about such-and-such things which are such that I could have avoided bringing them about.' I now know, for example, (1) that I see various books and other objects, (2) that I have a body that is sitting and is more than six feet in length, and (3) that I am writing certain things which seem to me to be important but which, had I chosen to do so, I would have refrained from writing.

I assume that most readers would assent to a similar set of propositions. (Perhaps there are philosophical sceptics who would not, but the reasonableness or unreasonableness of scepticism is not the subject matter of the present inquiry.) Perhaps there are some who would object to the way I have formulated the second item on the list. For the expression 'I have a body' (unlike 'I have an arm' and 'I have brown hair') is somewhat strange. One

INTRODUCTION

may contrast 'I have a body' with other statements of possession ('I have a green Chevrolet') where the object said to be possessed is something that is readily transferable. And so it might even be suggested that we should not say 'I have a body' at all.[2] But we need *some* way of expressing that intimate relation I bear to my body and 'I have a body' is as good a way of expressing this relation as any other. (It would be question-begging to assume at the outset that this relation is one of identity and that in consequence I *am* my body.)

Let us turn to the second part of our list. To formulate this we have only to look at the first part of the list and then to put similar but different facts in the past tense. '(1) At such-and-such times in the past, I had such-and-such other thoughts, beliefs, feelings, desires, attitudes. (2) I had a body of such-and-such a different sort. And (3) I intentionally brought about such-and-such other things which I could have avoided bringing about.' I know, for example, that earlier this morning I saw the sea, and that I subsequently brought it about that I am sitting here now.

The first type of fact in each half of the list is in part Cartesian, for it pertains to what are sometimes called 'states of mind'. (But I have not used the word 'mind' in setting forth these facts.) The second type of fact reminds us that we are very much in touch with material things and that we know that we are. And the third emphasises that we are active beings and that each of us is himself responsible for a part of the state of the world.

If we were to fill out our list (or, rather, our lists, one for each of us), we could formulate one long sentence using a single variable 'x' throughout: 'I am an x such that x thinks so-and-so, x has such-and-such a body, x is doing such-and-such things, x formerly thought such-and-such, x formerly had a body of such-and-such a different sort, and x formerly brought about such-and-such other things.' The use of the variable is not merely pedantic; it would indicate that the various items on our list pertain to *one and the same* entity throughout. We begin with the assumption that we are not here concerned with many different things, one thing that thinks, a second thing that has such-and-such a body, a third thing that is doing the various things, and a fourth, fifth and sixth thing to which our various statements in the past tense apply.

These different facts may have different degrees of justification. At the very least, each of them is something which, for me, has *some* presumption in its favour. That is to say, it is more reasonable to think it is true than to think it is false. Most of them, moreover, are epistemically acceptable; it is *not unreasonable* for me to accept them. Some are *beyond reasonable doubt*; it is more reasonable to accept them than not to accept them. Some, moreover, are *evident*; they are the ones I should appeal to when I wish to decide whether certain *other* things are reasonable. And some of them are *absolutely certain*; not only are they evident, but there is nothing that is *more* reasonable for us to believe than they are.[3]

Such facts as these, then, are what we have a right to take as data in our philosophy. They are a part of our pre-analytic or pre-philosophic data. Any philosophical theory which is inconsistent with any of these data is *prima facie* suspect. The burden of proof will be upon the man who accepts any such theory and not upon you and me. To show that he is justified in accepting his theory he must show that it is based upon data which are at least as respectable epistemically as the list of things that I have set forth.

3 Some Objections Considered

One may object; 'But people make mistakes about each of these things. Therefore you don't have a right to believe any of them.' We should reflect upon the appropriateness of the 'therefore'. The argument is like this one. 'People sometimes are subject to hallucinations and delusions. Therefore you have no right to think at the moment that you really are trying to read a book.' The argument is also like this. 'Every respectable encyclopaedia contains some erroneous statements. Therefore it is unreasonable of you to think that you can learn anything about the world by looking it up in the encyclopaedia.'

One may also object: 'But you are allowing yourself to be misled by grammar. To suppose, for example, that what is expressed by "I feel tired" really tells you something about yourself, about some individual thing, is merely to be taken in by the fact that the rules of our language require that every complete singular sentence have a subject-term as well as a predicate-term.' Now it doubtless is the case that the rules of our language require that every singular sentence have a subject-term as well as a predicate-term. But does this mean that when I say that what is expressed by 'I feel tired' says something about *me*, then I have been misled or taken in by grammar?

Could an investigation of language – of the English language or of Indo-European languages more generally – show us that we have gone wrong here? It is difficult to see how it could. The linguistic facts themselves are likely to have no implications at all about the nature of the self. It is only when they are taken in conjunction with some additional non-linguistic fact that they yield any such conclusions. And the reasonability of the conclusions will turn upon this non-linguistic fact and not upon what it is that the linguists have shown us.

I will illustrate this point by contrasting the following two arguments:

(A) The use of 'I' in 'I feel tired . . . (etc.)' is required by grammar.
Therefore, there is no reason to suppose it designates anything.

(B) The use of 'I' in 'I feel tired . . . (etc.)' is a *mere* requirement of grammar.
Therefore, there is no reason to suppose it designates anything.

In argument (A) the premise is restricted to certain facts about language, but the conclusion hardly follows from the premise. In argument (B) the conclusion does follow from the premise – if we give a suitable interpretation to the 'mere' – but the 'mere' takes us beyond the facts of language. To know that the use of 'I' in 'I feel tired' is a *mere* requirement of grammar one has to know that there is no person to whom it is used to refer. How, then, are we to justify the premise of (B)? Only by begging the question – and bringing to the study of language the information that there is no self.

It has often been pointed out that, although Indo-European languages have a subject-predicate grammar, there are other languages that do not. But what are we to do with this fact? Suppose anthropologists or linguists find a tribe that has no words for temperature – no words for hot and cold. And suppose a philosopher learns about this, and then argues as follows: 'You are complaining about the heat. But don't you know that it's a peculiarity of just a certain subset of languages that they have words ostensibly designating such things as heat and cold? Therefore you have no grounds for complaint.' Or, to make the analogy a little closer, suppose we find a language in which there is a present and future tense but no past tense. And then the philosopher argues: 'You are distressed about your past. But the past tense is a feature of only some languages, but not of all languages. Therefore there is nothing for you to be distressed about.'

Perhaps we are misled by our language when we suppose that

there *is* something which is our self. But this is something that has to be shown. It is not a point at which it is reasonable for us to begin.

4 Premature Speculations

I have said that any philosophical theory about the nature of the self – any philosophical theory about the nature of you or of me – should be adequate to our data. Either it should be consistent with our data, or if it is not, it should show us why we are wrong in appealing to such data. And to show this last, the philosophical theory must itself appeal to a set of data which is even *more* reasonable for us to accept than is the list of things with which we have begun. In other words, if a philosopher has a theory that seems to conflict with our data and if he wishes us to take his theory seriously, then there are two courses open to him. He could show us that, in fact, his theory does *not* conflict with our data. Or he could undertake the burden of proving that his theory is more reasonable than the data with which we have begun.

There are some very strange theories about the self or the person – such things as you and me. Some of these theories seem seriously to suggest that the self is an *abstract object* – for example, that I am a *class*, or a *property*, or a *function*. Some seem to imply that I am a *collection*, or a *bundle*, or a *structure*, or an *event*, or a *process*. (One writer has said: 'I am a verb – and so is God.') It is impossible to take such theories literally. The variable '*x*' in our formulation 'There exists an *x* such that *x* thinks so-and-so and *x* has a body of such-and-such a sort' cannot be taken to have as its value a class of things, or a structure, or an event, or a process. (William James said that the 'I' is 'a collection of feelings in his head and throat'; but, as Professor Geach has remarked, he didn't intend to imply that 'these head and throat feelings are getting into an awful muddle'.[4]

It may well be, of course, that when a philosopher tells us that the self is a bundle or a class or a structure or a process, he does not mean to be saying that *he himself* is a class or a structure or a process – he does not mean to be saying, for example, that there is a certain *process* which *has* a body that is more than six feet long and which *remembers* having *acted* in certain ways in the past. What he does mean to be telling us, he may explain, is that sentences ostensibly about the self, sentences ostensibly about him or about you or about me, can be paraphrased into other sentences wherein the variables refer, no longer to a self, no longer to him or to you and me, but to such entities as classes or structures or processes. In such a case, he will be saying that the relation that you and he and I bear to these entities is like the relation which, according to Frege and according to White-head and Russell, cardinal numbers bear to such entities as attributes or classes.

For all anyone knows, some such philosophical theory is true. But at the present time there is no positive reason whatever for accepting such a theory. Suppose, for example, a philosopher expresses himself by saying, 'The self is a bundle of sense impressions', and then explains to us that what he means by his assertion is this – that whatever is known about you and me can be paraphrased into true sentences wherein the substantival expressions refer only to sense impressions and not to you and me. If we are to take his theory seriously, then he must show, with respect to the sentences formulating our pre-philosophic data, exactly *how* those sentences may be paraphrased into sentences referring only to sense impressions. (Thus Russell and Whitehead could take the propositions of arithmetic – for example, the proposition that two and three is equal to five – and show, or attempt to show, how they can be paraphrased into sentences referring only to classes.) But if our philosopher cannot thus paraphrase our data, we may leave him with his theory and continue with our philosophical work. And it may safely be said that no philosopher has ever even begun to show how such facts as those comprising our provisional data can be paraphrased or re-expressed in statements that do not refer to persons or selves.[5]

5 A Minimum Philosophical Vocabulary

Many definitions will be formulated in what follows.[6] But it is necessary that some terms be undefined. The reader of any philosophical book has a right to know what the philosophical concepts are to which the author will appeal. And so I will now indicate briefly some of the technical expressions that will be used without definition in the present book. These fall within the following eight groups.

(1) I will speak of *things* and of the *properties* of things and of the *relations* in which things stand. But I will use 'thing' in a very broad sense. Whatever there is may be said, in this sense, to be a thing: hence properties and relations are themselves things, and so are physical objects, persons and shadows. (In the final chapter, I will propose a definition of *individual thing*.)

(2) I will make use of the concept of *de re* necessity – the concept that it is expressed by saying that a thing has a certain property necessarily. I will assume that properties and relations

are such that, whether or not they are exemplified or instantiated, they *exist* necessarily. Hence they might be called 'noncontingent things' or 'eternal objects'. The concept of necessity will be discussed in somewhat more detail in the following chapter.

(3) I will assume that there are such things as *propositions* and *states of affairs* and that these are noncontingent things. Thus there is the proposition that two and two are four and there is also the proposition that two and two are five. Both exist necessarily, although the first is true and the second is false. And there is that state of affairs which is there being horses and there is also that state of affairs which is there being unicorns. Both exist necessarily, although the first obtains (takes place, or occurs) and the second does not obtain (take place, or occur). These theses constitute the subject matter of Chapter IV; I there suggest that events and propositions constitute subspecies of states of affairs.

(4) I will make use of the intentional concepts of *believing*, *considering* and *endeavouring*, as expressed in 'He believes that Socrates is mortal', 'He is thinking about walking', and 'He is endeavouring to bring it about that he walks to Boston'. I will assume that the intentional attitudes to which these expressions refer take states of affairs as their objects.[7]

(5) I will make use of the concept of *physical necessity* and assume that some states of affairs are physically necessary (i.e. that they are such that it is a law of nature that they obtain). I will also make use of the concept of *causal contribution* (as expressed in 'The wood being dry contributed causally to the severity of the fire'). I will leave open the difficult question whether the second of these concepts might be explicated in terms of the first.

(6) I will make use of the epistemic locution 'more reasonable than', as used in the expression, 'Believing that the senses are generally reliable is *more reasonable than* believing that they are not generally reliable'.[8]

(7) I will make use of the expression 'proper part', as applied to individual things.[9]

And, finally, (8) I will allow myself to speak of *places* and *times*.

The principal philosophical theses of this book can be expressed by using this philosophical vocabulary and the locutions of logic. It is unfortunate to have to rely upon so many undefined concepts. But, I believe, every other treatment of these problems makes use of even more.

CHAPTER I

THE DIRECT AWARENESS
OF THE SELF

*I agree that in order to determine the concept of an
individual substance it is good to consult the concept
which I have of myself.*

Leibniz to Arnauld[1]

1 A Philosophical Question

Do we know ourselves directly and immediately? With respect
to this question, two of the great traditions of contemporary
Western philosophy – 'phenomenology' and 'logical analysis' –
seem to meet, unfortunately, at the extremes. The question is
whether one is ever directly aware of the *subject* of experience.
The question does not have to do with perception of one's *body*.
If it should happen to be the case that each of us is identical
with his body and if, as all but sceptics hold, we do perceive our
bodies, then, whether we realise it or not, we also perceive ourselves. Our question has to do with what we find when we consult
the data of immediate experience – when, as Hume puts it, we
enter most intimately into what we call ourselves. Thus Sartre
seems to say that, although we may apprehend things *pour soi*,
things that are manifested or presented to the self, we cannot
apprehend the self to which, or to whom, they are manifested or
presented – we cannot apprehend the self as it is in itself, as it
is *en soi*.[2] Russell frequently said that the self or subject is not
'empirically discoverable'.[3] And Carnap expressed what I take
to be the same view by saying 'the given is subjectless'.[4] I say it
is unfortunate that the members of the two great philosophical
traditions happen to meet at this particular point, of all places.
For at this particular point, if I am not mistaken, both groups
have lost their way.

We may put the question in Russell's early technical termin-
ology by asking, 'Are we ever directly acquainted with ourselves?'
I would say that the answer to Russell's question is obviously
'Yes'.

I will first describe acquaintance in a somewhat inexact and informal way and then I will attempt a more nearly exact statement. Given this statement, it should then be obvious that we are directly and immediately acquainted with ourselves – that we know ourselves directly and immediately. But the full import of this philosophical thesis may not be clear until we have replied to certain philosophical objections.

2 Acquaintance: A Preliminary Statement

The concept of the *direct acquaintance* of oneself presupposes that of the *direct knowledge* of a proposition. We could say that a proposition is known directly if, in Meinong's terms, it is 'self-presenting' or it 'presents itself'.[5] In order to have a preliminary foundation, let us say that a proposition 'presents itself' to a man, if, first of all, it is true, and if, secondly, it is necessarily such that, if it is true, then the man knows it is true. The proposition that I *seem* to see many people, for example, is one that is now self-presenting to me. This means, first, that I do in fact seem to see many people and, secondly, that it is necessarily true that, *if* I thus seem to see many people, then it is evident to me that I do. Of course I also know that there *are* many people here but this is not something that is self-presenting to me; for there *could* be many people here even if I didn't know that there were.

Among the propositions which are thus self-presenting for each of us at the present time are propositions about our state of mind at this time – our thinking certain thoughts, entertaining certain ideas and having certain sensory experience (or, as I would prefer to put it, our sensing in certain ways).

If a proposition is thus self-presenting to a man, then it is one that he *knows directly*. Now I suggest that whenever a person thus knows something directly then he may be said to have *direct knowledge of himself*; in Russell's terms, the man may be said to be *directly acquainted* with himself. For all the self-presenting states we have referred to are states of the knower himself. In knowing them directly, he knows himself directly. He is directly acquainted with certain of his states and also with himself.

To see that these states *are* states of the knower himself, we have only to ask ourselves: What state which is *not* a state of the man himself is one which is *necessarily* such that, if it were to obtain, then the man *knows directly* that it obtains? That there are many people in the room, as we have said, could obtain without my knowing about it; that there *seem to me* to be many people in the room couldn't possibly obtain without my knowing about it. Thus Brentano has held that the only individual thing which can be an object of such direct factual knowledge is the knower himself.[6]

If you are now awake and conscious, then you have certain properties such that you are now known directly by yourself to have those properties. Thus you may now be such that you seem to hear a voice, or you believe yourself to be in North America or in Great Britain, or you hope to receive some enlightenment from this book. If you do have such properties as these, then you have direct knowledge of yourself. And if you do have direct knowledge of yourself, as I am sure you do, then you are directly acquainted with yourself. This fact can also be put by saying that you are immediately aware of yourself.

I will now attempt to formulate this philosophical thesis somewhat more precisely.

3 Self-Presenting States

Can we now characterise 'self-presentation' more adequately? I suggest this definition:

> D.I.1 h is such that it is self-presenting to s at t =Df h occurs at t and is necessarily such that, whenever it occurs, then it is certain for s.[7]

Let us take *my feeling depressed* as a paradigm case of self-presenting state. I had said, in my preliminary formulation above, that the property of feeling depressed is one which is necessarily such that, if a person has it, then he knows directly that he has it. Let us now replace 'knows directly' by 'is certain'. Our assumption is, then, that people are *necessarily* such that, if they are depressed, then they are *certain* that they are depressed.

What it is for a state of affairs to be *necessarily* such that, if it occurs or obtains, then it is *certain* for a person that it occurs or obtains? Our question may be divided into two further questions. The first is: 'What is it to say of a thing that it is *necessarily* such that so-and-so?' And the second question is: 'What is it to say, with respect to a state of affairs, that it is *certain* for a man that it obtains?'

The first question – 'What is it to say of a thing that it is *necessarily* such that so-and-so?' – cannot be answered except by using expressions that are themselves as difficult to understand as is the locution 'x is necessarily such that it is F'. We might say: 'x is such that, if it were not F, it wouldn't exist'; or 'God couldn't have created x without making it such that it is F'; or

'x is such that in every possible world in which it exists it is F'. But if a person doesn't understand 'x is necessarily such that it is F', it is not likely that he will understand the expressions in terms of which we have attempted to clarify it. One should, however, be able to acquire the concept by considering examples. The 'F' in 'x is necessarily such that it is F' could be replaced by any of the following expressions, no matter what 'x' may designate: 'self-identical'; 'red or not red'; 'a musician if a violinist'; and 'such that two and two is four'. And for some but not all values of 'x' the following expressions would be true: 'x is necessarily an even number'; 'x is necessarily an abstract thing'; 'x is necessarily an individual thing'; and 'x is necessarily possibly red'.[8]

We are suggesting, then, that the property expressed by the phrase, 'being such that, if it feels depressed, then it is certain for it that it feels depressed', is a property that *everything* has necessarily. People have it necessarily and so do stones and abstract objects and everything else. Thus if a stone *were* to feel depressed, then it would be certain for it that it felt depressed. For such certainty is guaranteed by the very nature of the feeling. (This means that the property of feeling depressed has itself necessarily the property of being such that, if anything exemplifies it, then it is certain for that thing that it feels depressed. This property is had necessarily by the property of feeling depressed, and by any property that includes the property of feeling depressed.[9]

Let us now turn to the second question to which our definition of self-presentation gave rise: 'What is it to say, with respect to a thing, that it is certain for a man that the thing has a given property?'

We should distinguish between saying that a man *feels certain* about a given thing and saying that that thing is something which *is certain* for him. When we say that he *feels* certain ('He feels certain he will succeed'), we are saying something about the strength of his conviction or about the felt strength of his conviction. But when we say that something *is* certain for him ('That he feels depressed or seems – to himself – to have a headache is something that is certain for him'), we may, but of course we need not, be saying something normative and more objective. In such a case, we will be saying something, not about the strength of his convictions or about the way he feels and acts, but about what he has a right to believe, or what it is reasonable for him to believe. Let us here restrict the expression 'is certain for him' to this normative and objective sense.

We might define this sense approximately as follows: to say of something that it *is certain* for a man is to say that, for him, believing that something is at least as reasonable as believing anything else. A more exact definition is this:

> D.I.2   *h* is certain for s at *t* = Df (i) Accepting *h* is more reasonable for s at *t* than withholding *h* (i.e. not accepting *h* and not accepting not-*h*) and (ii) there is no *i* such that accepting *i* is more reasonable for s at *t* than accepting *h*.

The definition presupposes the normative epistemic concept here expressed by 'more reasonable than'.[10] This concept is discussed in detail in Appendix D of this book.

The first clause of the definiens ('Accepting *h* is more reasonable for s at *t* than withholding *h*') could be re-expressed by saying '*h* is beyond reasonable doubt for s at *t*'; for we may say that a proposition is beyond reasonable doubt if and only if accepting it is more reasonable than withholding it.

We are saying, then, that if a man feels depressed, then it is reasonable for him to believe he feels depressed and that, in such a case, there is nothing which is *more* reasonable for him to believe than that he feels depressed. Indeed, we are saying that no one can feel depressed and at the same time be such that it is not reasonable for him to believe that he feels depressed. And so, too, for the other states we have called 'self-presenting'.

There may be a certain oddity in saying 'If a man feels depressed, then it's reasonable for him to believe that he feels depressed'. But the oddness lies only in the fact that what such a statement says is obviously true. To realise this, we have only to consider that a man may appeal to his feeling depressed – or to any of his other self-presenting states – as a touchstone in assessing the reasonableness of *other* propositions. ('Has the drug taken effect? One reason to think so is the fact that I now feel depressed.') Indeed, we may say that one's ultimate appeal in any question of evidence is precisely to those states we have been calling 'self-presenting'.

4 *Direct Acquaintance*

We have been speaking of a cognitive relation that a person may bear to a state of affairs. What now of his direct acquaintance, or direct awareness, of *himself*? The states of affairs that are self-presenting to a person pertain to that person himself. It is obvious that that state of affairs which is my feeling

depressed pertains to me. But despite this obviousness, let us
spell out the relevant sense of the word 'pertain'.

Let us note first that a state of affairs may be said to entail
certain *properties*. Thus *my feeling depressed* may be said to
entail the property of *feeling depressed*, for it is necessarily such
that, if it obtains then something has the property of *feeling
depressed*. In this same sense, that state of affairs which is *some
dogs being brown* may be said to entail the property of *being
brown*, as well as the properties of *being canine* and *being both
brown and canine*. For it is necessarily such that, if it obtains,
then something has these properties. Let us say, then:

> D.I.3   *p* entails the property of being F = Df *p* is necessarily
> such that (i) if it obtains then something has the
> property of being F and (ii) whoever accepts *p* believes
> that something is F.

This definition is a schema in which the letter 'F' may be
replaced by any English predicate expression – e.g. 'red' or 'such
that Socrates is mortal'.[11] Thus the proposition that some men
are Greeks entails the properties of *being a man* and *being Greek*,
but the proposition that no men are Greeks does not entail
either of these properties. (The definition could be taken in such
a way that 'relation' may replace 'property'. Then that state of
affairs which is Phillip being father of Alexander could be said
to entail the relation *being father of*; for the state of affairs is
necessarily such that, if it obtains, then something bears the
relation *father of* to something, and whoever accepts it believes
that something is father of something.)

Let us next introduce the expression 'individual concept' and
use it to refer to a property that only one thing can have at a
time. Or more exactly:

> D.I.4   c is an individual concept = Df c is a property such
> that (i) it is possible that something has c and (ii) it
> is not possible that more than one thing has c at a
> time.

Thus the property of being the tallest man is an individual
concept; so, too, for the property of being President of the United
States; and so, too, I wish to urge, for the property of being
identical with me.

Let us note, in passing, that the term 'individual concept' is
sometimes used, more narrowly, to express what we will call an

'individual essence' or 'haecceity.'[12] This second concept, which we will use below, may be defined this way:

> D.I.5   G is an *individual essence* (or *haecceity*) =Df G is a property which is such that, for every *x*, *x* has G if and only if *x* is necessarily such that it has G, and it is impossible that there is a *y* other than *x* such that *y* has G.

Thus the individual essence or haecceity of Socrates, if there is such a thing, has the following characteristics. It is a property which is such that, if anything has it, then that thing has it necessarily; hence Socrates had it necessarily. (But it was not necessary that Socrates had it, for it was not necessary that there be a Socrates.) It is a property which everything other than Socrates necessarily fails to have. (Even if Socrates had not existed, no other thing could have had his haecceity.) According to the traditional account of individual essence, each thing has only one individual essence and it includes all the characteristics that the thing has necessarily.[13]

All individual essences or haecceities, then, are individual concepts, but not all individual concepts are individual essences or haecceities. Being the tallest man and being the President of the United States are individual concepts, but not haecceities. I will urge below that being identical with me *is* an individual essence or haecceity.[14]

Given the concept of an individual concept, we can say what it is for a proposition or state of affairs to imply, with respect to some particular thing, that that thing has a certain property. The President being in Washington may be said to imply, with respect to Mr Ford, that he has the property of being in Washington; and my feeling depressed may be said to imply, with respect to me, that I have the property of feeling depressed. This important concept may now be explicated in the following way:

> D.I.6   *p* implies *x* to have the property of being F =Df There is a property G such that (i) G is an individual concept, (ii) *p* entails the conjunction of G and the property of being F, and (iii) *x* has G.

(The letter 'F' in this definition is schematic and may be replaced by any predicate expression.) An alternative reading of the definiendum would be, '*p* implies, with respect to *x*, that it is F'. Consider, again, that state of affairs which is the President being in Washington. It does not logically imply that proposition or state of affairs which is Mr Ford being in Washington. But given the concept just defined, we may now say that the President being in Washington implies, with respect to Mr Ford, that *he* is in Washington. For it entails an individual concept, being President of the United States, and the state of affairs is necessarily such that, if it obtains, then whatever has that individual concept is in Washington. My feeling depressed implies the property of being identical with me; and my feeling depressed is necessarily such that, if it obtains, then whatever has that property feels depressed.

Definition D.I.6, then, tells us the sense in which a proposition or state of affairs may be said to *pertain* to a thing. The state of affairs pertains to a thing if it implies the thing to have a certain property.[15]

And now we may define direct acquaintance:

> D.I.7   s is acquainted with x at t =Df There is a p such that (i) p is self-presenting for s at t and (ii) there is a property that p implies x to have.

The second clause of the definiens may well be redundant; for, it would seem, every state of affairs that is self-presenting for a given person is one that implies him to have a certain property.

One has an individual concept of a thing if one knows a proposition implying that the thing has a certain property uniquely:

> D.I.8   s has an individual concept of x =Df There is a proposition p and an individual concept c such that (i) p implies x to have c and (ii) p is known by s.

Given this definition, we may say that, if a person is directly acquainted with himself then he has an individual concept of himself. For if he is directly acquainted with himself, then there is a state of affairs that is self-presenting for him; this state of affairs will imply the person to have a certain individual concept; and since the state of affairs is certain for him it will also be one that he knows.[16]

I would say, then, that if I feel depressed, or if I feel happy, or if I seem to see a sheep (seem to me, that is, to see a sheep), then I am directly acquainted with myself. For in each case, there is a self-presenting proposition which implies *me* to have a certain property. The individual concept implied by the proposition is that of *being I*, or *being identical with me*. And the proposition, since it is self-presenting, is *known* by me to be true.[17]

But let us defend the point in a somewhat different way.

5 *Individuation* Per Se

One may object: 'You cannot be directly aware of yourself unless you have an individual concept of yourself. But you can have an individual concept of a thing only if you have a way of individuating that thing. And you can individuate a thing only if you know something that is true of that thing and of nothing else. Hence you must be able to pick the thing out from among all other things. But this means that before you can individuate yourself you must be able to locate yourself within a certain class of things; you must pick out the members of that class and be able to specify the various ways in which each of them is uniquely related to you. The self-presenting states to which you refer hardly enable you to accomplish this.'

It would seem that, if we can individuate anything, if we can pick out anything, then it is *not* the case that the only way we have of individuating things is by relating them uniquely to still *other* things. And it may well be, in fact, that the only way we have, ultimately, of individuating *anything* is to relate it uniquely to *ourselves*.[18]

In order to deal adequately with these questions, we will first single out two of the concepts they presuppose. The one is the concept of individuating a thing, and the other is the concept of individuating a thing *per se* – without reference to any *other* individual thing. Let us say:

D.I.9   s individuates x = Df There is a p such that (i) p is known by s and (ii) there is a property p implies x to have.

Thus if we individuate a thing, we know a proposition entailing an individual concept of that thing. Our definition of individuation may be somewhat broad, but the above questions turn upon the much more narrow concept of individuation *per se*:

D.I.10   s individuates x *per se* = Df There is a p such that (i) p is known by s, (ii) there is a property p implies x to have, and (iii) there is no individual thing y such that y is other than x and there is a property p implies y to have.

If I individuate you *per se,* then there is some property which I know you to have uniquely – but the property is not one which consists in your being related uniquely to some other individual thing.

I have said that it is *not* the case that the only way we have of individuating a thing is that of relating it uniquely to some *other* thing. We may now prove this by a kind of Aristotelian argument.

The first premise of such an argument would be to assume that (1) we individuate or pick out certain individual things. This follows from what we have said at the outset, repudiating scepticism. There are many things that I can individuate or pick out. One of them, let us suppose, is you.

The second premise of our Aristotelian argument would be this: (2) there are three possibilities with respect to individuating any given thing: (a) we individuate in a circle (e.g. I individuate you by reference to Mr Jones, I individuate Mr Jones by reference to Mr Smith, and I individuate Mr Smith by reference to you); (b) we individuate by having individuated an infinite number of things (I individuate you by reference to Mr Jones, Mr Jones by reference to Mr Smith, Mr Smith by reference to the bookcase, and so on *ad infinitum*); or (c) we individuate some things without relating them uniquely to still other things and therefore individuate them *per se.*

Then the third premise in this Aristotelian argument would be: (3) the first two possibilities considered in the second premise – individuation in a circle and individuation into infinity – are each inconsistent with our first premise, with the fact that we do individuate certain things (with the fact that I have picked you out, for example).

And the conclusion of the argument would be: (4) we individuate some things without relating them uniquely to other things. There are some things that we identify *per se.*

I have no doubt whatsoever about the validity of this argument. The premises are true and the conclusion follows from the premises. We *do* individuate some things without relating them uniquely to other things.

What things do we individuate in this way?

There would seem to be three possible answers: (i) I am the only thing that I individuate *per se,* and I individuate all other things by relating them uniquely to me; (ii) I individuate myself *per se* and I also individuate certain other things *per se;* (iii) there are certain things other than myself that I individuate *per se,* and if I can pick out myself it is only by relating myself uniquely to some of these other things.

THE DIRECT AWARENESS OF THE SELF   33

(i) According to the first answer, then, I can pick *me* out *per se* and therefore without identifying myself as standing in some unique relation to some further thing, and anything else that I can identify I can identify *only* as being something that stands in some unique relation to some further thing. If I do thus pick me out *per se*, what do I identify myself as being? What is the individuating property that I can attribute to myself?

If I do individuate myself *per se* then there are propositions which are such that: I know them to be true; they imply some property that I have uniquely; and they do not imply any property that any *other* individual thing has uniquely. What property, then, could it be that I thus know myself to have uniquely and that does not pick me out merely by relating me uniquely to some *other* individual thing? It can only be the property of *being me*, or *being identical with myself*.[19]

The property of *being me*, of *being identical with myself*, can only be an individual essence or haecceity. It is a property I cannot fail to have. And it is a property that is 'repugnant to' all other things – 'repugnant' in the sense that nothing diverse from me could possibly have it.[20]

To say that I can pick me out as being this person, as being the thing that is identical with me, is *not* to say, of course, that I can pick me out as having those unique properties by means of which *others* pick me out. You may pick me out by means of properties that I don't even know I have. And if, as a result of amnesia, I forget the events of my past, I may still know that *I* am now in doubt about my past.[21]

There is a certain obviousness about this answer. If there is *something* that I individuate *per se*, then what better candidate could there be than myself? 'When a person tastes something, he can honestly swear that *he* knows it is sweet to *his* palate, and no trickery of the Greeks can dispossess him of that knowledge.[22] And the answer is confirmed by the implausibility of the other two possibilities.

(ii) The second possible view is that I individuate myself *per se* and also individuate certain other individual things *per se*.

Can we think of a situation in which I might be said to identify or individuate some individual thing other than myself and to identify or individuate it *per se*? If it *is* possible for me thus to pick you out *per se*, there would seem to be at most two ways in which I could do it.

One would be to pick you out as the only individual bearing a given relation to a certain abstract object. Thus I might pick out Pythagoras as the one who first thought of the Pythagorean theorem. If I can *know* that Pythagoras was the first to have the thought of this theorem, then the conditions of our definition of individuation *per se* are satisfied: I can individuate Pythagoras *per se*. But there are few individuals I can pick out as thus being uniquely related to a certain abstract object.

The only other way in which I might pick out an individual thing other than myself *per se* would seem to be something like this: I perceive the individual and pick it out as being *that* person or *that* individual. Thus if I see you approaching from the distance, like Coriscus, I can pick you as that thing that is approaching. If I try to express the way I pick you out, I will use demonstratives – just as I use the demonstrative 'I' to refer to myself. I will say you are 'that man' or 'that person' or 'that thing that is approaching'.

It is very tempting to say that, in the type of situation we are considering, the demonstrative expressions 'that person' and 'that thing that is approaching' are used only to express a certain relation that the thing in question bears uniquely to *me*. 'That person', for example, would be 'the person that *I* am now perceiving, or pointing at, or thinking about'; and analoguously for 'that thing that is approaching'. But *if* we should decide that, in such situations, I individuate *per se* some individual thing other than myself, then we would have to take a different view of such demonstrative expression.

We would have to say that these demonstrative expressions are like the word 'I' in that they may be used to intend certain individual essences or haecceities. This seems to have been the view of St Thomas and Duns Scotus.[23] According to this way of looking at the matter, if I pick you out as being *that* person or *that* thing, then I pick you out *per se*. For I pick you out as being something that has uniquely a certain property – the property of being that person or that thing. And this property, like the property of being identical with me, will be an individual essence or haecceity. In support of this latter point, one may urge: 'If you *are* that thing, then you are *necessarily* that thing. After all, that thing *has* to be that thing and it couldn't be anything *other* than that thing.'

But if today I individuate something *per se* as being *that thing* and if tomorrow I individuate something *per se* as being *that thing*, I may well have picked out two different things; whereas if today I individuate something *per se* as being identical with me and if tomorrow I individuate something *per se* as being identical with me, then I will have picked out one and the same thing.[24]

Let us note, moreover, that there are two ways of interpreting the expression 'that thing'. We could say that it intends a certain nonrelative property – namely, that of *being that thing*. And this property would be an individual essence or haecceity. Then the sentence 'That thing has to be that thing and couldn't be anything else' would tell us, with respect to the thing in question, that being that thing *is* its haecceity.

But 'that thing' could also be taken in a relational sense – as relating the thing in question to the one who is using the expression. So interpreted, it might be put as I have suggested, in some such phrase as 'the thing I'm now looking at' or 'the thing I'm concentrating on'. And when it is taken in this way, then, of course, it doesn't intend the individual essence or haecceity of the thing referred to.[25]

Which interpretation of 'that thing' is the correct one, and how are we to decide? The only way to decide, so far as I can see, is first to decide whether or not to accept the thesis that I can pick out *per se* certain entities other than myself. The thesis, then, seems to remain problematic.

(iii) But if this thesis is problematic, then, *a fortiori*, the third of our three possible views is also problematic. This is the view that the *only* things I can individuate *per se* are certain entities other than myself, and that I can pick me out only by reference to other things.

That I can pick me out only by reference to other things would seem to follow from a doctrine that has been accepted by a number of recent philosophers. The doctrine has been put this way by Vere Chappell: '. . . a necessary condition of our being able to distinguish persons as objects in the world, and so to refer to and identify them as such, is that they be uniquely and invariably associated with identifiable physical objects, in this case human bodies'.[26] Perhaps this is the only way we have of identifying *other* people, but is it the only way we have of identifying ourselves?

If what I have said is right, I identify myself without identifying myself by reference to my body and I indentify *my* body by reference to myself. 'I call mine the only body in which, for instance, my merely willing to raise an arm does, in normal circumstances, cause the arm to rise.'[27]

Those philosophers who seem to say I must identify me by reference to something other than myself *may* be concerned with a slightly different point. This is the point that I haven't identified myself *clearly* until I have contrasted myself with something else. But this point is quite consistent with saying that I individuate myself *per se*. Although I may individuate several different things obscurely, I don't individuate any of them clearly until I have contrasted them with each other. That is to say, I may pick out this object obscurely, then pick out that object obscurely, then see that this object is other than that object, and thereby pick out both objects clearly. This doctrine is suggested by St Thomas: 'what first comes to mind is being; secondly, that this being is not that being, and thus we apprehend division as a consequence; thirdly, comes the notion of one; fourthly the notion of multitude'.[28] Thus I first individuate myself obscurely and without reference to any other thing. Then I individuate other things by relating them uniquely to me. And finally, being able to contrast the other things with myself, I am able to individuate myself and the other things clearly and not merely obscurely.

That we individuate some things *per se* is inescapable and so, too, I would say, is the conclusion that we individuate ourselves *per se*. Of the three possible views we have distinguished, the third would seem clearly false.

Whether we accept the first or the second of the three possible views, we should remind ourselves of one point about the primacy of the self. Whenever I do identify *per se* some individual other than myself, then I am in a position also to identify that individual by reference to some unique relation that that individual bears to me. If I can now pick you out as being *that man,* then there is some way of perceiving which is such that I can now pick you out as being the thing I am now perceiving in that particular way. If I were *not* in a position to identify you by thus relating you uniquely to me, then I wouldn't be able to identify you *per se*. (But isn't it also true that, whenever I can pick you out, *per se,* as being *that man,* then I can pick *me* out, by reference to you, as being *the person who is perceiving that man?* No, for there be other people who are *also* perceiving you, in which case I will not be *the* person who is perceiving that man.)[29]

The theory of the use of the first person pronoun – for example, 'I' – that fits most naturally with what I have suggested is the following. Each person who uses the first person pronoun uses it to refer to himself and in such a way that, in that use, its *Bedeutung* or reference is himself and its *Sinn* or intention is his own individual essence. A corollary would be that, whereas each person knows directly and immediately certain propositions implying his own individual essence, no one knows any propositions implying the individual essence of anyone else.

There is still another consideration which provides a kind of

confirmation for this way of viewing self-reference. Castañeda
has shown that statement of self-attribution, such as 'Jones
believes that he himself is wise' (s), is not implied by the corresponding quantified statement, 'There is an x such that x is
identical with Jones and x believes that x is wise' (Q). Thus (Q)
might be true and (s) false if: Jones reads the lines on his hand
and takes them to be a sign of wisdom; he doesn't realise the
hand is his (for it is one of many protruding from a blanket);
and he is unduly modest and entirely without conceit.[30] What,
then, does (s) tell us that (Q) does not? I suggest it tells us this:
'Jones has an individual essence H; he accepts a proposition
which is self-presenting for him and necessarily such that it is
true if and only if whatever has H is wise.' Self-attribution, so
conceived, could be defined as follows in the terms we have been
using:

> D.I.11 s believes himself to be F =Df There is an individual
> essence C such that (a) a proposition implying s to
> have C is self-presenting for s and (b) s accepts a
> proposition which entails the conjunction of C and
> the property of being F.

If I am right in suggesting above that no one knows any propositions expressing the individual essence of haecceity of anyone
other than himself, then we may simplify D.I.11 by dropping
clause (a) altogether.

I would conclude, then, that I am able to individuate myself
per se. I do so in virtue of my awareness of being this particular
person. This awareness is a knowledge of propositions implying
my individual essence or haecceity and is implicit in each of my
self-presenting states. Every such state is necessarily such that,
if it obtains, then I am certain of my being this particular person.

To understand why many contemporary philosophers would
be inclined, all the same, to reject what I have said, let us turn
back to the doctrines of Hume and Kant, where we will find a
number of obvious but disastrous mistakes.

6 The Humean Tradition

I have said that the two great traditions in contemporary
philosophy tend to meet at the extremes and to share the doctrine
that may be put by saying 'the given is subjectless' or 'the self
is not to be found within experience'. Both traditions trace their
origins in part to Hume.[31] I suggest that, if we are to find out
what went wrong, we should turn first to the doctrine of Hume.

The essence of the Humean argument may be distilled in this way:

(1) I cannot be directly aware of any object unless that object is an impression,
But (2) I am not an impression,
Therefore (3) I cannot be directly aware of myself.

The conclusion of this argument follows from the two premises. And the second premise would seem to be beyond reasonable doubt. How, then, is the first premise to be defended?

Oddly enough, Hume does not explicitly defend the first premise.[32] If we try to find his reason for affirming it, we will find it in his theory of conception. And to see that the theory of conception is at least problematic, if not obviously false, we have only to formulate it and to consider it in the light of the philosophical data with which we began.

Hume summarises his theory in the following remark which may be found in his 'Abstract of a Treatise of Human Nature'. Hume wrote: 'As our idea of any body, a peach, for instance, is only that of a particular taste, color, figure, size, consistency, etc., so our idea of any mind is only that of particular perceptions without the notion of anything we call substance, either simple or compound.'[33] This seems to me to be very obviously false, but many philosophers, I am afraid, tend all too easily and unthinkingly to assume that it is true.

Is it true that our idea of a peach is an idea only of a particular taste, colour, figure, size, consistency and the like, and analogously that our ideas of such things as ships, trees, dogs and houses are ideas only of the particular qualities or attributes that these things are commonly said to have? One is tempted to say instead that our idea of a peach is an idea of *something that has* a particular taste, colour, figure, size and consistency; and analogously for the other familiar physical things. But even this is not quite right. Our idea of a peach is not an idea of something that *has* the particular qualities, say, of sweetness, roundness and fuzziness, but the concrete thing that *is* sweet and round and fuzzy. We also make clear, what is essential to our idea of a peach, that the thing that is round is the *same* thing as the thing that is sweet and also the *same* thing as the thing that is fuzzy.

Leibniz saw the point very clearly when he criticised Locke's *Essay Concerning Human Understanding*. When we consider any person or thing, he said, what comes before the mind is always a *concretum* and not a set of abstract things or qualities; we may consider something as knowing, or something as warm, or something as shining, but we do not thereby consider knowledge or warmth or light. The abstract things, he noted, are far more difficult to grasp than are the corresponding *concreta*.[34]

I cannot help but think that the point is a simple-minded one. 'Our idea of a peach is not an idea of sweetness, roundness and fuzziness . . . ; it is an idea of something that is sweet and also round and also fuzzy . . .' One would not have even thought of mentioning it, had not philosophers denied it and constructed fantastic systems on the basis of its negation. A small mistake at the outset, as the Philosopher said, turns out to be a great one in the end.

If the first part of Hume's observation is wrong, then so is the second. Our idea of 'a mind' (if by 'a mind' we mean, as Hume usually does, a person, or a self) is not an idea only of 'particular perceptions'. It is not the idea of the perception of love or hate and the perception of cold or warmth, much less an idea of love or hate and of heat or cold. It is an idea of that which loves or hates, and of that which feels cold or warm (and, of course, of much more besides). That is to say, it is an idea of an x such that x loves or x hates and such that x feels cold or x feels warm, and so forth.

I would say that a second error we find in Hume's writings, and in the writings of those who follow him with respect to our immediate acquaintance with ourselves, has to do with the interpretation of certain data or evidence. Thus Hume argues that he and most of the rest of mankind are 'nothing but a bundle or collection of different perceptions'. And in support of this 'bundle theory', he cites a kind of *negative* evidence. He tells us, with respect to a certain proposition, that he *has* certain evidence for saying that he has *no* evidence for that proposition. But when he cites the evidence he *has* for saying that he has *no* evidence for the proposition, he seems to presuppose, after all, that he *does* have evidence for the proposition.

What Hume said was this: 'For my part, when I enter most intimately into what I call *myself*, I always stumble on some particular perception or other, of heat or cold, light or shade, love or hatred, pain or pleasure. I never can catch *myself* at any time without a perception, and never can observe anything but the perception.'[35] As Professor Price once observed, it looks very much as though the self that Hume professed to be unable to find is the one that he finds to be stumbling – to be stumbling on to different perceptions.[36] How can he say that he doesn't find himself – if he is correct in saying that he finds himself to be stumbling and, more fully, that he finds himself to be stumbling on to certain things and not to be stumbling on to certain other things?

We must take care not to misinterpret the difficulty. The difficulty is *not* that, in formulating his evidence for the 'bundle theory' of the self, Hume presupposes that there *is* a self. For this presupposition, that there is a self, is not contrary to what Hume wishes to say. The 'bundle theory', after all, is not intended to *deny* that there is a self. It is intended merely to say *what* the self is and what it is not. There is a self, or there are selves, according to Hume, and what selves are are 'bundles of perceptions'.

The difficulty is that Hume appeals to certain evidence to show that there are only impressions or perceptions, and that when he tells us what this evidence is, he implies not only (i) that there is, as he puts it in his example, heat or cold, light or shade, love or hatred, but also (ii) that there is *someone* who finds heat or cold, light or shade, love or hatred, and moreover (iii) that the one who finds heat or cold is *the same as* the one who finds love or hatred and *the same as* the one who finds light or shade, and finally (iv) that this one does not in fact stumble upon anything but perceptions. It is not unreasonable to ask, therefore, whether Hume's report of his fourth finding is consistent with his report of the second and third. If Hume finds what he says he finds, that is to say, if he finds not only perceptions, but also that *he* finds them and hence that there is *someone* who finds them, how can his premises be used to establish the conclusion that he never observes anything but perceptions?

One may protest: 'But this is not fair to Hume. It is true that, in reporting his data, he used such sentences as "I stumble on heat or cold" and "I never observe anything but perceptions". He didn't need to express himself in this way. Instead of saying "I stumble on heat or cold" or "I find heat or cold", he could have said, more simply, "Heat or cold is found". And instead of saying "I never observe anything but perceptions", he could have said, more simply, "Nothing but perceptions are found". He could have reported his data in this way; and had he done so, he would not have presupposed that there exists an x such that x succeeds in finding certain things and such that x fails to find certain others.'

But *could* Hume have reported his data in this selfless way? Let us recall that his findings are both positive and negative and let us consider just the negative ones. It is one thing to say, modestly and empirically, 'I find nothing but impressions or perceptions'. It is quite another thing to say, rashly and non-empirically, 'Nothing but perceptions or impressions are found'. The point will be clearer, perhaps, if we consider another type of example. I may look around the room and, from where I stand, fail to see any cats or dogs in the room. If I express this negative finding modestly and empirically, I will simply say 'I do not see any cats or dogs'. But if I say, solely on the basis of my negative observation, 'No cats or dogs are seen', then I will be speaking rashly and non-empirically and going far beyond what my data warrant. How do I know what other people or God may find? And how can I be sure that there are no unseen dogs or cats? Clearly Hume would not have been justified in saying, 'Nothing but impressions are to be found'. And in fact he made no such subjectless report. He said, referring to himself, that *he* found nothing but impressions.

The difficulty may be put briefly. It is essential to Hume's argument that he reports not only what it is that he finds but also what it is that he fails to find. But the two types of report are quite different. The fact that a man finds a certain proposition p to be true does warrant a subjectless report to the effect that p is true. For finding that p is true entails that p is true. But the fact that he fails to find a certain proposition q to be true does not similarly warrant any subjectless report about q. For one's failure to find that q is true entails nothing about the truth of q. The fact that a man fails to find that q is true entitles him to say only that *he*, at least, does not find that q is true. And this would not be a subjectless report.

What Hume found, then, was not merely the particular impressions, but also the fact that *he* found those impressions as well as the fact that *he* failed to find certain other things. And these are findings with respect to himself.

7 *The Kantian Considerations*
There are considerations in the *Critique of Pure Reason*, in particular in the discussion of what Kant calls the first of the 'paralogisms of pure reason', which may suggest we have gone wrong, for Kant seems to take them to show that we cannot have any direct awareness of ourselves. Doubtless we cannot do full justice to Kant's discussion unless we present it within the framework of the system of philosophy that he develops. But we can and should ask: does Kant point out anything which should give us pause with respect to what we have been saying? And

we can discuss this question without going into the details of the Kantian system.

I believe that Kant does not point out anything that should give us pause. Let us recall briefly what it is that he may have to tell us.

Consider the following three sentences:

    (1) I feel depressed.
    (2) I seem to see a dog.
    (3) I don't seem to hear anything.

According to what I have said, these sentences may express what is known to be true on a given occasion. If they are uttered by me on that occasion they will express what I know to be true. And they will express three different things about one and the same thing. The thing that the 'I' in the first sentence refers to is the same as the thing that the 'I' in each of the other sentences refers to, and the three sentences tell us three different things about that thing.

According to Kant, however, all this is a mistake. The word 'I', he would say, doesn't refer to anything in these three sentences. (But Kant expresses himself in a most misleading way. Instead of saying merely that the expression 'I' doesn't designate anything, he introduces the substantival expression 'transcendental subject' and seems to say that what the 'I' designates is *a transcendental subject* or *transcendental ego*. But he doesn't profess to show that there *is* such a subject. He means to tell us rather that, although we can't express our thoughts without using a term ostensibly designating the subject, and although we cannot help thinking that there *is* such a subject, nevertheless, the word 'I' in such sentences as the three we have set forth above doesn't designate anything at all. We will do well to avoid saying that, according to Kant, the 'I' designates a transcendental subject.) Kant writes:

> . . . the 'I' is indeed in all our thoughts, but there is not in this representation the least trace of intuition, distinguishing the 'I' from other objects of intuition . . . We do not have and cannot have, any knowledge whatsoever of any such subject.[37]

(The observation that 'there is not in this representation the least trace of intuition' should remind us of the Humean doctrine that the subject of experience is not a sense-impression.) *Why* does Kant say 'we cannot have any knowledge whatsoever of any such subject'? Don't our three sentences above express three things I can know directly and immediately about myself?

We can, I think, construct two different arguments which are adequate to Kant's thought. The first is simply absurd and the second seems only to repeat the errors that had been made by Hume.

The first argument is suggested by passages such as the following:

> Through this I or he or it (the thing) which thinks, nothing further is represented than a transcendental subject of the thoughts $= x$. It is known only through the thoughts which are its predicates, and of it, apart from them, we cannot have any concept whatsoever . . . It is obvious that in attaching 'I' to our thoughts we designate the subject of inherence only transcendentally, without knowing anything of it either by direct acquaintance or otherwise.[38]

The first argument, then, might be formulated this way:

(1) We cannot really know anything about a thing unless we can know what it is apart from the predicates it has.

(2) If we can know the self or subject at all, we can know it only by knowing what predicates it has.

Therefore

(3) We cannot really know anything about the self or subject.

The second premise would seem to be beyond question. For it tells us that, to the extent that we know the self or subject, we know something about it. And the conclusion follows from the premises. What then, of the first premise?

To see that the first premise is absurd, we have only to try to put it more clearly. Among the more obvious interpretations that suggest themselves are these three:

'We cannot know anything about a thing unless we know something about it other than what we do know about it';
'We cannot know anything about a thing if the only things we know about it are things we do know about it';
'Since there is a distinction between a thing and its properties, the thing that *has* the properties is itself a bare particular that does *not* have any properties, and so we can't know anything about *it* merely by knowing what properties it has'.

I assume it is not necessary to criticise these possible interpretations explicitly. And the other possibilities that suggest
themselves do not seem to be any more plausible than
these.[39]

During the latter part of the nineteenth century and the early
part of the twentieth century, there were philosophers in the
idealistic tradition who reasoned in a similar way. They seemed
to say that we can never hope to have any genuine knowledge
of reality. The most we can hope to know about any particular
thing is to know what some of its properties or attributes are.
But, they said, we can never know what the thing is that has
those properties or attributes.[40] In the present century, Jean-Paul
Sartre has despaired because we seem to have no access to the
en-soi – to the self as it is in itself. What ever we find is at best
only *pour-soi* – the self as it manifests itself to itself.[41] Russell has
written: 'One is tempted to regard "This is red" as a subject-
predicate proposition, but if one does so, one finds that "this"
becomes a substance, an unknowable something in which predicates inhere . . .' [42] And a number of contemporary philosophers
seem to have argued that, if we distinguish between a thing
and its properties, then we must say that the thing is a 'bare
particular' that doesn't have any properties.[43] (Compare: 'If we
distinguish between a child and its parents, then we
must say that the child is an orphan that doesn't have
any parents.')

Despite the impressive tradition, shouldn't we say that this
is simply a muddle?

The second argument that we may reconstruct from Kant's
discussions resembles the one we have attributed to Hume, in
that it presupposes a theory of conception. We may put it this
way:

(1)   I cannot be directly aware of any thing unless I have
      a concept of that thing (or: unless that thing can be
      the subject of an intuition).
(2)   The I cannot be a predicate of anything.
(3)   If I had a concept of the I (or: if the I were an object
      of intuition), then the I could be a predicate or of
      other things.
Therefore
(4)   I do not have a concept of the I (or: the I is not an
      object of intuition).
Therefore
(5)   I cannot be directly aware of the I.

We have put the argument in such a way that the conclusions do follow from the premises.

The first premise is not implausible. At least, it can be interpreted in such a way that, in *that* interpretation, it is true. For example, we could take it to say: 'I cannot be directly aware of anything unless I'm aware of that thing as being something or other – and so I must be able to conceive what it is to *be* such a something-or-other.' This interpretation of Kant's first premise accords with what we have said. I can't be directly aware of myself, for example, unless I can be directly aware of myself as being in some state or other – say, as being depressed, or as being appeared to, or as loving or hating. And perhaps we may say, as Kant's first premise suggests, that if I am thus aware of myself, then I know what it is (I have a concept of what it is) for a thing to be depressed, or to be appeared to, or to love or hate.

The second premise – 'I cannot be a predicate of anything' – also accords with what we have said. Indeed, the fact to which it refers gives us a good *prima facie* reason for saying that the I is what Aristotle called a substance – for one mark of a thing's being a substance is that the thing cannot be predicated of any *other* thing.[44]

The crux of this Kantian argument, then, would seem to lie with the second premise. Here we have a theory about what it is to *conceive* a thing. Kant's scepticism about our direct apprehension of ourselves, like that of Hume, rests upon a theory of conception.

Kant's theory has the consequence that we cannot conceive of any individual thing – a particular peach, for example. It implies that, one can have a concept of a peach, only if a peach is capable of being predicated of other things. But what could it mean to say that a *peach* is a predicate of anything? Now if Hume were right in what *he* said about our idea of a peach ('our idea of a peach is only that of a particular taste, colour, figure, size, consistency, etc.'), then one could say that the things we think of when we think of a peach (taste, colour, figure, size, consistency) *are* capable of being predicates of other things. But Hume, as we have tried to show, was mistaken. And I think it is fair to say that Kant gives us no positive reason (unless the entire system set forth in *Critique of Pure Reason* is itself such a reason) for supposing that *his* theory of conception is correct. I would conclude, therefore, that he has given us no positive reason for his scepticism with respect to our apprehension of ourselves.[45]

Let us now consider this apprehension in somewhat more detail.

8 Inner Perception

We may say, following one important philosophical tradition, that the self is an object of 'inner perception'. And this would be to say that each of us is directly acquainted with himself, in the way that we explicate this exposition in D.I.7 above.[46] But we should contrast such inner perception with outer perception – with the way in which we perceive the familiar physical things around us.

Thus whenever we perceive a spatial object, then the object that we perceive has certain proper parts that we perceive and certain proper parts that we do not perceive. Suppose, for example, that I see a cat. Then that side of the cat that faces me is such that I see certain parts of *it*. But I do not see *all* the parts of the side that faces me (I do not see those parts I would see if I took a closer look or used a microscope) and I do not see *any* of the parts of the insides or any of the parts of the sides that face away. One of the results in changes of spatial perspective is that certain parts become seen that had not been seen before and certain parts cease to be seen that had been seen before. And so if the distance between our body and the perceived object is not too great, we may now look over this part and now look over that. We may look more closely and scrutinise – and this means that we may now see smaller parts that we had not seen before. And analogously for the nonvisual senses. But whatever our perspective upon the perceived object may be, there will always be certain parts of the perceived object that we do perceive and certain other parts of the perceived object that we do not perceive. Moreover, and this is the important point about external perception, if we know that we are perceiving a certain physical thing, then we are also capable of knowing that we are perceiving something that is just a proper part of that thing. But the situation is different when we perceive ourselves to be thinking.[47]

I may perceive myself to be thinking and know that I am doing so and yet be unable to know whether I am perceiving any proper part of anything that I am perceiving. It may be, for all anyone knows, that whenever I perceive myself to be thinking, I *do* perceive some part of myself. This would be the case, for example, if I could not perceive myself to be thinking without perceiving some part of my body, and if, moreover, I were identical with my body or with that part of my body. But it is not true that, whenever I perceive myself to be thinking I thereby perceive what I can *know* to be a part of myself. (Whether or not I am identical with my body or with some part of my body, I do not *know* that I am.) In short, to know that I perceive the cat to be standing, I must know that I perceive a proper part of the cat, or of the cat's body; but to know that I perceive myself to be thinking I need *not* know that I perceive what is a proper part of myself. Sartre said that the ego is 'opaque'; I would think it better to say that the ego is 'transparent'.[48]

Ordinarily if a man can be said to perceive *that* the cat is standing, then he may also be said, more simply, to perceive *the cat*. But the locution 's perceives that *a* is F' does not entail the simpler locution 's perceives *a*'.[49] Compare 'Jones perceives that Smith is no longer in the room' and 'Jones perceives that the lights are on next door'. Could it be, then, that a man might be aware of himself as experiencing *without* thereby being aware of himself? Let us approach this question somewhat obliquely, by recalling still another familiar source of philosophical perplexity.

During the first third of this century, British and American philosophers were perplexed about the status of what they called 'sense-data' or 'appearances'. They thought, for example, that if a man were to walk around a table, while focusing upon the white tablecloth on the top, he could experience a great variety of sense-data or appearances. Some of these entities would be rectangular like the table-top itself; they would be the ones he would sense if he were to get his head directly above the table and then look down. Most of them, however, would be rhomboids of various sorts. If the lighting conditions were good and the man's eyes in proper order, most of the appearances would be white, like the tablecloth. But if the man were wearing rose-coloured glasses, he might sense appearances that were pink, or if he were a victim of jaundice, he might sense appearances that were yellow. The other senses, as well as imagination, were thought to bring us into relation with still other types of appearances or sense-datum.

The nature and location of these strange entities, as we know, caused considerable puzzlement, and imposing metaphysical systems were constructed to bring them together with the rest of the world. I am sure that it is not necessary now to unravel all the confusions that were involved in this kind of talk, for the sense-datum theory has been ridiculed about as thoroughly as any philosophical theory can be ridiculed. But we should remind ourselves of one of these confusions – another very simple mistake. It was the mistake that H. A. Prichard had in mind, I think, when he used the expression, 'the sense-datum fallacy'.[50]

It was assumed that, if a physical thing appears white or rhom-

boidal or bitter to a man, then the man may be said to sense or
to be aware of an appearance that *is* white, or an appearance
that *is* rhomboidal, or an appearance that *is* bitter. It was
assumed that if a dog presents a canine appearance, then the
dog presents an appearance that *is* canine. (Thus Professor Lovejoy wrote in his Carus Lectures: 'No man doubts that when he
brings to mind the look of a dog he owned when a boy, there
is something of a canine sort immediately present to and there-
for compresent with his consciousness, but that it is quite
certainly not that dog in the flesh.')[51] And it was assumed, more
generally, that whenever we have a true statement of the form
'Such-and-such a physical thing appears, or looks, or seems so-
and-so to Mr Jones', we can derive a true statement of the form
'Mr Jones is aware of an appearance which is in fact so-and-so'.
But this assumption is quite obviously false.[52] Consider the
following reasoning, which would be quite sound if the assumption were true: 'That man looks Italian and more than seventy
years old. Therefore he presents an appearance which *is* Italian
and he presents an appearance which is more than seventy years
old.' It is absurd to suppose that an appearance, like a man, may
be Italian or more than seventy years old; it is absurd to suppose
that an appearance may be a dog; and, I think, it is equally
absurd to suppose that an appearance, like a tablecloth, may be
rectangular, or pink, or white.

When the philosophers thus talked about sense-data or appearances, they were, however inadequately, reporting *something*
that is very familiar to us all, and we should not let their philosophical theories blind us to the fact that there *are* sensation
and imagination and that the experiences we have when we
observe the familiar things around us may be varied merely by
varying the conditions of observation. Suppose now we were
considering this fact on its own, and without any thoughts about
Hume's theory or about Hume on the observability of the self.
How would we describe it if we are to avoid the absurdities of
the sense-datum fallacy?

We would do well to compare the 'grammar' of our talk about
appearances with that of our talk about feelings. Consider the
sentence 'I feel depressed'. It does not imply that there is a
relation between me and some other entity; it simply tells one
how I feel. The adjective 'depressed', in other words, does not
describe the *object* of my feeling; rather, if I may put the matter
so, it describes the *way* in which I feel. It could be misleading,
therefore, to use the longer sentence 'I have a depressed feeling'
in place of the shorter 'I feel depressed'. For the longer sentence,

'I have a depressed feeling' has a syntactical structure very much like that of 'I have a red book'. Hence one might be led to suppose, mistakenly, that it implies the existence of *two* entities, one of them *had* by the other. And taking 'a depressed feeling' as one would ordinarily take 'a red book', one might also be led to suppose, again mistakenly, that the feeling which the person is said to have resembles the person in being *itself* depressed. I say one *might* be misled in these ways by the sentence 'I have a depressed feeling' though I don't know of anyone who ever *has* been misled by it.

It is quite obvious, I think, that in such sentences as 'I feel depressed', the verb is used to refer to a certain type of *undergoing*. This undergoing is what traditionally has been called being in a conscious state, or being in a sentient state. And the adjective is used to qualify the verb and thus to specify further the *kind* of undergoing to which the verb refers. The adjective could be said to function, therefore, as an adverb. Thus the sentences 'I feel depressed' and 'I feel exuberant' are related in the way in which 'He runs slowly' and 'He runs swiftly' are related, and not in the way in which 'He has a red book' and 'He has a brown book' are related. In short, *being depressed* is not a predicate of the feeling; rather *feeling depressed* is a predicate of the man.

I suggest that the sentences 'I am aware of a red appearance' and 'I am experiencing a red sensation' are to be interpreted in the way in which we interpreted 'I have a depressed feeling' and 'I feel a wave of exuberance'. Despite their grammatical or syntactical structure, neither sentence tells us that there are *two* entities which are related in a certain way. They, too, ascribe a certain type of undergoing to the person. The adjective 'red', in 'I am aware of a red appearance' and 'I am experiencing a red sensation', is used adverbially to qualify this undergoing.[53] Thus we might say 'I am appeared to redly'. It would be useful, at least for the purposes of philosophy, if there were a verb – say, the verb 'to sense' – which we could use to refer to this type of undergoing. Then we could say that such a sentence as 'I am aware of a red appearance' tells us *who* the subject is sensing. Or, better perhaps, it tells us in what *way* he is sensing. For to be aware of 'a red appearance', presumably, is to sense in one of the ways that people do, when under favourable conditions, they look at objects that are red.

To be sure, *this* way of describing being appeared to fails to capture the self-evident character of appearance. Or, in the terms that we have been using, it fails to capture that certain ways of being appeared to are self-presenting. For 'I am appeared to redly' (or 'I sense redly'), so interpreted, makes reference to a certain contingent fact about the way in which *red* things appear, and such facts are not self-presenting. But we can accommodate our description to the facts of self-presentation. One way of expressing the self-evident fact involved in being appeared to redly would be to say: 'There is a way of appearing which is such that (i) I believe it is the way in which red things appear when they are perceived under conditions which are optimum for perceiving them to be red and (ii) I am being appeared to in that way.'[54]

If we say that a man 'senses redly', may we also say that he 'senses rhomboidally', or 'senses rectangularly'? There is no reason why we may not. Thus we might identify one's sensing rhomboidally, or one's sensing rectangularly, with one of the ways in which a person might be expected to sense if, under favourable conditions, he were to observe objects that are rhomboidal, or rectangular. Or we could identify sensing rhomboidally or sensing rectangularly with a way of sensing which is such that one *believes* it is the way in which rhomboidal or rectangular things appear when they are perceived under conditions which are optimal for perceiving them.

And what of the sort of thing the sense-datum philosopher is trying to describe when he says 'I sense a triangular red sense datum located to the left of a circular blue one'? We needn't coin an adverb to describe the situation. We could say merely: 'There is a way of appearing which is such that (i) it is the way one is appeared to under optimum conditions for perceiving that a red triangle is to the left of a blue circle and (ii) I am appeared to in that way.' Or, if we wish to capture the self-presenting factor in being thus appeared to, we might say: 'There is a way of appearing which is such that (i) I believe it to be the way one is appeared to under optimum conditions for perceiving that a red triangle is to the left of a blue circle and (ii) I am appeared to in that way.' This latter sentence, it should be noted, does not imply anything about the ways in which red triangles and blue circles actually do appear.

We may summarise this way of looking at appearing by saying that so-called appearances or sense-data are 'affections' or 'modifications' of the person who is said to experience them.[55] The sentences in which we seem to predicate properties of appearances can be paraphrased into other sentences in which we predicate properties only of the self or person who is said to sense those appearances. If this is correct, then appearances would be paradigm cases of what the scholastics called 'entia per alio' and what we might call 'ontological parasites'. They are not entities in their own right; they are 'parasitical upon' other things. And what they are parasitical *upon* are persons or selves. (We will return to this concept of an ontological parasite in Chapter III.)

It is interesting to note, in passing, that Hume himself criticises the view that appearances are modifications of persons or selves – and that, in doing so, he provides us with an excellent example of the sense-datum fallacy. First he notes the absurdity of Spinoza's view, according to which such things as the sun, moon and stars, and the earth, seas, plants, animals, men, ships and houses are in fact only 'modifications' of a single divine substance. And then he concludes that, if this Spinozistic view is absurd, then so, too, is the view that 'impressions' or 'ideas' are only modifications of the self. But in drawing this conclusion he seems clearly to have committed the sense-datum fallacy. For, he says, when I consider 'the universe of thought, or my impressions and ideas', I then 'observe *another* sun, moon, and stars and earth, and seas, covered and inhabited by plants and animals; towns, houses, mountains, rivers . . .' [56] In other words, if a real dog cannot be a modification of God, then an appearance of a dog cannot be a modification of me!

What is the reasoning behind the present way of interpreting appearances? For one thing, it seems to me, we multiply entities beyond necessity if we suppose that, in addition to the person who is in a state of undergoing or sensing, there is a certain *further* entity, a sense-datum or an appearance, which is the object of that undergoing or sensing. And for another thing, when we do thus multiply entities beyond necessity, we entangle ourselves in philosophical puzzles we might otherwise have avoided. ('Does the red sense-datum or appearance have a back side as well as a front side? Where is it located? Does it have any weight? What is it made of?')

And now we may return to the question that brought us to this consideration of appearances: 'Could it be that a man might be aware of himself as experiencing without thereby being aware of himself?' If what I have suggested is true, then the answer should be negative. For in being aware of ourselves as experiencing, we are, *ipso facto*, aware of the self or person – of the self or person, as being affected in a certain way.

This is not to say, of course, that we do not *also* perceive or observe external physical things. It is in virtue of the ways in which we are 'appeared to' by the familiar things around us, of the ways in which we are affected or modified by them, that we perceive them to be what they are. If, under the right conditions, the fields should appear green to me, then I would *see* the fields to be green.[57] And at the same time I could become directly aware of – immediately acquainted with – the fact that I myself am modified or affected in a certain way.

If what I have been saying is true, then there are two rather different senses in which we may be said to apprehend ourselves.

The first type of apprehension was what Hume himself reported – that *he* found heat or cold, that *he* found light or shade, and that *he* did not find himself, at least in the sense in which he found heat or cold and light or shade. He found, to repeat, that there was *someone* who found heat or cold, that this same someone found light or shade, and that this same someone did not in the same sense find himself. That we apprehend ourselves in this first sense would seem to be clear whatever view we may take about the nature of appearances, or of being appeared to.

And if the particular view of appearances that I have proposed is true, then we apprehend ourselves in still another sense. For if appearances, as I have said, are 'parasites upon' or 'modifications of' the one who is appeared to, then *what* one apprehends when one apprehends heat or cold, light or shade, love or hatred, is simply oneself. Whether one knows it or not, one apprehends *oneself* as being affected or modified.

The two points may be summarised by returning to the figure of the bundle theory. One may ask, with respect to any bundle of things, what is the nature of the bundle and what is the nature of the bundled. What is it that holds the particular items together, and what are the particular items that are thus held together? Now, according to the second of the two points that I have just made, the items within the bundle are nothing but states of the self or the person. And according to the first point, as we may now put it, what ties these items together is the fact that the same self or person apprehends them all. Hence, if these two points are both correct, the existence of particular bundles of perceptions presupposes in two rather different ways the existence of selves or persons that are not mere bundles of perceptions.

Referring to the view that the self is a substance, Hume said that we have no 'idea of self, after the manner it is here explain'd. For from what impression cou'd this idea be derived?' Might not the proper reply be this – that we can derive the idea of such a self from any impression whatever?[58]

CHAPTER II

AGENCY

Moreover, the particular and the individual are found in a more special and perfect way in rational substances, which have dominion over their own actions and which are not only acted upon, like others, but which can act of themselves. Actions belong to individuals. And thus among substances individuals of a rational nature have a special name: this name is person.

St Thomas Aquinas [1]

1 'He Could Have Done Otherwise'

Sometimes we refrain from doing things we could have done, and sometimes we do things we could have refrained from doing. What does it mean to say that one could thus do otherwise?

Suppose one were to say to a man: 'This morning you could have arranged things with the result that you would be in Boston now, but you didn't', meaning thereby that he had it within his power this morning so to arrange things, and that he did not exercise this power. How is one to understand this sense of 'could' and of 'in his power'?

First I shall note certain things we need *not* be implying when we thus say of a man that he could have done otherwise.

When we say that sometimes a man does things he could have refrained from doing, we do not imply that *everything* he does is something he could have refrained from doing. For many of the things we do are things we cannot help doing.

When we say, 'This morning you could have arranged things with the result that you would be in Boston now', we are not implying that the act in question was in any sense morally or legally *permissible*. For having said, 'You could have arranged things with the result that you would be in Boston now', we may add, quite consistently: 'And it is a very good thing that you didn't, since, as you well knew, that was about the worst thing you could have done this morning.' (In this case, one might *also* say, 'This morning you *could not* have done it', but taking 'could' in its moral or legal sense and not in the sense that now concerns us.)

Nor does 'He could have done it this morning', in our present sense of this expression, imply that the man was able to do this at any other time. Conceivably he will have had only one opportunity in his life to arrange things so that he would be in Boston now, or even to arrange things so that he would ever be in Boston. And so we are not predicating of him a 'general ability' to get to Boston, as one might say, in the case of a lady who lives in Newton.[2]

We are not implying that he *knew how* to exercise this power effectively. For we could consistently add: 'What a pity you didn't know you should have travelled toward the east, for had you done so you would be in Boston now.' (In this case, he may have known that he had the power without having known how to exercise it. For he may have known that he could travel in any direction and that one of them was such that if he were to travel in that direction, he would be in Boston now; but he may not have known which direction it was.) This point is essential to marking off the sense of 'could' and 'can' that is implied by 'ought'. Consider a man in the position of Jimmy Valentine, for whom it is imperative to open the safe in the shortest time possible: he has it directly within his power to turn the dials to any one of the 10,000 possible combinations within 10 seconds (there being 100 positions for the left dial and 100 for the right) but he has no idea at all of what the proper combination is. The man *could* turn the dials to the proper combination within 10 seconds; for if he undertook to set the dials to $L - 84$ and $R - 32$, then he would have the proper combination. But it would be unjust to say to him: 'You could have done it within 10 seconds; therefore you *ought* to have.'

When we say, of our agent, that he *could have* arranged things in a certain way, we are not implying, then, that he *knew that* he had the power. For 'He could have' does not imply that he knew that he could have. When we say, 'You could have arranged things with the result that you would be in Boston now', we may add, quite consistently: 'And what a pity that you had no idea at the time that you could have.' (In this case, although we can say 'You could have', we cannot say 'You could have if you had chosen'. The latter statement, as Kurt Baier points out, would be true only if the agent's success would be due to his 'skill, know-how, or practical knowledge, and not to luck'.[3] But we can say to the man who didn't realise that getting to Boston had been in his power: 'There were things such that, if you had chosen to bring *them* about, then you would be in Boston now.') Indeed, *most* of the things that are within our agent's power are things he knows nothing whatever about.

And let us take note of what we might call *the principle of the diffusiveness of power*. If being in Boston was within our agent's power, then *ipso facto* indefinitely many conjunctive states of affairs were also within his power – for example, that state of affairs which is his being in Boston and Boston being the capital of Massachusetts. For if he had it within his power to make it true that he is in Boston, then he also had it within his power to make true the conjunctive proposition that he is in Boston *and* Boston is the capital of Massachusetts.

Shall we say, then, that if a certain state of affairs *p* is within an agent's power, and if a certain other state of affairs *q* obtains, then the conjunction, *p&q*, is within the agent's power? The answer isn't entirely clear. What if it is in the power of *another* agent to prevent *q* from obtaining – and therefore to prevent the conjunction, *p&q*, from obtaining? Consider, for example, a second man who is now in Boston but who had it within his power this morning to arrange things in such a way that he would *not* now be in Boston. Was it within our first man's power this morning to arrange things in such a way that both men would be in Boston now? (This latter certainly was not 'entirely up to him'. But it may well be doubted whether *anything* is entirely up to him.) However these questions are to be answered, the following principle, at least, would seem to be true:

If (I) *q* is within s's power at *t*, (II) *p* occurs, and (III) not-*p* is not within the power of anyone other than s, then *p&q* is within s's power at *t*.

This principle, which is important to the theory of agency, might be called 'the principle of the diffusiveness of power'.

2 Some Unsatisfactory Answers

Let us remind ourselves of certain familiar but (so it seems to me) obviously unsuccessful attempts to explicate the present sense of 'could' and 'within his power'. In considering these attempts, we may contrast our original 'could have' statement, which we are assuming to be *true*, with a second 'could have' statement, which we will assume to be *false*. The second statement will be: 'This morning you could have arranged things with the result that you would be in Vladivostok now, but you didn't.' In this way we will be able to see that, whereas some of the proposed answers to our questions are overly restrictive, others are overly permissive. The restrictive ones will be those which are such that, if they were true, then this morning our man could *not* have arranged things in such a way that he would be in Boston now. The permissive ones will be those which are such that, if they were true, then this morning he *could* have arranged things in such a way that he would be in Vladivostok now.

We will consider five different ways of answering the question.

(i) Our 'could' is not the could of logical possibility. If it were, we could say of the man we are now considering, 'This morning he could have arranged things with the result that he would be in Vladivostok now', since what such a statement expresses is something that is logically possible. But the man *we* are considering could not have so arranged things this morning. Hence this first answer is too permissive.

(ii) Nor is our 'could' the 'could' of epistemic possibility. To say 'You could have arranged things with the result that you would be in Boston now' is not to say 'Your having so arranged things with the result that you would be in Boston now is consistent with everything that is known'.[4] For we may truly say that he *could* so have arranged things even though we know in fact that he did *not* so arrange them. Nor does 'You could so have arranged things this morning' mean the same as 'Your having arranged them this morning is consistent with everything that was known this morning'. Suppose that, unknown to everyone this morning, the man had been locked in his room, sound asleep and unable to move. In such a case it would be false to say that he could then have arranged things with the result that he would be in Boston now; but it might be true to say that his having so arranged them is consistent with everything that was known this morning.

(iii) Are we dealing, then, with a 'could' that is 'constitutionally iffy'? In saying 'You could have arranged things this morning so that you would be in Boston now', are we saying: 'If you had undertaken (chosen, willed, tried, set out) to bring it about that you are in Boston now, you would have succeeded.' No, for our agent might not have had the requisite information. Suppose, for example, he had been confused about directions. If he had undertaken to go to *Boston* he would have gone to New London. Yet he *could* have arranged things with the result that he would be in Boston. For if he had undertaken to go to New London, and he could have undertaken that, then he would be in Boston now.

Are we saying, then, something like this: 'There are certain things such that, if this morning he had undertaken (chosen, willed, tried, set out) to bring it about that those things would occur, then he would be in Boston now'? This formula, unlike the preceding one, could be applicable to the man who didn't know this morning that he could then arrange things so that he would be in Boston now.[5]

Whichever of the two types of 'if' statement we choose, there would seem to be things consistent with the 'if' statement that are not consistent with our 'could' statement. If this is true, the 'could' statement cannot have the same meaning as the 'if' statement. Consider, for example, those things which are such that, if this morning our agent had undertaken (chosen, willed, tried, set out) to bring them about, then he would be in Boston now. And let us suppose (i) that he *could not* have undertaken (chosen, willed, tried, set out) to bring any of those things about and (ii) that he would be in Boston now only if he *had* undertaken (chosen, willed, tried, set out) to bring them about. These suppositions are consistent with saying that he *would* be in Boston now *if* he had undertaken those things, but they are not consistent with saying that he *could* then have arranged things so that he would be in Boston now.[6]

There are, of course, many things we cannot even try or undertake to do. A man cannot undertake to pray or to swim if he doesn't know what it *is* to pray or to swim. For we cannot undertake to do a thing unless we have a concept of what it is to do that thing. Again, most of us cannot try to undertake certain things we find abhorrent – killing our friends or our families. At least, we cannot undertake these things without having some reason or motive *for* undertaking them. When such a reason or motive is lacking, the undertaking will not be within our power. Again, we all have repressions that prevent us from undertaking still other sorts of things.

Any theory of agency should be adequate to the fact that some undertakings are within our power and others are not. But the view that 'cans' and 'coulds' are constitutionally iffy – at least in the forms in which we have considered it – would seem not to be adequate to this fact.

We could say with von Wright: 'Although doing does *not* entail trying to do, it would seem that ability to do entails capacity for trying to do. If I *can do*, I also *can try*.'[7] Or we might say, more fully: although doing a given thing doesn't entail trying to do that thing, it does entail (in the present broad sense of 'try') trying to do *something*. For everything I can do, there is something I can try to do.

(iv) Is our 'could' the 'could' of physical possibility? Making use of the concept of *physical necessity* or *law of nature*, we may characterise physical possibility in the following way and distinguish it from the related concept of causal possibility:

D.II.1 p is *physically possible* $=$ Df It is not physically necessary that p does not occur.

D.II.2 p is *causally possible* $=$ Df There does not occur an event q such that it is physically necessary that, if q occurs, then p does not occur.

'Law of nature' may replace 'physically necessary' in these two definitions.

If we say that an event is physically possible, in the sense defined, we are saying that the event is one such that the assumption that it obtains is, by itself, consistent with the laws of nature. In *this* sense of 'physically possible', it is physically possible not only that our man this morning arranged things in such a way that he is in Boston now, but also that he then arranged them in such a way that he is in Vladivostok now. For one can hardly say that it is a *law of nature* that the man did not so arrange things. But although his arranging things in such a way that he would be in Vladivostok now is therefore 'physically possible' in the sense in question, it is quite certain that, in our present sense of 'could', the man *we* are talking about *could* not so have arranged things this morning.

(v) Let us consider causal possibility, then. If we say of an event that it is causally possible, where causal and physical possibility are distinguished in the way described above, we are saying in effect that there occurs *no sufficient causal condition* for the event in question *not* occurring. For the concept of sufficient causal condition may be understood in this way:

D.II.3 p is a *sufficient causal condition* of q $=$ Df p and q are events which are such that it is physically necessary but not logically necessary that, if p occurs at any time t, then q occurs at t or after t.

We have been assuming that our agent did *not* in fact arrange things with the result that he is in Boston now. Hence the suggestion that his arranging things was causally possible implies that there occurred a certain event this morning – the agent not making the arrangements in question – which is such that there occurred *no* sufficient causal condition for that event. And this would mean, in turn, that *determinism* is false (or, alternatively, that *indeterminism* is true). For determinism may be characterised this way:

D.II.4   Determinism =Df The proposition that, for every event that occurs, there occurs a sufficient causal condition of that event.

Is our 'could' thus one of simple indeterminism? In saying 'You could have arranged things with the result that you would be in Boston now', are we saying merely: 'Your *not* being in Boston now has no sufficient causal condition'? It would seem not. For it may well be that, although this morning the man could have arranged things so that he would be in Boston now, he has been in Chelmsford for the past fifteen minutes. And this will mean that for the past fifteen minutes, if not for considerably longer, there has occurred a set of conditions constituting a sufficient causal condition for his not being in Boston now.

Could we modify this indeterministic answer by saying: 'Even though for the past fifteen minutes there has occurred a sufficient causal condition for your not being in Boston now, there *was* a time (say, 10 o'clock this morning) when there occurred *no* sufficient causal condition for your not being in Boston now'? This, too, seems wrong. Suppose that between 9 and 11 o'clock this morning a certain *other* man had had it within *his* power, in this present indeterministic sense, to render our agent incapable of moving from the place where he then happened to be and that our agent was incapable of depriving him of this power; and suppose further that at 11 o'clock the other man exercised this power but without there occurring any sufficient causal condition for his so doing. These suppositions would be consistent with saying to our agent, 'At 10 o'clock this morning there occurred no sufficient causal condition for your not being in Boston now'. But they are not consistent with saying 'At 10 o'clock this morning you could have arranged things with the result that you would be in Boston now'.

We should remind ourselves, finally, that these indeterministic answers may be criticised in still another way. It is possible that there are cases of indeterminism that are not cases of ability to do otherwise. Suppose that an atomic particle is so situated that there is a place such that there has occurred no sufficient causal condition for the particle *not* now being in that place. This fact alone would hardly imply that the particle *could* have made it happen that it is now in a place other than where it is in fact.

3 A Proposed Solution

I suggest that any adequate analysis of what is intended by 'He could have done otherwise' must make use of the following three concepts: (a) that of *physical necessity*, expressible in the locutions '*p* is physically necessary' or '*p* is a law of nature', where the expression replacing '*p*' designates a state of affairs; (b) that of *causal contribution*, expressible in the locutions '*p* contributes causally to *q*' or 'the occurrence of *p* contributes causally to the occurrence of *q*'; and (c) that of *undertaking* or *endeavour*, expressible in the locutions '*s acts with the intention of* contributing causally to the occurrence of *p*' or '*s undertakes*, or *endeavours*, to contribute causally to the occurrence of *p*'. I will comment briefly on each of these concepts.

(a) It is generally agreed, I think, that the concept of physical necessity, or a law of nature, is fundamental to the theory of causation and, more generally, to the concept of nature. Some universal generalisations, expressible in the form, 'For every *x*, if *x* is F, then *x* is G' are nomic, or lawlike, and some are not. (A mark of a nomic, or lawlike, generalisation is the fact that the corresponding, singular counterfactual, 'If *a* were F, then *a* would be G', is also true.)[8] The lawlike generalisations may be said to express laws of nature – the physical necessity of certain states of affairs.

The physical necessity that pertains to states of affairs is analogous, in two fundamental respects, to the logical necessity that pertains to propositions. Thus we may say these two things about logical necessity: (i) if a proposition is logically necessary then it is true; and (ii) if a conditional proposition is logically necessary and if its antecedent is logically necessary, then its consequent is logically necessary. And we may say these two analogous things about physical necessity: (i) if a state of affairs is physically necessary then it occurs; and (ii) if a conditional state of affairs is physically necessary and if its antecedent is also physically necessary, then its consequent is physically necessary. But a state of affairs may be physically necessary, without it being logically necessary that that state of affairs occur. The latter point may be put by saying that the laws of nature of this world are not laws of nature in every possible world.

(b) The concept of *causal contribution* is to be distinguished from that of a *sufficient causal condition*. If *c* is a sufficient causal condition of *e*, then it is physically necessary that if *c* occurs then *e* occurs. But *c* may contribute causally to *e* without it being physically necessary that if *c* occurs then *e* occurs. If we say, for example, that the presence of oxygen in the room contributed causally to the fire, we do not imply that it is physically necessary, or a law of nature, that if there is oxygen in the room then there is a fire. A sufficient causal condition may be thought of as a conjunction of events. If it occurs, then some of its conjuncts may be said to contribute causally to its effect.[9] And so when we speak of one event *contributing causally* to another, we presuppose that the first event is a part of a sufficient causal condition of the second and that this sufficient causal condition in fact occurs.

(c) I will discuss *undertaking*, or *endeavouring*, in detail below. The concept in question is sometimes expressed by means of the word 'trying', as in the following quotation from G. E. Moore: 'That the bird's *body* moves away, owing to its wings moving in a certain way, is not *all* we mean by saying it *flies* away: as Wittgenstein says, if *I raise* my arm, something else happens *beside* that *my* arm is raised: that *I raise* it is a *Handlung*, and this is what we mean by saying that the raising is due to my *will*, though I neither *choose* nor *decide*. When I *choose* or *decide*, all that happens may be that I *try* to raise it.' [10] But our expression 'to undertake' should not be taken to connote the effort or the doubt that is sometimes associated with 'to try'.

Let us now turn to the analysis of 'He could have done otherwise'.

The 'could' that I will attempt to explicate is *indeterministic* in this respect: our definitions will imply, in effect, that if our agent had it within his power at 10 o'clock this morning to arrange things with the result that he would be in Boston now, then there were certain things such that at 10 o'clock this morning there had occurred no sufficient causal condition for his not then *undertaking* those things. (But presumably in the case of the undetermined subatomic particle, the absence of the equipment necessary for undertaking or endeavouring constitutes a sufficient causal condition for *its* not undertaking anything, and our definitions, therefore, will not apply to it.)

In addition to being thus indeterministic, our 'could' will also be constitutionally iffy. For the definitions will imply that *if* our agent had undertaken some of the things just referred to, and *if* further conditions, which I shall try to specify, had obtained, then he *would* be in Boston now. (We will not, however, make use of any contrary-to-fact conditional in the formulation of our definitions.)

What we say must be consistent with the possibility that, for the past fifteen minutes, there has occurred a sufficient causal condition for the fact that our agent has not been in Boston now.[11] To ensure this consistency I will attempt to make a technical distinction between what we may describe as being 'directly' in our agent's power and what we may describe as being 'indirectly' in his power. Thus he may have had it *directly* within his power at 10 o'clock this morning to take the first step in a journey towards Boston, but he may have had it only *indirectly* in his power then to arrange things with the result that he would be in Boston now. And perhaps, although he then had it directly within his power to take the first step, he had it only indirectly in his power to take the second, and only indirectly in his power to take any of the others. But he may have been so situated that, if he *had* taken the first step, then he *would* have had it directly within his power to take the second, and if he had then taken the second then he would have had it directly within his power to take the third, and so on, until he stepped into Boston. One could say that the first step 'directly enabled' him to take the second (since taking the first put taking the second directly within his power) and that each step, had he continued the journey, would have directly enabled him to take the next.

I shall formulate three definitions: first, a definition of what it is for our agent to be *free to undertake* a certain activity; second, a definition of what it is for a state of affairs to be *directly within his power*; and third, a definition of the more general concept of what it is for a state of affairs to be *within his power*. By making use of the third of these definitions, we will be able to explicate 'He could have done otherwise' as 'Doing otherwise was within his power'.

Our first definition, then, will be this:

> D.II.5   s is *free at t to undertake* p =Df There is a period of time which includes, but begins before, t and during which there occurs no sufficient causal condition either for s undertaking p or for s not undertaking p.

Why not say, more simply, that the agent is free to undertake p provided only there is no sufficient causal condition for his *not* undertaking p? The answer is suggested by St Thomas, in commenting on Aristotle's remark that 'where it is in our power to act it is also in our power not to act, and vice versa'. St Thomas writes: 'If the capacity to act is within us, the capacity not to act must also be in our power. If the capacity not to act were not in our power, it would be impossible that we would not act. Therefore, it would be necessary that we act, and so the capacity to act would not come from us but from necessity.'[12]

The things that are directly within a man's power are his free undertakings and anything that *they* would cause. If a state of affairs is directly within an agent's power, then something he is free to undertake is such that his undertaking it would bring about that state of affairs. In other words:

D.II.6 p is directly within s's power at t =Df There is a q such that: s is free at t to undertake q; and either (a) p is s undertaking q or (b) there occurs an r at t such that it is physically necessary that, if r and s-undertaking-q occur, then s-undertaking-q contributes causally to p.[13]

Perhaps we should remind ourselves that, when we say 'there *is* a q such that he is free to undertake q', we do not mean that q *occurs*, or *obtains*. For many of the states of affairs that our agent is free to undertake are states of affairs that do *not* occur or obtain.[14]

It may be that our agent is free, in the sense just defined, to undertake to get himself to the piano. It may also be that, if he were now to undertake to get to the piano, then he would cause himself to be three feet closer to Boston. Our definition would allow us to say, therefore, that getting three feet closer to Boston is now directly within his power. But if he does not know that there is such a place as Boston, then he will not know that getting three feet closer to Boston is directly in his power. Or if he knows that there is such a place but does not know where it is, then he may know that getting three feet closer to Boston is directly in his power (for he knows that going three feet in any direction is directly in his power) but he may not know what it is that he needs to undertake. It is quite possible, therefore, that, although there are various things such that his undertaking any one of them would get him three feet closer to Boston, his undertaking to get three feet closer to Boston is not among them.

Unless our agent is very close indeed to Boston, it is not likely that getting to Boston is directly within his power in the sense just defined. But there is a clear sense in which it may be *indirectly* within his power. For, as we have noted, if he takes the first step, which is directly within his power, then he will put taking the second step directly within his power, and if he takes the second, then taking the third will become directly within his power, and so on until the trip is completed. Each step, as we have said, directly enables him to take the next.

Our example should suggest, then, how to explicate the broader concept of being *either directly or indirectly in one's power* – or, as we may put it more simply, the concept of *being within one's power*. Roughly, we may say that a state of affairs is within our agent's power if it is one of a series of states of affairs such that the first is directly within his power and each of the others is such that it would be made possible by its predecessor. More exactly:

> D.II.7 p is within s's power at t =Df p is a member of a series such that (i) the first is directly within s's power at t and (ii) each of the others is such that its predecessor in the series is a sufficient causal condition of its being directly within his power.

Since a series of states of affairs may have just one member, our definition allows us to say, as obviously we should be able to say, that the things that are thus within an agent's power include the things that are directly within his power.

To understand what these concepts involve, let us change our example for the moment. We may imagine an oversized grasshopper who finds himself in an uncomfortable situation in Cleveland. He has it directly within his power at 2 o'clock to jump in one or the other of two different directions; if he jumps in the one direction, he will land in Chicago at 2:05, and if he jumps in the other direction, he will land in Detroit at 2:05. We will suppose, then, that these two states of affairs – landing in Chicago at 2:05 and landing in Detroit at 2:05 – are each *directly* within his power at 2. Let us suppose further that if he were to bring it about that he is in Chicago at 2:05, he would then have it directly within his power to be in Minneapolis at 2:10 and he would also have it directly within his power to be in St Louis at 2:10. But if he were to bring it about that he is in Detroit at 2:05, then he would have it directly within his power to bring it about that he is in Toronto at 2:10 and also to bring it about that he is in Buffalo at 2:10. Hence among the states of affairs that are within his power at 2 o'clock, but not then directly within his power, are these: being in Minneapolis at 2:10; being in St Louis at 2:10; being in Toronto at 2:10; and being in Buffalo at 2:10. Our definition of 'within his power' is intended to be adequate to this type of situation.

We will now try to illustrate the definition with respect to just the last of these possibilities: it is within the power of the grasshopper at 2 o'clock to arrange things in such a way that he will be in Buffalo at 2:10. We may say that, in accordance with the terms of the definition, this last state of affairs – his being in Buffalo at 2:10 – is the final member of a series of three states of affairs which are such that: the first is directly within the grasshopper's power at 2 o'clock; the first would be a sufficient causal condition of the second; and the second would be a sufficient causal condition of the third.

What would be the first and second members of this series? It would not be enough to say, of the first member of the series, merely that it is the grasshopper being in Detroit at 2:05; for the first must be a sufficient causal condition of the second. And it will not be enough to say of the second merely that it is the grasshopper jumping toward the south-east at 2:06; for the second must be a sufficient causal condition of the third. The second state of affairs could be expressed only in a long conjunctive statement, one that included information about the force and speed of the jump and the flight conditions between Detroit and Chicago. And the first state of affairs would be even more extensive, for it would include enough to constitute a sufficient causal condition for the second.

But isn't there a difficulty in supposing that such comprehensive states of affairs as these are within the power of the grasshopper – and that the first one, the most comprehensive of the three, is *directly* within his power? Let us remind ourselves of what we have called the principle of the diffusiveness of power:

If (I) q is within s's power at t, (II) p occurs, and (III) not-p is not within the power of anyone other than s, then $p \& q$ is within s's power at t.

If being in Detroit by 2:05 is directly within the grasshopper's power at 2 o'clock, then so, too, is that comprehensive state of affairs we have imagined to be the first member of our series of three.

What do we mean, then, when we say to a man, 'This morning you could have arranged things in such a way that you would be in Boston now, but you didn't do so'? We mean that, although the man did not make it happen this morning that he had so arranged things, nevertheless it was then within his power so to arrange them. The 'could' is constitutionally iffy, as may be seen by unpacking D.II.7, and the proposed explication is consistent with saying that, for some time now, there has been a sufficient causal condition for the agent's *not* being in Boston now. But the 'could' is also indeterministic. For we are saying that this morning the man was free to undertake such arrangements. And this means, according to D.II.5, that there was no sufficient causal condition for his undertaking them at that time and also no sufficient causal condition for his not undertaking them at that time.

4 Freedom and Indeterminism

I have said that, if there is anything that is within an agent's power, then there is something that he is 'free to undertake' – there is something such that there occurs no sufficient causal condition for his undertaking it and there occurs no sufficient causal condition for his not undertaking it. I have not used the expression 'free will', for the question of freedom, as John Locke said, is not the question 'whether the will be free'; it is the question 'whether a man be free'.[15] The question is whether the man is free to undertake any of those things he does *not* undertake and whether he is free not to undertake any of those things he *does* undertake.

Nor is the metaphysical question of freedom: 'Is the man free to bring about what it is that he undertakes to bring about?' Using the verb 'to will' where I have used 'to undertake', Jonathan Edwards and other philosophers have tried to restrict the question of freedom to 'Is the man free to do what it is that he wills to do?' and then to answer the question affirmatively by pointing out that on occasion people do do the things that they will to do (that on occasion people do bring about what it is that they undertake to bring about).[16] Using St Thomas's terms, we could say that these philosophers have restricted themselves to questions about the success of the *actus voluntatis imperatus*; they have tried to bypass the more fundamental question of the freedom of the *actus voluntatis elicitus*.[17] They have asked 'Do we ever bring about the things we will?' but not 'Are we free to will the things we will?'

But we have spoken of undertakings or endeavours rather than of acts of will. Our basic intentional locution is:

s undertakes (endeavours) at t to contribute causally to the occurrence of p.

If we carry St Thomas's distinction over into our terminology, we may say that, on any occasion when an instance of this expression is true, the object of the *actus elicitus* is the undertaking or endeavour itself, and the object of the *actus imperatus* is the agent contributing causally to that state of affairs which is p. In D.II.5 we have defined the freedom of the *actus elicitus* – what it is to be free to undertake something.

This freedom, we have said, is essentially indeterministic: there occurs no sufficient causal condition for the agent undertaking that thing and there occurs no sufficient causal condition for his not undertaking it.

One familiar objection to any such indeterministic account may be put this way: '(i) According to your account, if anything is ever within anyone's power, then certain events occur which are not preceded or accompanied by any sufficient causal conditions. But (ii) if an act which is within an agent's power is thus indeterministic, it is not possible for another person to exert any influence upon such an act. Yet (iii) we do exert influence upon the actions of other people, including those actions they could have refrained from performing. We do this, for example, by giving them motives or reasons. And so (iv) your theory is false.'

The error in the argument lies in the second premise: 'if human action is thus indeterministic, it is not possible for us to exert any influence upon the actions of other people'. Let us consider once again our oversized grasshopper who found himself in an unbearable situation in Cleveland and was thus compelled to jump – either toward Chicago or toward Detroit. Let us now imagine further that *we* compelled him to jump. Had we not made it unbearable for him in Cleveland he would have remained where he was. But we brought about a sufficient causal condition for his jumping. Now saying that there occurred a sufficient causal condition for his jumping is entirely consistent with saying that there occurred *no* sufficient causal condition for his jumping in the direction he did jump. Perhaps there were only two things he was able to do – to jump toward the west or to jump toward the north – and we compelled him to choose between those alternatives. But if each of them was within his power we did not compel him to jump toward the west and we did not compel him to jump toward the north. In controlling his behaviour, we restricted his options, but we left him with two.

One way, then, of affecting another person's behaviour is to restrict his options. We prevent him from making choices he otherwise could have made. We may indeed thus cause him to act in a certain general way and leave the further particulars up to him – as we caused the grasshopper to jump and left him with the choice of north or west.

But *restricting* his options is not the only way we can affect another person's free behaviour. We can also affect him by *enabling* him to do what he otherwise could not have done. For if he then does what we have enabled him to do, we have brought about some *necessary* causal condition of his act.

I have said that one event is a *sufficient* causal condition of another provided it is physically necessary (or a law of nature) that, if the first event occurs, then the second occurs, either at the same time or later. We may also say, analogously, that one event is a necessary causal condition of another provided it is physically necessary (or a *law of nature* that, if the second has occurred, then the first has also occurred, either at the same time or before). The definition is:

> D.II.8 *p* is a *necessary causal condition* of *q* =Df *p* and *q* are events such that it is physically necessary but not logically necessary that, if *q* occurs at any time *t*, then *p* occurs at *t* or prior to *t*.

Now even if a man's undertaking has no sufficient causal condition, it has indefinitely many necessary causal conditions, indefinitely many conditions each of which is a *sine qua non* of his undertaking what he does.

Our abilities are thus necessary causal conditions of what we do. Therefore if you provide me with the necessary *means* for getting to Boston, means without which I wouldn't have been able to get there, then, if I do go there, you can be said to have contributed causally to what I do. And this will be true even though my undertaking the trip had no sufficient causal conditions. Or perhaps I could not have undertaken the trip unless I had thought it would involve something pleasurable or worthwhile. If now you had persuaded me that the trip *would* be pleasurable or worthwhile, then you gave me a *motive* or *reason* for going, a motive or reason without which I would not have been able to undertake the trip. And so, once again, if I did go, then you contributed causally to my act even though there occurred no sufficient causal condition for my doing what I did. This last example makes clear one way in which our reasons and motives can be said to contribute causally to what we do.

And, of course, I can also affect *my own* subsequent free behaviour in these ways. Thus with every act I perform, I restrict my subsequent activity. (At 2 o'clock our grasshopper could have arranged to be in any one of four different places by 2:10. But when he took the first step, he eliminated two of the possibilities, and when he took the second step, he eliminated still another.) Moreover, in planning ahead and taking preliminary steps, I *enable* myself to do things I otherwise could not have done. I may even supply myself with reasons and motives by trying to ensure that the subsequent act, if it is performed, will be pleasureable or worthwhile.

Let us remind ourselves that I can *have* a reason or motive for doing a certain thing even though I do *not* undertake to do that thing. This is evident from the fact that, in the case of any difficult decision, I may have reasons both *pro* and *con*. In such cases, whatever choice I make, I will have had reasons or motives for doing something else instead. And these reasons or motives, as Leibniz said, can 'incline but not necessitate'.

What would it be for a reason or motive to incline but not necessitate? We could say that a man's desire for a certain state of affairs *p* is one that *inclines but does not necessitate* provided these conditions hold: he desires *p*; it is not within his power to undertake not-*p*; but it is within his power not to undertake *p*. Consider a public official of this sort: (a) his scruples are sufficiently strong that he would never undertake to bring it about that he is offered a bribe; but (b) his desire for money is sufficiently strong that, if he were offered a bribe, he would be unable to refuse it. His desire for money could be said to incline but not necessitate. He can prevent himself from bringing about the tempting state of affairs, but if it presents itself he will be unable to resist it. The situation is, of course, a familiar one and is one reason why people pray to be delivered from temptation. Kant remarks: 'And how many there are who may have led a long blameless life, who are only *fortunate* in having escaped so many temptations.' [18]

5 *The Agent as Cause*

What is it for an *agent* to bring about a state of affairs?

Sometimes a distinction is made between 'event causation' and 'agent causation' and it has been suggested that there is an unbridgeable gap between the two. But if we take the standard concept of 'event causation' – the concept of one event contributing causally to another – along with the concept of undertaking, or endeavouring, then we can say what it is for an agent to contribute causally to the occurrence of an event or state of affairs.

The concept of event causation, as we have said, may be expressed in the locution '*p* contributes causally to *q*' – or, if one prefers, 'the occurrence of *p* contributes causally to the occurrence of *q*'.[19] (The latter locution has the advantage of enabling us to say 'the occurrence of *p* at *t* contributes causally to the occurrence of q at t'; but for simplicity we will ignore such temporal references in much of what follows.)

In terms of event causation, so considered, and our undefined concept of undertaking, we may now define agent causation.

We will say first that, if a man's undertaking contributes causally to something, then the man *does* something which contributes causally to that something:

> D.II.9   s does something at t which contributes causally to p =Df There is a q such that s's undertaking q at t contributes causally to p.

Given the concept just defined, let us now attempt to characterise a broader concept of agent causation that we may express by saying 's contributes causally to p'. We wish to construe this broader concept in such a way that we may say each of these things:

(a) If a person does something that contributes causally to p, then *he* contributes causally to p.[20]
(b) If a person undertakes something, then he contributes causally to his undertaking that something.
(c) If a person does something that contributes causally to p, then he contributes causally to his thus doing something that contributes causally to p.

I would propose, then, the following definition of this broader concept of agent causation:

> D.II.10   s contributes causally at t to p =Df Either (a) s does something at t that contributes causally to p, or (b) there is a q such that s undertakes q at t and s-undertaking-q is p, or (c) there is an r such that s does something at t that contributes causally to r, and p is that state of affairs which is s doing something that contributes causally to r.

(Should we also be able to say that the agent contributes causally to some of his own *omissions*? We will provide for this possibility in the following section.)

We assume that, if a state of affairs p occurs and if an agent s contributes causally to a *necessary* causal condition of p, then s contributes causally to p. This fact, as we have noted, enables us to say that an agent may contribute causally to subsequent free actions of other agents and of himself.

We may now formulate and reply to still another familiar objection to the type of theory here defended. The objection is:

'Your account presupposes that there are certain events which men, or agents, cause to happen. Suppose, then, that on a certain occasion a man does cause an event p to happen. What now of *that* event – that event which is his thus causing p to happen? Your account implies that there occurs no sufficient causal condition for his causing p to happen. Will you say, then, that it's not caused by anything at all? But if you say that, then how can you ever hold *him* responsible for his causing an event to happen?'

The answer to this objection will be clear if we consider certain schematic theorems about agency. The theorems are consequences of: the ontology of events and states of affairs we have presupposed; the interpretation we have given to the undefined concept of undertaking; and what we have said about event causation.

T1 If s contributes causally to p, then p.

T2 If s does something that contributes causally to p, then s contributes causally to his doing something that contributes causally to p.

T3 If s contributes causally to p, then there exists a q such that s undertakes q.

T4 If s undertakes p, then s contributes causally to s undertaking p.

But the following principles, it should be noted, are *not* consequences of what we have said:

If s undertakes p, then p.

If s contributes causally to p, then s undertakes p.

If s undertakes p, then s undertakes s's undertaking p.

And so we may reply to the above objection by saying this: 'If a man does something that causes a certain event p to happen, then, *ipso facto,* he contributes causally to his doing something that causes that event p to happen. It is a mistake, therefore, to say that nothing causes his causing that event to happen.'

The schematic letters in our formulae, then, may be replaced by expressions designating actions; e.g. 'His raising his arm', 'His stealing the money', and 'His breaking his promise'.[21] And we may say that, whenever an agent performs such an act, he contributes causally to the fact that he performs that act.

I believe that Suarez would agree with us on this point. He says: 'If we understand the term "effect" so that it includes not only the thing produced, but also everything that flows from the power of the agent, then we may say that the action itself is in a certain sense the effect of the agent.' [22]

But one may object: 'What you say means that, no matter what I do, I have to bring myself to do it. Some things, yes, I do have to bring myself to do, but not everything.' To answer this objection, perhaps it is enough to note that, although we are saying that the agent causes his undertakings, we are not saying that he undertakes his undertakings ('. . . to say I can will if I will, I take to be an absurd speech'.) [23] But we will consider this objection more fully below, after distinguishing means and ends.

We next introduce an expression fundamental to the theory of agency:

> D.II.11   By contributing causally at t to p, s contributes
> causally at t to q =Df s contributes causally at t to p,
> and that event which is s contributing causally at t
> to p also contributes causally to q.

Thus we may say that, by contributing causally to the replenishment of the water-supply, the worker contributed causally to the household being poisoned. The second clause of the definiens ('that event which is s contributing causally to p contributes causally to q') assures us that things needn't be the other way around. We needn't say that, by contributing causally to the household being poisoned, the worker contributed causally to the replenishment of the water-supply. We may also say that, by contributing causally (by making it happen) that his hand was extended out the car window, the driver contributed causally to his signalling. And to say this is *not* to say that his extending his hand out the window caused him to signal. Other replacements for 'p' and 'q', respectively, might be: 'His jumping 6 feet 3 inches' and 'His outjumping George'; 'His moving his Queen to King-knight 7' and 'His checkmating his opponent'; and 'His trying to save Jones's life' and 'His doing his duty'.[24] (It should be noted, in connection with the final example, that one of the consequences of what we have said is that an agent contributes causally to his own undertakings.)

We next comment briefly on those acts that are deliberate omissions.

6 A Note on Deliberate Omission
Doesn't a person also contribute causally to some of his own *omissions* – those omissions he may be said deliberately to com-

mit? Suppose one man greets another and the second man does not respond. If the second man was unaware of the fact that he was addressed by the first, then his failure to respond may have been a mere omission. But if he intended to snub the first man, to insult him by failing to respond to his greeting, then he could be said to have *committed the omission*; he omitted the act *deliberately*.

We may characterise deliberate omission in this way:

> D.II.12   s deliberately omits undertaking p at t =Df s considers at t undertaking p and s does not undertake p at t.

(Here we appeal once again to the concept of *considering*, or *entertaining*, a state of affairs – a concept that is essential to any adequate theory of thought.)

Now our definition D.II.9, above, of 's does something that contributes causally to p', does not cover those cases in which a person s may be said to do something by committing an omission. But if we choose, we may remedy this defect by replacing D.II.9 by the following:

> D.II.9.1   s does something at t which contributes causally to p =Df There is a q which is such that either (a) s undertaking q at t contributes causally to p, or (b) s deliberately omits q at t and p is that state of affairs which is s deliberately omitting q.

If we make use of this revised definition, then we may say, in accordance with D.II.10, that s contributes causally to his own deliberate omissions and to their results. (He may be *morally* responsible for the results of some of his non-deliberate, or uncommitted omissions – those omissions he should not have made. But, I assume, it would not be accurate to say that he is *causally* responsible for such results.)[25]

Let us now look more closely at positive endeavour.

7 *Endeavouring*

What more can we say about the nature of undertaking or endeavouring? 'He undertakes p' abbreviates the longer locution: 'He undertakes to contribute causally to the occurrence of p.' We have noted that, for the word 'undertakes', in this undefined locution, we may substitute 'endeavours'. Or we may read the locution, perhaps more naturally, as

He acts with the intention of contributing causally to the occurrence of p.

This latter formulation may be the least misleading. For it does not suggest a conscious effort (as does 'endeavour') and it does not suggest commitment (as does 'undertake'). Using this formulation, then, let us make some general points about the meaning of our intentional locution. We will permit ourselves the shorter form:

He acts with the intention of bringing about p.

Let us note, first, that a person may act with the intention of bringing about a given state of affairs without feeling any *desire, urge* or *compulsion* to bring about that state of affairs. The ordinary things we try to bring about from one moment to another are not themselves objects of felt wants or desires. One may act with the intention of getting across the street without being troubled or titillated by any *desire* to get across the street.[26]

Secondly: from the fact that a man acts with the intention of bringing about a certain state of affairs, it does not follow that that state of affairs occurs or ever will occur, and therefore it does not follow that the man's act is a success. ('Hobbes acted with the intention of bringing it about that he square the circle.')

Thirdly: if a man acts with the intention of bringing about a certain state of affairs, then there *is* a certain state of affairs he is acting with the intention of bringing about. ('There is a certain impossible state of affairs such that Hobbes and others have acted with the intention of bringing them about.')

Fourthly: from the facts that (i) there is a certain state of affairs p such that a man acts with the intention of bringing it about that p occurs, and (ii) that state of affairs p entails or includes a certain other state of affairs q, and furthermore (iii) the man in question knows or believes that p entails q and (iv) he is completely rational, it does *not* follow that (v) he acts with the intention of bringing it about that q occurs. One might speak here of '*the principle of the nondivisiveness of intention*'. Suppose a man who is completely rational acts with the intention of bringing about that state of affairs which is his being in Washington while the President is there and that he knows that that state of affairs entails the President being in Washington. It may well be that the man does not thereby act with the intention of bringing it about that the President be in Washington. In this respect, intending is like desiring, hoping, fearing, doubting and wondering, and unlike knowing and believing.

The fifth point is closely related to the fourth and presents, so to speak, the other side of the coin. If a rational man *believes* that he is about to visit Washington and if he knows that the President will then be there, then he will also believe that he will visit Washington while the President is there. May we make an analogous point about *intending*? If a man acts with the intention of bringing it about that he will visit Washington and if he knows that the President will be there, does he act with the intention of bringing about that state of affairs which is his being in Washington while the President is there? It seems to me that the answer is yes.

I would say that, if a rational man acts with the intention of bringing about a certain state of affairs p and if he believes that by bringing about p he will bring about the conjunctive state of affairs, p and q, then he *does* act with the intention of bringing about the conjunctive state of affairs, p and q.[27] One might speak here of 'the principle of the diffusiveness of intention', and note the analogy with our earlier principle of the diffusiveness of power.

Thus if a man acts with the intention of bringing it about that he drive off in the car that is parked on the corner and if he knows that the car that is parked on the corner belongs to another man, then he acts with the intention of bringing it about that he drive off in the car that is parked on the corner and belongs to another man. But we should remind ourselves of the fourth point above: in saying that he acts with the intention of bringing it about that he drive off in the car that is parked on the corner and belongs to another man, we are *not* committed to saying that he acts with the intention of bringing it about that he drive off in a car that belongs to another man. This point is relevant, of course, to the problem of distinguishing those consequences which are intended from those which are *consented to but not intended*. (Our man might plead: 'I didn't intend to steal. If I drove off in a car that belonged to someone else, that was only a *side effect* of what I was doing.' Most thieves, of course, would be equally justified in entering such a plea.)

Finally, what of our *awareness* of our endeavours? Do we always know what it is that we are undertaking? The question may be taken in two ways.

One might take it to be: 'When we undertake a certain state of affairs, do we thereby think about that state of affairs and our undertaking it – do we take note of and contemplate these things?' The answer to this question is obviously 'No'. Most of the things we undertake in the course of our daily activities we don't take note of or contemplate at all.

But in asking whether we are always aware of our endeavours one might mean this: 'When we undertake a certain state of affairs are we in a *position* to know that we are undertaking that state of affairs?' And the answer to *this* question, I suggest, is 'Yes'. If I am in fact undertaking to bring about a certain state of affairs *p*, and if I think about the question whether I *am* then undertaking *p*, then I can know, directly and immediately, that I am undertaking *p*.

Given the concepts that we have here been concerned to explicate, we could reformulate the last point as follows: if a man is undertaking a certain state of affairs *p*, and if it is directly within his power to consider or entertain the proposition that he is undertaking that state of affairs *p*, then it is also directly within his power then to make it immediately and directly evident to himself that he is undertaking *p*.

Thus many of our undertakings could be said to be 'unconscious' in that we do not contemplate or think about them. But we are, presumably, always in a position to know what they are – and in this sense they differ from those drives that are said to be 'subconscious'.

8 Purposive Activity

We are now in a position to look somewhat more deeply into the structure of purposive activity and into some of the philosophical questions to which this concept gives rise.

Let us begin with the distinction between means and ends:

> D.II.13 s undertakes *p* and does so for the purpose of bringing about *q* = Df s undertakes to bring about (i) *p* and (ii) his-undertaking-*p* contributing causally to *q*.

We may also say that s undertakes *p* as a *means* to bringing about *q*. We will assume that, if he thus undertakes one thing as a means to a second thing, then he also undertakes the second thing. Suppose a man is trying to blow up the palace and his purpose in so doing is to bring about the death of the king. He has two intentional objects, one of them subordinate to the other. In such a case he is undertaking to blow up the palace and doing so (i.e. undertaking this) *for the purpose of* bringing about the death of the king. To say that he does this is not to say that he succeeds – either in blowing up the palace or in bringing about the death of the king.

A simpler definition would be obtained if the above definiens were revised to read:

s undertakes to bring about that state of affairs which is: (i) p and (ii) p contributing causally to q.

To see the disadvantage of this simpler definition, we should consider a somewhat different type of case. Consider a man who dislodges a stone at the top of the hill and aims it toward a certain cabin below. He endeavours to bring it about that the stone will hit the cabin, but his purpose in so doing is to bring it about that the stone traverses a certain intermediate place between himself and the cabin. (The only way he can assure himself that the stone *will* traverse this intermediate place is by assuring himself that the stone will hit the cabin.) We may say, of this situation, that the agent undertook to destroy the cabin in order that the stone would traverse a certain area. Or, in our terminology, he undertook to make it happen that the cabin was destroyed and did so for the purpose of making it happen that the stone traversed a certain area. But the simpler definition would not capture this situation. The simpler definition would require us to say that he undertook to make it happen that the cabin was destroyed and that the destruction of the cabin would cause the stone to traverse the area in question. But the destruction of the cabin, as he knew, would be subsequent to the traversal of the area and therefore, being rational, he was not undertaking to make the destruction of the cabin cause the traversal of the area. What he was undertaking to do was, rather, to bring about that his endeavour to destroy the cabin would bring about the traversal of the area.[28] This is why we need the more complex definition.

Other examples of this need are provided by the following: the man who undertakes to bring it about that a tree will grow next year for the purpose of collecting his pay next week; and the man who undertakes to make his arm go up for the purpose of activating those causes in his brain that will bring it about that his arm goes up.

Causation, then, is an essential part of the *object* of purposive activity. If we intend one thing as a means to another, then we intend that a certain causal relation obtain. But we should not misconstrue the *way* in which causation thus enters into the object of intention. Annette Baier has proposed this objection to a version of the above definition: 'I intend to examine Chisholm's definition of purposive activity in order to test the adequacy of his assumptions. Do I, therefore, intend that my examining it shall causally contribute to my testing the assumptions? . . . No causal chain runs from the examination to the test. What is needed if my examination is to serve my purpose, is that it *count* as a test, not that it cause a test.'[29] But the definition does not require us to say that the *examining* is intended to cause the testing.[30] It requires us to say, rather, that her *undertaking* the examining is intended to cause the testing. If the act is successful, then that event which is her undertaking to make an examination will contribute causally to that event which is a test being performed. To be sure, if the examination itself *counts as* a test, then the *examination* does not thereby contribute causally to the test. But whatever contributes causally to the occurrence of the examination *does* thereby contribute causally to the occurrence of the test.[31] And, if the act is successful, then the undertaking does contribute causally to the examining and therefore also to the test.

The expression we have just been considering – 's undertakes *p* and does so for the purpose of bringing about *q*'– is intentional with respect to both variables; it does not imply that either of the states of affairs, *p* or *q*, obtains. But the following expression is intentional only with respect to the second variable: 's contributes causally to *p* for the purpose of bringing about *q*.' This concept is, of course, readily reducible to the terms we have been using.[32]

We may now consider once again an objection alluded to above. The objection may be put this way: 'Your view commits you to saying that, whenever a man makes anything happen, then he makes it happen that he makes that thing happen. But that is absurd. To be sure, there are *some* occasions on which I may cause myself to do something. Tonight I may leave a reminder on the table in order to bring it about that I will do a certain thing tomorrow. But ordinarily I do not need to act on myself in this way. Ordinarily I do *not* thus cause myself to do the things I do; I just do them. And so you are certainly mistaken in saying that, whenever a man makes a certain thing happen, he makes it happen that he makes that thing happen.'[33]

When a man thus leaves a reminder on the table, he does something for the purpose of influencing himself to do a certain other thing later. It is true to say that, in *that* sense, a man does not ordinarily cause himself to do the things he does. For a man's ordinary actions are such that it is usually not necessary for him to do *other* things for the purpose of causing it to happen that he performs those acts. As we have just seen, it is one thing to say merely that a man makes a certain event *p* happen, and it is quite another thing to say that he makes something happen for the purpose of making *p* happen. From the fact that he makes *p* happen, it does not follow that he makes anything happen for the purpose of making p happen. And so a man may make it happen that he performs a certain action without thereby doing anything for the purpose of causing himself to perform that action. Therefore, from the fact that most acts are such that the agent does not do anything for the purpose of causing himself to get them done, it does not follow that there are certain things a man makes happen without thereby making it happen that he makes those things happen.

Any account of purposive activity ought to be adequate to the following distinctions. Thus (1) there are certain things we bring about merely in order to bring about certain other things; we submit to an unpleasant remedy, for example, for the sake of a subsequent cure. (2) There are certain things we bring about 'for their own sakes', or 'for themselves alone'; certain pleasurable activities are obvious examples. And it would seem that (3) on occasion there are certain things we undertake *both* in order to bring about still other things *and also* as 'ends in themselves' or 'for their own sakes'. Deprecating amusement as an end in itself, Aristotle quotes Anacharsis who said that it is proper 'to amuse oneself in order that one may exert oneself'.[34]

Suppose a man could choose between two ways of bringing it about that he could exert himself later: one of them a regimen indifferent in itself and the other a matter of amusing himself, and the two methods being equally harmless. In such a case, a reasonable man would be likely to choose the second method: he would amuse himself for the sake of amusing himself and also for the sake of exerting himself later. Again, of two medicines that are equally effective, a reasonable man would choose the one that is pleasant rather than the one that is not – in which case, he would take the pleasant medicine partly just for the sake of taking the medicine and partly for the sake of the subsequent cure.[35]

Were it not for the third category, those things we bring about both for their own sakes and also for the sake of certain other things as well, we could formulate a relatively simple definition of bringing about something for its own sake. We could say merely that those things we undertake to bring about for the sake of other things are those things which we undertake to bring about for the purpose of bringing about some other thing; and then we could say that those things we undertake to bring about for their own sakes are those things which we undertake to bring about, but which we do not undertake to bring about for the purpose of bringing about some other thing. But such a definition would not allow us to say that a man takes a pleasant medicine both for the sake of taking it and also for the sake of the subsequent cure.

A man undertakes one thing as a *means* to another, we have said, if he undertakes the one thing for the purpose of bringing about the other. But what he undertakes as a means he may not undertake *merely* as a means, since of the various ways of bringing about a given end, he may choose the one he feels to be worth pursuing on its own account. Of the various ways of preserving his health, a man may choose walking on the ground that it is worth doing for its own sake, whereas taking an unpleasant medicine would not be worth doing for its own sake. Where the means is thus something that is also chosen for its own sake, the agent undertakes a certain causal chain, not only in order that the final member of that chain be realised, but *also* in order that one of the earlier members be realised. But where a thing p is a mere means, it is a part of a causal chain that the agent is undertaking – and he is not undertaking the causal chain for the purpose of bringing about p. Let us say, then:

> D.II.14 p is for s a *mere means* to something else $=$ Df (i) There is a q such that p is for s a means to q and (ii) for every r, if p is for s a means to r, then it is false that s undertakes r for the purpose of bringing about p.[36]

The ultimate goal or end of a man's activity at any time, then, is something that he then undertakes but does not undertake as a mere means.

> D.II.15 p is an *ultimate end* or *end in itself* for s $=$ Df (i) s undertakes p and (ii) it is false that p is for s a mere means to something else.

Thus if walking is undertaken, not only as a means to health but as an ultimate end or end in itself, then the agent undertakes a certain chain of events, not only in order that he may be healthy, but also in order that he may walk.

In considering the morality of intention, we may wish to distinguish between the preliminary steps that a man makes toward a certain goal (his goal, say, is the death of another man and he now loads his gun, or he hires an assassin) and what he takes to be the final step (he pulls the trigger). Consider a man who takes several steps with the intention of bringing about the death of the king: stealing money to buy a gun; buying a gun; loading the gun; and then travelling with the gun to the place where he expects to find the king. It would hardly do to say that, with each of these steps, he made an attempt upon the life of the king, for then we would be saying incorrectly and unjustly, that he made *four* attempts upon the life of the king.[37] What we should say is that he took several *preliminary steps*. With each of these steps he acted with the intention of putting himself in a position wherein he would then be able to bring about something else (ultimately, the gun being fired) for the purpose of bringing about the death of the king. His state of mind, therefore, differed from that of the man who fired a shot and intended that the bullet hit and kill the king. This second man was not taking a *preliminary* step towards killing the king. He had arrived at 'the moment of consummation': he was acting with the intention of killing the king and not acting with the intention of putting himself in a position wherein he could subsequently kill the king.

Or, again, consider the man who hired an assassin. The *final* step in hiring the assassin was for him only a *preliminary* step in bringing about the death of his victim, even though there may have been nothing further that he himself intended to do to bring about this end.

I propose then this definition of a preliminary step:

D.II.16   s intends p as a *preliminary step* towards bringing about q =Df s undertakes p and does so for the purpose of bringing it about that someone bring about q.

The 'someone' here referred to may be the agent himself or it may be someone else. In the former case, the agent is acting with the intention of contributing causally to his own subsequent endeavours. Let us remind ourselves again that there is no contradiction in saying that one may contribute causally to an agent's free endeavours. One may do this by putting certain attractive ends in another agent's power and thus creating a necessary causal condition for his bringing them about.

A final step would be a step that is not thus preliminary. When the agent takes a final step, then we may say that he has made an attempt:

D.II.17   s *makes an attempt* to bring about p =Df s undertakes p and does not undertake anything as a preliminary step toward p.

When the assassin buys his gun or when he loads it, he has not yet made an attempt to kill his victim; but, in the normal case, he does make such an attempt when he pulls the trigger.

We may now make six observations about this concept of making an attempt. (1) Making an attempt, in the present sense of the term, is quite consistent with success – this despite the fact that we are not likely to *say* 'He made an attempt' if we know both that he succeeded and that he was confident of success.[38] (2) To take a preliminary step toward a given end is not to make an attempt to bring about that end, but it will be to make an attempt to bring about a certain *means* to that end. Our agent who took only a preliminary step toward killing the king did make an attempt to bring it about that his gun was loaded. (3) Attempts, as here defined, may be 'half-hearted' or 'confident', the difference being a matter of the agent's own confidence in his success. (Sometimes, of course, 'half-hearted attempt' may be used merely for 'pretended attempt'.) (4) We said that an agent who makes an attempt has arrived at 'the moment of consummation'. Possibly, however, he has not reached the point of no return. A man who shoots at the king in the ordinary way will have arrived at the latter point. But not so for the man who makes an attempt by putting a bomb in the king's carriage – if there is still time for him to remove the bomb or to prevent the king from entering the carriage. (5) Although an attempt is a non-preliminary step, a man may make an attempt toward a certain end while also taking a preliminary step towards that same end. Thus he may fire the pistol with one hand while reaching for ammunition with the other. He takes the latter step as a precautionary measure – in case he should miss.[39] (6) We could not ordinarily say 'The assailant made an attempt upon the life of the king' unless we could also affirm the *de re* statement that 'The king was such that the assailant made an attack upon him'. But we may say 'The assailant made an attempt to bring about the death of the king', in our sense of these terms, without thus being able to say 'The king was such that the assailant made an attempt to bring about his death'. (Perhaps the assailant attacked a post, thinking it was the king, or perhaps there *was* no king.) And we might be able to affirm the *de re* statement 'The king was such that the assailant made an attempt to bring about his death' without being able to affirm the *de dicto* 'The assailant made an attempt to bring about the death of the king'. (Oedipus did not attempt to kill his father, but his father was such that he, Oedipus, attempted to kill him.) The logical relations betweeen such *de re* and *de dicto* concepts will be discussed in Appendix C.

Finally, consider the concept of a *successful endeavour*. We could define a very broad sense of this concept by saying simply this: a man is successful in his endeavour to bring about a certain state of affairs p provided that (i) he does endeavour to bring about p and (ii) his endeavour to bring about p contributes causally to the occurrence of p. But this interpretation of 'successful endeavour' is very broad and allows for the possibility of what we might call 'inadvertent successes' and 'happy failures'.

An example of an 'inadvertent success' is provided by this would-be assassin: he is driving to his victim's home with the intent of killing him there; *en route,* he accidentally runs over and kills a pedestrian; and the pedestrian turns out to be none other than the intended victim. The assassin had undertaken his victim's death and in fact he brought it about. But was his undertaking successful?

An example of a 'happy failure' is provided by the prospective assassin who does everything that he believes to be necessary for the complete execution of his plan and who does indeed succeed despite a crucial failure. In shooting at his victim, he causes him to make an escape and then, in the course of this escape, the intended victim is killed by an unexpected stroke of lightning. The undertaking was hardly a complete success.

If a man is *completely* successful in the endeavours he makes at a certain time to bring about a certain state of affairs, then *everything* he undertakes at that time to bring about that state of affairs is something he successfully brings about. And so we should say:

> D.II.18   s is *completely successful* in his endeavour at t to bring about p =Df (i) s makes an attempt at t to bring about p and (ii) everything he then undertakes for the purpose of bringing about p contributes causally to p.

Consider once again an assassin who achieved an inadvertent success: he shot at the victim and accomplished his goal, not because the bullet hit the mark, as he intended, but because the firing of the gun caused some paint cans to fall on the victim's head and kill him. This act was not a complete success by our present definition, for in the endeavour to bring about the death of his victim, there was something the agent undertook to bring about – the bullet hitting the mark – which was not successful.

But is the definition too rigid? Suppose that, as a good marksman, the assassin did succeed in shooting the victim, but that, as a man of caution, he acted at the same time upon an alternative method. And what if the alternative method failed? (As he fired at the victim, he stepped on a lever to activate a trap door but the lever didn't work.) In such a case, we cannot say, as our definition would have it, that *everything* he undertook for the purpose of bringing about the victim's death was successful. Yet, wasn't he completely successful in what he endeavoured to do with the gun? For the definition to be adequate to the successful phase of our assassin's activity, we have only to fill the blank, not by 'the victim dies', but by 'the victim dies as a result of being shot'.

Any adequate theory of intention, I believe, should be constructed upon concepts such as those that have been explicated here. Further development of the theory would involve concepts and questions of law and morality that are beyond the scope of the present book.

Let us turn back to our metaphysical questions about the agent.

9 Some Further Philosophical Questions

We undertake certain things p by undertaking certain other things q; in such cases, we undertake q for the purpose of bringing about p. And so it must also be the case that we undertake certain things p without undertaking certain *other* things q for the purpose of bringing about p. The things p that we thus undertake could be said to be things we *undertake directly*.

When we are successful with respect to the things we undertake directly, we may be said to perform certain *basic actions*. These are the things we succeed in doing without undertaking still other things to get them done. For most of us, raising our arms and blinking our eyes are thus basic. But people have different 'repertoires' of basic acts and what one person can perform as a basic act another may be able to bring about only by undertaking a lengthy chain of causes.[40]

We may characterise the present sense of basic act as follows:

D.II.19 s brings about p as a *basic act* at t = Df (i) s undertaking p contributes causally at t to p and (ii) there is no q such that s undertakes q at t for the purpose of bringing about p.

In other words, our agent performed as a basic act provided he brought about something he *undertook* to bring about and provided further there was nothing he undertook for the *purpose* of bringing that thing about.

Given this definition of basic action, we need not say, as some have said, that a man's basic actions are actions 'which he cannot be said to have caused to happen'.[41] And we may say, if we choose, that a man may undertake a basic act on a certain occasion and fail. (Presumably this would happen, if unknown to himself, the man had lost some member of his 'repertoire' of basic actions and then discovered the loss.)

Let us now contrast the things we thus *undertake directly* with the things we *bring about directly*.

We bring about some things by bringing about other things that cause them. Or, in other words, we bring about certain things p by bringing about certain other things q such that q brings about p. Therefore, it would seem, we also bring about certain things p *without* bringing about certain other things q such that q brings about p. Let us say:

D.II.20   s brings about p *directly* at t =Df (i) s contributes causally at t to p and (ii) there is no q such that (a) s contributes causally at t to q and (b) q contributes causally to p.

If a man brings about anything at all, then, presumably, he brings about some things as *basic acts* and he also brings about some things *directly*. But we must distinguish the things he brings about as basic acts, and the things he brings about directly.

If what I have been saying is true, then a man's undertakings are things he brings about directly. But, given our definitions, we cannot say that undertakings are basic acts; for basic acts are undertaken and undertakings are not. The mark of a basic act is that, although it is undertaken, nothing is undertaken as a *means* to bringing it about. And the mark of what one brings about directly is that, although it is brought about, it is not brought about by some *other* thing the agent brings about.

I think we can say that anything an agent brings about directly is an internal change, a change within himself. Using a scholastic term, we could say that the things he causes directly are *immanently* caused; as states of the agent himself, they may be said to 'remain within the agent'.[42]

This way of looking at direct causation should be contrasted with that suggested by H. A. Prichard: 'Where we have willed some movement of our body and think we have caused it, we cannot have directly caused it. For what we have directly caused, if anything, must have been some change in our brain.' Prichard's

view would be compatible with that suggested here if our undertakings could be said to *be* 'changes in our brain'.[43] But whether
or not our undertakings are themselves changes in our brains, it
would seem that they contribute causally to certain changes in
our brains that we know next to nothing about.

I will note, finally, how the answers that we have given to our
philosophical questions will help us in answering still *other*
philosophical questions. I will consider five such questions and
put them in the form of puzzles.

(1) 'A responsible act is an act such that, at the time at which
the agent undertook to perform it, he had it within his power
not to perform the act. But physiology seems to tell us that what
the agent thus accomplishes is caused by certain physiological
events. (The man raises his arm; certain cerebral and muscular
events cause the arm to go up.) How, then, can the act be said to
be something that was then in his power not to perform?'

The agent was such that, in the endeavour to make it happen
that his arm go up, he made it happen (i) that the various physiological states, including the cerebral and muscular events,
occurred and also (ii) that his arm went up. Since he made (i)
occur, and since (i) contributed causally to the occurrence of (ii),
he may also be said to have contributed causally to the occurrence
of (ii). Making the physiological states happen *was* something
that it was within his power not to perform; and since, we may
suppose, his arm would not have gone up if he had not made
those states happen, the act was something that was within his
power not to perform.

(2) 'If a man has learned what the muscle motions are that
cause his arm to go up, and if, in the course of a physical examination, he wishes to move those muscles, then he can do so by
raising his arm. Physiology tells us, however, that the muscle
motions cause the arm to go up. And causation is asymmetrical:
if a particular event p is the cause of a particular event q, then q
cannot be the cause of p. The cause, moreover, cannot occur
after the effect. How, then, can he move his muscles by raising
his arm?'

The man who 'moves his muscles by raising his arm' makes it
happen that his arm goes up *for the purpose of* making it happen
that his muscles move. This means he endeavoured to make it
happen that *by making it happen* that the arm goes up he would
make it happen that the muscles move. See D.II.13. It does *not*
mean he endeavoured to make it happen that *his arm going up*
would make it happen that the muscles move. Recall the phy-
sician who endeavoured to bring it about that the patient would

be recovered in six months and did so in order that he, the doctor, might receive his pay next week.

(3) 'Oedipus's father was identical with Laius, the offensive traveller. Oedipus intended to kill the offensive traveller, but he certainly did not intend to kill his own father. Yet the killing of the offensive traveller *was* the killing of Oedipus's father. Hence we must say of this event both that it was intentional and that it was not intentional. How can this be?'

That state of affairs which was the killing of the offensive traveller was not the same as that state of affairs which was the killing of Oedipus's father. The former, for example, implies that someone was an offensive traveller, but the latter does not. And the latter implies that Oedipus had a father, but the former does not. Yet there was a sense in which we may say that Oedipus's act was both intentional and nonintentional. But in this sense the terms 'intentional' and 'nonintentional' are not contraries, since the sentence 'Oedipus's act was both intentional and nonintentional' is elliptical for 'Oedipus's act was intentional with respect to one thing and nonintentional with respect to another thing'. What Oedipus did was intentional with respect to the killing of the unfriendly traveller and nonintentional with respect to the killing of his father. And this is only to say that he acted with the intention of killing the unfriendly traveller and did not act with the intention of killing his father.[44]

(4) 'If there are any states of affairs that the man himself causes to happen, then there must be certain states of affairs q which are such that he causes q to happen without *first* causing still *other* states of affairs p such that p causes q to happen. If there are such "basic actions", then raising the arm must be among them, since (if our agent is like most of the rest of us) there is nothing else he needs to *do* in order to raise his arm. But if the motion of the arm is caused by physiological events, then there are no "basic actions". And therefore there is nothing that the agent himself causes to happen.'

The final premise is false. It is not the case that, if the motion of his arm is caused by physiological events, then there are no basic actions. Saying that the motion of his arm is a basic act is quite consistent with saying that physiological events cause his arm to go up. For when we say that the motion of his arm is a basic act, we are saying only that when he makes it happen there is nothing else that he makes happen *for the purpose* of making it happen. But this is not to say that there are no physiological events that cause it to happen.

(5) ' " . . . if there are any actions at all, there must be two

distinct *kinds* of actions: those performed by an individual M, which he may be said to have *caused* to happen; and those actions, also performed by M, which he cannot be said to have caused to happen. The latter I shall designate as *basic actions.*" Occasionally people discover that they have lost the ability to perform basic acts; a man discovers, for example, that one of his limbs has become paralysed. How *can* a man discover such a thing unless he does what he usually does for the purpose of performing the act in question and then finds that his attempt is a failure? But if there is something a man usually does for the purpose of performing the supposed " basic act", then the act in question is not a basic act. How can this be?' [45]

When a man discovers such a thing, he has not *done* what he usually does for the purpose of performing the basic act in question; that is to say, he has not undertaken anything for the purpose of performing the basic act. But he did undertake to perform the basic act and failed. There were certain things, entirely unknown to him, that he made happen as a result of undertaking to move his limb. And although he made those things happen, he didn't make it happen that he moved his limb.

I would suggest to the reader that, in evaluating the present way of dealing with such questions, he do so in part by comparing it with the available alternatives.

CHAPTER III

IDENTITY THROUGH TIME

> *The identity of a person is a perfect identity; wher-*
> *ever it is real, it admits of no degrees; and it is*
> *impossible that a person should be in part the same,*
> *and in part different . . . For this cause, I have first*
> *considered personal identity, as that which is perfect*
> *in its kind, and the natural measure of that which is*
> *imperfect.*
>
> Thomas Reid [1]

1 The Ship of Theseus

To understand the philosophical problems involved in persistence, in the fact that one and the same thing may endure through a period of time, we will begin with what Reid would have called the 'imperfect' cases and remind ourselves of some ancient philosophical puzzles. One such puzzle is suggested by the familiar dictum of Heraclitus: 'You could not step twice in the same river; for other and yet other waters are ever flowing on.' [2] Another is the problem of the Ship of Theseus. [3]

Updating the latter problem somewhat, let us imagine a ship – the Ship of Theseus – that was made entirely of wood when it came into being. One day a wooden plank is cast off and replaced by an aluminum one. Since the change is only slight, there is no question as to the survival of the Ship of Theseus. We still have the ship we had before; that is to say, the ship that we have now is identical with the ship we had before. On another day, another wooden plank is cast off and also replaced by an aluminum one. Still the same ship, since, as before, the change is only slight. The changes continue, in a similar way, and finally the Ship of Theseus is made entirely of aluminum. The aluminum ship, one may well argue, *is* the wooden ship we started with, for the ship we started with survived each particular change, and identity, after all, is transitive.

But what happened to the discarded wooden planks? Consider this possibility, suggested by Thomas Hobbes: 'If some man had kept the old planks as they were taken out, and by putting them afterwards together in the same order, had again made a ship of them, this, without doubt, had also been the same numerical ship with that which was at the beginning; and so there would have been two ships numerically the same, which is absurd.' [4] Assuming, as perhaps one has no right to do, that each of the wooden planks survived intact throughout these changes, one might well argue that the reassembled wooden ship *is* the ship we started with. 'After all, it is made up of the very same parts, standing in the very same relations, whereas that ugly aluminum object doesn't have a single part in common with our original ship.'

To compound the problem still further, let us suppose that the captain of the original ship had solemnly taken the vow that, if his ship were ever to go down, he would go down with it. What, now, if the two ships collide at sea and he sees them start to sink together? Where does his duty lie – with the aluminum ship or with the reassembled wooden ship?

'The carriage' is another ancient version of the problem. Socrates and Plato change the parts of their carriages piece by piece until, finally, Socrates's original carriage is made up of all the parts of Plato's carriage and Plato's carriage is made up of all the parts of Socrates's original carriage. Have they exchanged their carriages or not, and if so, at what point?

Perhaps the essence of the problem is suggested by an even simpler situation. Consider a child playing with his blocks. He builds a house with ten blocks, uses it as a garrison for his toy soldiers, disassembles it, builds many other things, then builds a house again, with each of the ten blocks occupying the position it had occupied before, and he uses it again as a garrison for his soldiers. Was the house that was destroyed the same as the one that subsequently came into being?

These puzzles about the persistence of objects through periods of time have their analogues for the extension of objects through places in space. Consider the river that is known in New Orleans as 'the Mississippi'. Most of us would say that the source of the river is in northern Minnesota. But what if one were to argue instead that the source is in Montana, where it is known as 'the Missouri'? Or that its source is in Pittsburgh, where it is known as 'the Ohio', or that its source is farther back where it is called 'the Allegheny', or in still another place where it is called 'the Monongahela'? [5]

The accompanying diagram provides us with a schematic illustration.

```
        (a)        (b)        (c)
         x          x          x
              x     x     x
                  x x x
                    x
                    x
                    x
                   (d)
```

Of the river that has its central point at (d), one might wonder whether it flows south-easterly from (a), or due south from (b), or south-westerly from (c). (For simplicity, we ignore the Allegheny and the Monongahela.) If we are puzzled about the beginning of the Mississippi, we should be equally puzzled about the end of the Rhine. Reading our diagram from bottom to top (and again oversimplifying), we could say that if the Rhine begins at (d), then it ends either with the Maas at (a), or with the Waal at (b), or with the Lek at (c).[6]

Perhaps we can imagine three philosophers looking down at the river(s) that end(s) at (d). One insists that the river flows between (a) and (d), another that it flows between (b) and (d) and the third that it flows between (c) and (d); and each insists that, since the arms (or tributaries) to which the other two philosophers refer are distinct not only from each other but from the river itself, neither of the other two can be right. Their dispute, clearly, would be analogous in significant respects to the problem of the Ship of Theseus.

What are we to say of such puzzles? We might follow the extreme course that Carneades took and simply deny the principle of the transitivity of identity.[7] In other words we might say that things identical with the same thing need not be identical with each other. But if we thus abandon reason and logic at the very outset, we will have no way of deciding at the end what is the most reasonable thing to say about ourselves and *our* persistence through time.

We might be tempted to deny the possibility of alteration. Thus one could say: 'Strictly speaking, nothing alters – nothing is such that at one time it has one set of properties and at another time it has another set of properties. What happens is, rather, that at one time there is a thing having the one set of properties and at the other time there is another thing having the other set of properties.' But this supposition, if we apply it to ourselves, is inconsistent with the data with which we have begun. Each of us knows with respect to himself that he now has properties he didn't have in the past and that formerly he had properties he doesn't have now. ('But a thing x isn't identical with a thing y unless they have all their properties in common. And if the present you has one set of properties and the past you another, how can they be the same thing?') The answer is, of course, that there aren't two you's, a present one having one set of properties, and a past one having another. It is rather that you *are* now such that you have these properties and lack those, whereas formerly you *were* such that you had those properties and lacked these. The 'former you' *has* the same properties that the 'present you' now has, and the 'present you' *had* the same properties that the 'former you' then had.[8]

Bishop Butler suggested that it is only in 'a loose and popular sense' that we may speak of the persistence of such familiar things as ships, plants and houses. And he contrasted this 'loose and popular sense' with 'the strict and philosophical sense' in which we may speak of the persistence of *persons*.[9] Let us consider these suggestions.

2 *Playing Loose with the 'Is' of Identity*
We will not pause to ask what Butler meant in fact. Let us ask what he could have meant. He suggested that there is a kind of looseness involved when we say that such things as the Ship of Theseus persist through time. What kind of looseness is this?

It could hardly be that the Ship of Theseus, in contrast with other things, is only loosely identical with itself. Surely one cannot say that, while some things are only loosely identical with themselves, other things are tightly identical with themselves.[10] The statement 'This thing is more loosely identical with itself than that thing', if it says anything at all, tells us only that the first thing is more susceptible than the second to loss of identity, and this means only that the first is more readily perishable than the second.

We should construe Butler's remark as saying, not that there is a loose kind of identity, but rather that there is a loose sense of 'identity' – a loose (and popular) use of the 'is' of identity.

What would be a *loose* sense of 'A is B', or 'A is identical with B' – a sense of 'A is B' which is consistent with a denial of the *strict* sense of 'A is B'? I suggest this: we use the locution 'A is B', or 'A is identical with B', in a *loose* sense, if we use it in such a way that it is consistent with saying 'A has a certain property that B does not have' or 'Some things are true of A that aren't true of B'.

Do we ever use the locution 'A is B' in this loose way? It would seem, unfortunately, that we do.

I will single out five different types of such misuse.

(1) One may say: 'Route 6 is Point Street in Providence and is Fall River Avenue in Seekonk.' Here we would seem to have the 'is' of identity, since it is followed in each occurrence by a term ('Point Street' and 'Fall River Avenue') and not by a predicate expression. But since Point Street and Fall River Avenue have different properties (one is in Providence and not in Seekonk and the other is in Seekonk and not in Providence), the statement may be said to play loose with 'is'.

As our brief discussion of the rivers may make clear, this use of 'is' is readily avoided. We have only to replace 'is' by 'is part of' and then switch around the terms, as in: 'Point Street in Providence is part of Route 6 and Fall River Avenue in Seekonk is part of Route 6.' Or we could also say, of course: 'Point Street is part of Route 6 in Providence and Fall River Avenue is part of Route 6 in Seekonk.' [11]

(2) One may say 'This train will be two trains after Minneapolis', or, travelling in the other direction, 'Those two trains will be one train after Minneapolis'. In the first case ('fission'), we are not saying that there is one thing which will subsequently be identical with two things. We are saying, rather, that there is one thing which will be divided into two things, neither of them being identical with the original thing, but each of them being a part of the original thing. And in the second case ('fusion'), we are not saying that there are two things which are subsequently to become identical with each other, or with a third thing. We are saying rather that there are two things which will both become parts of a third thing. (Why not cite an amoeba as an instance of 'fission'? There is the off-chance that amoebas are persons, or at least may be thought to be persons, and in such a case, as we shall see, our treatment would have to be somewhat different.)

(3) One may say: 'The President of the United States was Eisenhower in 1955, Johnson in 1965 and Ford in 1975.' [12] Here one may seem to be saying that there is, or was, something – namely, the President of the United States – which was identical with Eisenhower in 1955, with Johnson in 1965 and with Ford in 1975. And so, given that Eisenhower, Johnson and Ford were three different people, one may seem to be saying that there is one thing which has been identical with three different things. But this talk, too, is readily avoided. We have only to reformulate the original sentence in such a way that the temporal expression

('in 1955', 'in 1965' and 'in 1975') may be seen to modify, not the verb 'was', but the term 'the President of the United States'. Thus we could say: 'The President of the United States in 1955 (the person who officially presided over the United States in 1955) was Eisenhower; the President of the United States in 1965 was Johnson; and the President of the United States in 1975 was Ford.' [13]

(4) Pointing to a musical instrument, one man may say to another: 'What you have there is the same instrument that I play, but the one that I play isn't as old as that one.' The first 'is' might be taken to be the 'is' of identity, for it would seem to be followed by a term ('the same instrument that I play'), but the man is saying, of the thing designated by the first term ('what you have there'), that it is older than the thing designated by the second. But of course he didn't need to talk that way. He could have said: 'What you have there is an instrument of the same sort as the one that I play.'

We note a second example of this way of playing loose with 'is' – not because the example introduces any new considerations (for it doesn't), but because it has attracted the attention of philosophers.

Consider the following list:

Socrates is mortal.
Socrates is mortal.

How many sentences have been listed? We could say either 'exactly one' or 'exactly two'. That these incompatible answers are both possible indicates that the question is ambiguous. And so it has been suggested that, to avoid the ambiguity, we introduce the terms 'sentence-token' and 'sentence-type' and then say 'There are two sentence-tokens on the list and one sentence-type'. But if we say this, then we can say: 'The first item on the list is the same sentence-type as the second (for they are syntactically just alike and say the same thing), but the two are different sentence-tokens (for they are two, one being in one place and the other in another).' Here, once again, we are playing loose with 'is'.[14] We *needn't* speak this way in order to deal with the ambiguity of 'How many sentences are there?' We could say there *are* two sentence-tokens and they are tokens *of* the same (sentence-) type. The example does not differ in principle, then, from 'The instrument Jones plays is the same as the one Smith plays but is somewhat older'.

It is sometimes said that we should distinguish the two locutions 'A is identical with B and A is a so-and-so' and 'A is the same so-and-so as B'. It has even been suggested that, for purposes of philosophy, the first of these two locutions should be abandoned in favour of the second.[15] According to this suggestion, we should never say, simply and absolutely, 'A is identical with B'; we should 'relativise the ascription of identity to a sortal' and say something of the form 'A is the same so-and-so as B', where the expression replacing 'so-and-so' is a count-term, or sortal, such as 'man', 'dog', 'horse'. But this suggestion has point only if we can find instances of the following:

> A is the same so-and-so as B, and A is a such-and-such but is not the same such-and-such as B.

Are there really any such As and Bs?

What would be an instance of the above formula? In other words, what would be an instance of an A which is 'the same so-and-so' as something B, but which is not 'the same such-and-such' as B? The only instances which have ever been cited, in defending this doctrine of 'relativised identity', would seem to be instances of one or the other of the four ways of playing loose with 'is' that we have just distinguished. For example: 'Different official personages may be one and the same man' or 'This is the same word as that'. What the suggestion comes to, then, is that we abandon the strict use of 'is' and replace it by one or more of the loose uses just discussed. There may be advantages to this type of permissiveness, but it will not help us with our philosophical problems.[16]

Do these ways of playing loose with 'is' suggest a true interpretation of the thesis we have attributed to Bishop Butler – the thesis according to which it is only in 'a loose and popular sense' that we may speak of the persistence through time of such familiar physical things as ships, plants and houses? Is it only by playing loose with 'is' that we may say, of the Ship of Theseus, that it is one and the same thing from one period of time to another?

We *can*, of course, play loose with 'is' in one or another of these ways when we talk about the Ship of Theseus. Knowing that it is going to be broken up into two ships, we might say: 'It's going to be two ships.' Or knowing that it was made by joining two other ships, we might say: 'Once it had been two ships.' Or knowing that it makes the same ferry run as does the Ship of Callicles, we might say: 'The Ship of Theseus and the Ship of Callicles are the same ferry.' But the Ship of Theseus doesn't have to be talked about in these loose and popular ways any more than anything else does.

(5) It may be that the Ship of Theseus and the carriage and other familiar things involve still another way of playing loose with 'is'. Thus Hume said that it is convenient to 'feign identity' when we speak about things which, though they 'are supposed to continue the same, are such only as consist of succession of parts, connected together by resemblance, contiguity, or causation'.[17] What Hume here has in mind by 'feigning' may have been put more clearly by Thomas Reid. (Though Reid and Hume were far apart with respect to most of the matters that concern us here, they seem to be together with respect to this one.) Reid wrote:

> All bodies, as they consist of innumerable parts that may be disjoined from them by a great variety of causes, are subject to continual changes of their substance, increasing, diminishing, changing insensibly. When such alterations are gradual, because language could not afford a different name for every different state of such a changeable being, it retains the same name, and is considered as the same thing. Thus we say of an old regiment that it did such a thing a century ago, though there now is not a man alive who then belonged to it. We say a tree is the same in the seed-bed and in the forest. A ship of war, which has successively changed her anchors, her tackle, her sails, her masts, her planks, and her timbers, while she keeps the same name is the same.[18]

I believe that Reid is here saying two things. The first is that, whenever there is a change of parts, however insignificant the parts may be, then some old thing ceases to be and some new thing comes into being. This presupposes that, strictly speaking, the parts of a thing are essential to it, and therefore when, as we commonly say, something loses a part, then that thing strictly and philosophically ceases to be.[19]

The second thing I take Reid to be saying is this. If, from the point of view of our practical concerns, the new thing that comes into being upon the addition of parts is sufficiently similar to the old one, then it is much more convenient for us to treat them as if they were one than it is for us to take account of the fact that they are diverse. This point could also be put by saying that such things as the Ship of Theseus and indeed most familiar physical things are really 'fictions', or as we would say today, 'logical constructions'. They are logical constructions upon things which *cannot* survive the loss of their parts.

If Reid is right, then, 'The Ship of Theseus was in Athens

last week and will be in Kerkyra Melaina next week' need not be construed as telling us that there *is* in fact a certain ship that was in Athens last week and will be in Kerkyra Melaina next week. It does not imply that any ship that was in the one place is identical with any ship that will be in the other place. And so if this is true, and if all the same we say 'A ship that was in Athens last week is identical with a ship that will be in Kerkyra Melaina next week', then, once again, we are playing loose with the 'is' of identity.

3 An Interpretation of Bishop Butler's Theses

We have found a way, then, of interpreting Bishop Butler's two theses.

According to the first, familiar physical things such as trees, ships, bodies and houses persist 'only in a loose and popular sense'. This thesis may be construed as presupposing that these things are 'fictions', logical constructions or *entia per alio*. And it tells us that, from the fact that any such physical thing may be said to exist at a certain place P at a certain time t and also at a certain place Q at a certain other time t', we may *not* infer that what exists at P at t is identical with what exists at Q at t'.

According to the second thesis, persons persist 'in a strict and philosophical sense'. This may be construed as telling us that persons are not thus 'fictions', logical constructions or *entia per alio*. And so it implies that, if a person may be said to exist at a certain place P at a certain time t and also at a certain place Q at a certain other time t', then we *may* infer that something existing at P at t is identical with something existing at Q at t'.

We now consider the two theses in turn.

4 Feigning Identity

Could we think of familiar physical things, such as ships and trees and houses, as being logical constructions? Let us consider just one type of physical thing, for what we say about it may be applied, *mutatis mutandis,* to the others.

Mon	AB
Tue	BC
Wed	CD

Consider the history of a very simple table. On Monday it came into being when a certain thing A was joined with a certain other thing B. On Tuesday A was detached from B and C was joined to B, these things occurring in such a way that a table was to be found during every moment of the process. And on Wednesday B was detached from C and D was joined with C, these things, too, occurring in such a way that a table was to be found during every moment of the process. Let us suppose that no other separating or joining occurred.

I suggest that in this situation there are the following three wholes among others: AB, that is, the thing made up of A and B; BC, the thing made up of B and C; and CD, the thing made up of C and D. I will say that AB 'constituted' our table on Monday, that BC 'constituted' our table on Tuesday and that CD 'constituted' our table on Wednesday. Although AB, BC and CD are three different things, they all constitute the same table. We thus have an illustration of what Hume called 'a succession of objects'.[20]

One might also say, of each of the three wholes, AB, BC and CD, that it 'stands in for' or 'does duty for' our table on one of the three successive days. Thus if we consider the spatial location of the three wholes, we see that the place of the table was occupied by AB on Monday, by BC on Tuesday, and by CD on Wednesday. Again, the table was red on Monday if and only if AB was red on Monday, and it weighed 10 pounds on Monday if and only if AB weighed 10 pounds on Monday. And analogously for BC on Tuesday and for CD on Wednesday.

The situation may seem to involve two somewhat different types of individual thing. On the one hand, there is what might be called the *ens successivum* – the 'successive table' that is made up of different things at different times.[21] And on the other hand, there are the things that do duty on the different days for the successive table: namely, AB, BC and CD. But any *ens successivum* may be viewed as a logical construction upon the various things that may be said to do duty for it.

Considering, then, just the simple situation I have described, can we express the information we have about the *ens successivum* in statements that refer only to the particular things that stand in or do duty for it? It should be clear that we can, but let us consider the situation in some detail.

Looking back to our diagram, we can see that Monday's table evolved into Tuesday's table and that Tuesday's table evolved into Wednesday's table. We began with AB; then A was separated from B and replaced by C, but in such a way that there was a table to be found at every moment during the process; then, in a similar way, B was separated from C and replaced by D. We could say, then, that BC was a 'direct table successor' of AB, and that CD was a 'direct table successor' of AB.

Making use of the undefined concept of *part*, or *proper part*, we may define the concept of 'table successor' in the following way:

> D.III.1 x is at t a direct table successor of y at t' =Df (i) t does not begin before t'; (ii) x is a table at t and y is a table at t'; and (iii) there is a z, such that z is a part of x at t and a part of y at t', and at every moment between t' and t, inclusive, z is itself a table.

Thus z is a table which is a proper part of a table. (If we cut off a small part of a table, we may still have a table left. But if the thing that is left is a table, then, since it was there before, it was then a table that was a proper part of a table.) The concept *part*, as it is understood here, will be discussed in detail in Appendix B ('Mereological Essentialism').

We may also say, more generally, that the CD of Wednesday is a 'table successor' of the AB of Monday, even though CD is not a *direct* table successor of AB. The more general concept is this:

> D.III.2 x is at t a table successor of y at t' =Df (i) t does not begin before t'; (ii) x is a table at t and y is a table at t'; and (iii) x has at t every property P such that (a) y has P at t' and (b) all direct table successors of anything having P have P.

The definition assures us that a direct table successor of a direct table successor is a table successor; so, too, for a direct table successor of a direct table successor . . . of a direct table successor.[22]

We may now say that things that are thus related by table succession 'constitute the same successive table'.

> D.III.3 x constitutes at t the same successive table that y constitutes at t' =Df Either (a) x and only x is at t a table successor of y at t', or (b) y and only y is at t' a table successor of x at t.

Each such thing may be said to 'constitute a successive table'.

D.III.4   *x* constitutes at *t* a successive table =Df There are a
y and a *t'* such that *y* is other than *x* and *x* constitutes
at *t* the same table that *y* constitutes at *t'*.

We are on the way, then, to reducing our successive table to
those things that are said to constitute it.

Certain propositions, ostensibly about the successive table, may
be reduced in a straightforward way to propositions about the
things that are said to constitute it. For example:

D.III.5   There is exactly one successive table at place P at
time *t* =Df There is exactly one thing at place P at
time *t* that constitutes a successive table at *t*.

Our definition of 'constituting the same successive table' (D.III.3)
assures us that nothing will constitute more than one successive
table at any given time.

Some of the properties that the table has at any given time
are thus such that the table borrows them from the thing that
constitutes it at that time; but others are not. An example of a
property of the first sort may be that of *being red*; an example
of a property of the second sort may be that of *having once been
blue*. How are we to mark off the former set of properties?

Some properties may be said to be 'rooted outside the times
at which they are had'. Examples are the property of *being a
widow* and the property of *being a future President*. If we know
of anything that it has the former property at any given time,
then we can deduce that the thing existed prior to that time.
And if we know of anything that it has the latter property at
any given time, then we can deduce that the thing continues to
exist after that time. Let us say:

D.III.6   G is rooted outside times at which it is had =Df
Necessarily, for any *x* and for any period of time
t, *x* has the property G throughout *t* only if *x* exists
at some time before or after *t*.

Some properties may – but need not – be rooted outside the
times at which they are had. An example is the property of
being such that it is or was red. Our successive table may derive
this from its present constituent – if its present constituent is
red. But it may derive it from a former constituent – if its present
constituent is not red. The definition of this type of property
is straightforward:

D.III.7   G may be rooted outside times at which it is had
       =Df G is equivalent to a disjunction of two properties
       one of which is, and the other of which is not, rooted
       outside times at which it is had.

Some properties, finally, are *not* such that they may be rooted
outside the times at which they are had.[23] An example is *being
red*.

Of the properties that our successive table has at any given
time, which are the ones that it borrows from the thing that
happens to constitute it at that time? The answer is: those of its
properties which are *not* essential to it, and those of its properties which are *not* such that they may be rooted outside the times
at which they are had. But the essential properties of the successive table – e.g. that it *is* a successive table – and those of its
properties which may be rooted outside the times at which they
are had – e.g. that it was blue or that it was or will be blue – are
not such that, for any time, they are borrowed from the thing
that constitutes the successive table at that time.

We may say, more generally, of the *ens successivum* and the
thing that constitutes it at any given time, that they are exactly
alike at that time with respect to all those properties which are
such that they are not essential to either and they may not be
rooted outside the times at which they are had.

Consider now the following definitional schema:

D.III.8   The successive table that is at place P at time *t* is F
       at *t* =Df There is exactly one thing at place P at *t*
       that constitutes a successive table at *t* and that thing
       is F at *t*.

This definition is applicable only if the predicates that replace
the schematic letter 'F' are properly restricted. For the properties
designated by such predicates should be those which are not
essential to either and are not such that they may be rooted
outside the times at which they are had. Hence acceptable
replacements for 'F' would be: 'red', '10 feet square', and 'such
that it weighs 10 pounds'.

But not all the properties of the successive table are derivable
in this straightforward way from the properties of things that
constitute it. For example, if AB ceased to be after Monday, we
could say of the successive table on Monday, but not of AB, that
it was going to persist through Wednesday. Or if CD came into
being on Wednesday, we could say of the successive table on

Wednesday, but not of CD, that it is at least two days old. Moreover, on Monday, the successive table, but not AB, was such that it would be constituted by CD on Wednesday; while on Wednesday, the successive table, but not CD, was such that it was constituted by AB on Monday.

Nevertheless all such truths about the successive table may be reduced to truths about AB, BC and CD. That this is so should be apparent from these definitions.

> D.III.9   The successive table that is at place P at time t has existed for at least 3 days $=$Df There is exactly one x such that x is at place P at time t and x constitutes a successive table at t; there are a y and a time t' such that x is at t a table-successor of y at t'; and t and t' are separated by a period of three days.

This definition tells us, then, what it is for a successive table to persist through time. And the following definition suggests the way in which, at any time, the successive table may borrow its properties from things that constitute it at *other* times:

> D.III.10   The successive table that is at place P at time t is constituted by x at t' $=$Df There is a y such that y is at place P at time t; y constitutes a successive table at t; and either x is identical with y and t is identical with t', or y constitutes at t the same successive table that x constitutes at t'.

It should now be obvious how to say such things as 'the successive table is red on Monday and green on Wednesday'.

One may object, 'You are committed to saying that AB, BC, CD, and our table are four different things. It may well be, however, that each of the three things AB, BC, CD satisfies the conditions of any acceptable definition of the term 'table'. Indeed your definitions presuppose that each of them *is* a table. Hence you are committed to saying that, in the situation described, there are *four* tables. But this is absurd; for actually you have described only *one* table.'

We will find a reply to this objection, if we distinguish the strict and philosophical sense of such expressions as 'There are four tables' from their ordinary, or loose and popular, sense. To say that there are four tables, in the strict and philosophical sense, is to say that there are four different things, each of them a table. But from the fact that there are four tables, in this strict and philosophical sense, it will not follow that there are four tables in the ordinary, or loose and popular, sense. If there are to be four tables in the ordinary, or loose and popular, sense, it must be the case that there are four things, not only such that each constitutes a table, but also such that no two of them constitute the same table. In other words, there must be four *entia successiva*, each of them a table.

We may, therefore, explicate the ordinary, or loose and popular, sense of 'There are n so-and-so's at t' (or 'The number of so-and-so's at t is n') in the following way:

> D.III.11 There are, in the loose and popular sense, n so-and-so's at t =Df There are n things each of which constitutes a so-and-so at t, and no two of which constitute the same so-and-so at t.

The term 'so-and-so' in this schematic definition may be replaced by any more specific count-term, e.g. 'table' or 'ship'. And the definiendum could be replaced by 'The number of successive so-and-so's at t is n'.

Hence the answer to the above objection is this: in saying that there are exactly *three* tables in the situation described one is speaking in the strict and philosophical sense and not in the loose and popular sense. In saying that there is exactly *one* table one is speaking in the loose and popular sense and not in the strict and philosophical sense. But the statement that there are *four* tables – AB, BC, CD and the successive table – is simply the result of confusion. One is trying to speak both ways at once.[24] The sense in which we may say that there *is* the successive table is not the sense in which we may say that there *is* the individual thing AB, or BC, or CD.[25]

The foregoing sketch, then, makes clear one way in which we may feign identity when what we are dealing with is in fact only a 'succession of related objects'. The ways in which we do thus feign identity are considerably more subtle and complex. Playing loose with 'is' and 'same', we may even speak of the sameness of a table when we are dealing with successions of objects which are related, not by what I have called table succession, but in much more tenuous ways. Nevertheless it should be clear that if we are saying something we really know, when we thus speak of the sameness of a table, what we are saying could be re-expressed in such a way that we refer only to the related objects and not to the ostensible entities we think of them as making up. And so, too, for other familiar things – ships and trees and houses – that involve successions of related objects that stand in or do duty for them at different times.

We could say, then, that such things are *entia per alio*. They are ontological parasites that derive all their properties from other things – from the various things that do duty for them. An *ens per alio* never is or has anything on its own. It is what it is in virtue of the nature of something other than itself. At every moment of its history an *ens per alio* has something other than itself as its stand-in.

But if there are *entia per alio*, then there are also *entia per se*.

5   The Persistence of Persons through Time

Am I an *ens per alio* or an *ens per se*?

Consider the simplest of Cartesian facts – say, that I now hope for rain. Hoping for rain is one of those properties that are rooted only in the times at which they are had. And so if I am an *ens per alio*, an *ens successivum*, like our simple table or the Ship of Theseus, then I may be said to hope for rain only in virtue of the fact that my present stand-in hopes for rain. I borrow the property, so to speak, from the thing that constitutes me now.

But surely *that* hypothesis is not to be taken seriously. There is no reason whatever for supposing that *I* hope for rain only in virtue of the fact that some *other* thing hopes for rain – some stand-in that, strictly and philosophically, is not identical with me but happens to be doing duty for me at this particular moment.

If there are thus two things that now hope for rain, the one doing it on its own and the other such that its hoping is done for it by the thing that now happens to constitute it, then I am the former thing and not the latter thing. But this is to say that I am *not* an *ens successivum*.[26]

But might I not be a constituent of an *ens successivum*?

If I am a constituent of an *ens successivum*, then there have been other things that once constituted the same person that I do now and presumably there will be still others in the future. But if this is so, then the things I think I know about my past history may all be false (even though they may be true of the person I happen now to constitute) and I may have no grounds for making any prediction at all about my future. *Is* this the sort of thing I am?

Let us recall the data with which we began, the list of things we have a right to believe about ourselves. Among those things, we said, is the fact that we do undergo change and persist through time. Each of us is justified in believing a great variety of things about his past. We are justified in believing these things until we have found some reason to doubt them. It is reasonable to treat these beliefs as being innocent, epistemically, until we have found some positive reason for thinking them guilty.

What would such a positive reason be?

It is important to remind ourselves that we do *not* find any such positive reason in the writings of those philosophers who have professed to be sceptical about the persistence of persons through time.

Consider, for example, Kant's discussion of what he calls 'the third paralogism of transcendental psychology'. For all I can know, Kant there says, the thing that calls itself 'I' at one time may be other than the thing that calls itself 'I' at another time. There might be a series of different subjects which make up my biography, each of them passing its thoughts and memories on to its successor – each subject would 'retain the thought of the preceding subject and so hand it over to the subsequent subject'.[27] The relation between the successive subjects, he says, could be like that of a set of elastic balls, one of which impinges on another in a straight line and 'communicates to the latter its whole motion, and therefore its whole state (that is, if we take account only of the positions in space)'. Kant goes on to say: 'If, then, in analogy with such bodies, we postulate substances such that the one communicates to the other representations together with the consciousness of them, we can conceive a whole series of substances of which the first transmits its state together with its consciousness to the second, the second its own state with that of the preceding substance to the third, and this in turn the states of all the preceding substances together with its own consciousness and with their consciousness to another. The last substance would then be conscious of all the states of the previously changed substances, as being its own states, because they would have been transferred to it together with the consciousness of them. And yet it would not have been one and the same person in all these states.'[28]

Does *this* give us a reason for wondering whether we have in fact persisted through time? Surely not. What Kant has pointed out to us, in these speculations, is simply that the following is logically possible: instead of there being just one person who makes up my biography, there was a succession of different persons, all but the first of them being deluded with respect to its past. It is also logically possible, as Russell pointed out, that the universe came into being three seconds ago with all its ostensible traces and relics of the past. And it is logically possible that a malicious demon is deceiving each of us with respect to what we think are the external physical things around us. But the fact that these are logically possible is itself no reason for thinking that they actually occur.

'Given the transitory nature of the ultimate particles that make up the physical universe, isn't it reasonable to suppose that, if I do persist through time, then my consciousness may be transferred, as John Locke seemed to suggest, from one substance or individual thing to another? And if my consciousness is thus transferred, wouldn't I, too, be transferred from one substance to another?'

The supposition, I am certain, is not only untenable but also incoherent. Philosophers have taken it seriously, however, and so we should consider it briefly.

Is it possible to transfer my consciousness from one substance to another with the result that, whereas the former substance but not the latter was I, the latter substance but not the former is now I? In such a case, I could truly say: 'This is other than that, but once I was that and now I'm this.'

Locke said that, 'it being the same consciousness that makes a man be himself to himself, personal identity depends on that only, whether it be annexed solely to one individual substance, or can be continued in a succession of several substances'.[29] The same consciousness, he said, *could* be thus continued in a succession of several substances, if it were 'transferred from one thinking substance to another', and if this does happen then the different 'thinking substances may make but one person' [30] And these different thinking substances will all be 'the same self'.[31] (In fairness to Locke, we should note that he does not quite bring himself to say that I might now be identical with this but not with that and then later identical with that but not with this. Although he suggests that it is possible to transfer my consciousness from one substance to another, he does not explicitly say that, whereas the former substance *was* I, the latter substance is *now* I. It may very well be that he, too, was playing loose with 'is'.)

A *part* of a thing or an *appendage* to a thing may be transferred to another thing, as an organ may be transplanted from one body to another. The *contents* of a thing may be transferred to another thing, as apples may be moved from one bag to another.

Speaking somewhat more metaphorically, we might also say that the *properties* of one thing may be transferred to another thing. If you are infected by my contagious disease and if I then recover, one *could* say that my sickness *including my aches and*

and pains has been transferred from me to you. But the disease or sickness will not be transferred in the literal sense in which, say, its carriers might be transferred.

My personality traits could be said to be transferred to you if you acquire the kind of complexes and dispositions that are characteristic of me. My beliefs could be said to be transferred to you, if you begin to believe the same things I do. And my memories could even be said to be transferred from me to you, if you remember, or think you remember, the same things I do. (But if I remember or think I remember *my* doing the deed, the content of that memory could *not* be transferred to you.) [32] By thus acquiring my properties – or, more accurately, by thus instantiating some of the properties that I do – you may become so much like me that others will have difficulty in telling us apart – in that they are unable to decide, with respect to certain things that have happened, whether they belong to your biography or to mine. Perhaps the courts will have to make a decree. Perhaps it will even be reasonable for them to decide, with respect to some of the things that only I did in the past, that you and not I are responsible for them, and then they might decide, with respect to the name I formerly had, that you should be the one who bears it.

But none of these possibilities, perplexing as they may be, justifies us in saying that there could be *two* different substances which are such that *I* am transferred from one to the other.[33]

There is still another type of transfer which is quite naturally described in the way in which Locke described 'transfer of self'. This is illustrated in the transfer of a shadow ('the shadow of his hand moved from the wall to the table and became larger but more faint in the process'). But a shadow is an *ens per alio*; it borrows its properties from other things (most notably from shadowed objects). The kind of transfer that is involved in the passage of a shadow from one object to another, to the extent that it differs from the types of transfer we distinguished above, is typical of *entia per alio*. But persons, we have seen, are *entia per se*.

What could it mean, after all, to say that I might be 'annexed to' or 'placed in' a thinking thing or individual substance?

Whatever it might mean, either I am identical with the thinking substance in which I am thus placed or I am not identical with it.

If I am identical with the thinking substance in which I am thus placed, then I cannot be transferred *from* that substance to another thinking substance.

But if I am placed in a certain thinking substance and am not identical with that thinking substance, then there are *two* different things – the thinking substance and I. But if there are two things, which of us does the thinking? There are exactly four possibilities.

(1) Neither of us does the thinking – that is to say, neither of us thinks. But this we know is false.

(2) I think but the thinking substance does not think. Why call the latter a 'thinking' substance, then? (It would be like calling an elevator a thinking substance because it contains someone who thinks.) And what relation do I bear to this thinking substance? I'm not a *property* of it, since properties do not think. Am I a proper *part*, then, of the thinking substance? But proper parts of substances are themselves substances. And so if I am myself a thinking substance, what is the point of saying there is *another* thinking substance in which I am 'placed' or to which I am 'annexed'?

(3) The thinking substance thinks but I do not. But isn't this absurd? 'It's not really I who think; it is some *other* thing that thinks in me – some other thing that does what I mistakenly take to be my thinking.' (Or should the latter clause have been: 'some other thing that does what *it* mistakenly takes to be my thinking'?)

(4) Both the thinking substance and I think. Isn't this multiplying thinkers beyond necessity? If I want my dinner, does it follow that two of us want my dinner? Or does the thinking substance want its dinner and not mine?

I think we may reasonably conclude that there is no significant sense in which we may speak of the transfer of a self from one substance or individual thing to another.

6 'Will I Be He?': Truth-Conditions and Criteria

Suppose that there is a person x who happens to know, with respect to a certain set of properties, that there is or will be a certain person y who will have those properties at some future time, and x asks himself: 'Will I be he?' Either x is identical with y, or x is diverse from y.

We cannot find the *answer* to the question, 'Is x identical with y?', merely by deciding what would be practically convenient. To be sure, if we lack sufficient evidence for making a decision, it may yet be necessary for the courts to *rule* that x is the same person as y, or that he is not. Perhaps the ruling will have to be based upon practical considerations and conceivably such considerations may lead the court later to 'defeat' its ruling.

But one may always ask of any such ruling 'But is it *correct*, or *true*?' For a ruling to the effect that x is the same person as y will be correct, or true, only if x is identical with y.

We should remind ourselves, however, that the expression 'x is the same person as y' also has a use which is not this strict and philosophical one. Thus there are circumstances in which one might say: 'Mr Jones is not at all the same person he used to be. You will be disappointed. He is not the person that you remember.' We would not say this sort of thing if Mr Jones had changed only slightly. We would say it only if he had undergone changes that were quite basic and thorough-going – the kind of changes that might be produced by psychoanalysis, or by a lobotomy, or by a series of personal tragedies. But just *how* basic and thorough-going must these changes be if we are to say of Mr Jones that he is a different person? The proper answer would seem to be: 'As basic and thorough-going as you would like. It's just a matter of convention. It all depends upon how widely it is convenient for you to construe the expression "He's the same person he used to be". In so far as the rules of language are in your own hands, you may have it any way you would like.' [34] (Compare 'Jones is not himself today' or 'Jones was not himself when he said that'.)

This, however, is only playing loose with 'same' – or, more accurately, it is playing loose with 'not the same'. When we say, in the above sense, 'Jones is no longer the person he used to be', we do not mean that there is, or was, a certain entity such that Jones was formerly identical with that entity and is no longer so. What we are saying does not imply that there are (or have been) certain entities, x and y, such that at one time x is, or was, identical with y, and at another time x is not identical with y. For this is incoherent, but 'Jones is no longer the person he used to be' is not.

Nor do we mean, when we say 'Jones is no longer the person he used to be', that there *was* a certain entity, the old Jones, which no longer exists, and that there is a certain *different* entity, the new Jones, which somehow has taken his place. We are not describing the kind of change that takes place when one President succeeds another. In the latter case, there is a clear answer to the question 'What happened to the old one?' But when we decide to call Jones a new person, we are not confronted with such questions as: 'What happened, then, to the old Jones? Did he die, or was he annihilated, or disassembled, or did he retire to some other place?'

The old Jones did not die; he was not annihilated or disassembled; and he did not retire to any other place. He *became* the new Jones. And to say that he 'became' the new Jones is *not* to say that he 'became identical' with something he hadn't been identical with before. For it is only when a thing comes into being that it may be said to become identical with something it hadn't been identical with before. To say that our man 'became the new Jones' is to say that he, Jones, *altered* in a significant way, taking on certain interesting properties he had not had before. (Hence we should contrast the 'became' of 'Jones then became a married man', said when Jones ceased to be a bachelor, with that of 'The President then became a Republican', said when President Johnson retired.) When we say of a thing that *it* has properties that *it* did not have before, we are saying that there is an x such that x formerly had such-and-such properties and x presently has such-and-such other properties.

It will be instructive, I think, to consider two somewhat different examples.

The first is suggested by C. S. Peirce.[35] Elaborating upon his suggestion, let us assume that you are about to undergo an operation and that you still have a decision to make. The utilities involved are, first, financial – you wish to avoid any needless expense – and, secondly, the avoidance of pain, the avoidance, however, just of *your* pain, for pain that is other than yours, let us assume, if of no concern whatever to you. The doctor proposes two operating procedures – one a very expensive procedure in which you will be subjected to total anaesthesia and no pain will be felt at all, and the other of a rather different sort. The second operation will be very inexpensive indeed; there will be no anaesthesia at all and therefore there will be excruciating pain. But the doctor will give you two drugs: first, a drug just before the operation which will induce complete amnesia, so that while you are on the table you will have no memory whatever of your present life; and, secondly, just after the agony is over, a drug that will make you completely forget everything that happened on the table. The question is: given the utilities involved, namely, the avoidance of needless expense and the avoidance of pain that *you* will feel, other pains not mattering, is it reasonable for you to opt for the less expensive operation?

My own conviction is that it would *not* be reasonable, even if you could be completely certain that both amnesia injections would be successful. *You* are the one who would undergo that pain, even though you, Jones, would not know at the time that it is Jones who is undergoing it, and even though you would never remember it. Consider after all, the hypothesis that it would *not* be you. What would be your status, in such a case, during the time of the operation? Would you have passed away? That is to say, would you have *ceased to be*, but with the guarantee that you – you, yourself – would come into being once again when the agony was over?[36] And what about the person who *would* be feeling the pain? Who would he be?

It may well be that these things would not be obvious to you if in fact you had to make such a decision. But there is one point, I think, that ought to be obvious.

Suppose that others come to you – friends, relatives, judges, clergymen – and they offer the following advice and assurance. 'Have no fear', they will say. 'Take the cheaper operation and we will take care of everything. We will lay down the convention that the man on the table is not you, Jones, but is Smith.' What *ought* to be obvious to you, it seems to me, is that the laying down of this convention should have no effect at all upon your decision. For you may still ask, 'But won't that person be I?' and, it seems to me, the question has an answer.

I now turn to the second example. Suppose you know that your body, like that of an amoeba, would one day undergo fission and that you would go off, so to speak, in two different directions. Suppose you also know, somehow, that the one who went off to the left would experience the most wretched of lives and that the one who went off to the right would experience a life of great happiness and value. If I am right in saying that one's question 'Will that person be I?' or 'Will I be he?' always has a definite answer, then, I think, we may draw these conclusions. There is no possibility whatever that *you* would be *both* the the person on the right and the person on the left. Moreover, there *is* a possibility that you would be *one or the other* of those two persons. And, finally, *you* could be one of those persons and yet have no memory at all of your present existence. In this case, there may well be no *criterion* by means of which you or anyone else could decide which of the two halves was in fact yourself. Yet it would be reasonable of you, if you were concerned with *your* future pleasures and pains, to hope that you would be the one on the right and not the one on the left. It would also be reasonable of you, given such self-concern, to have this hope even if you knew that the one on the right would have no memory of your present existence. Indeed it would be reasonable of you to have it even if you know that the one on the *left* thought he remembered the facts of your present existence. And it seems to me to be absolutely certain that no fears that you might have, about being the half on the left, could reasonably be allayed by the adoption of a convention, even if our procedure were endorsed by the highest authorities.[37]

In trying to *decide* which one of the two persons, if either, you will be, you will, of course, make use of such *criteria* that you have and are able to apply. As we all know, there are intriguing philosophical questions about the criteria of the identity of persons through time. ('How are we to make sure, or make a reasonable guess, that that person at that time is the same as that person at the other time?')[38] What are we to do, for example, when bodily criteria and psychological criteria conflict? Suppose we know that the person on the left will have certain *bodily* characteristics that we have always taken to be typical only of you – and that the person on the right will have certain *psychological* characteristics that we have always taken to be typical only of you. In such a case there may be no sufficient reason at all for deciding that you are or that you are not one or the other of the two different persons. But from this it does not follow that you *will* not in fact be one or the other of the two persons.

We should remind ourselves of a very simple and obvious point. When you ask yourself, 'Will I be the person on the right?' your question is *not* 'Will the person on the right satisfy such criteria as I have, or such criteria as someone or other has, for deciding whether or not a given person is I?' To be sure, the best you can do, by way of answering the first question, is to try to answer the second. But the answers to the two questions are logically independent of each other.

What is a *criterion* of personal identity? It is a statement telling what constitutes evidence of personal identity – what constitutes a good reason for saying of a person x that he is, or that he is not, identical with a person y. Now there is, after all, a fundamental distinction between the *truth-conditions* of a proposition and the *evidence* we can have for deciding whether or not the proposition is true. The *truth-conditions* for the proposition that Caesar crossed the Rubicon consist of the fact, if it is a fact, that Caesar did cross the Rubicon. The only *evidence* you and I can have of this fact will consist of certain *other* propositions – propositions about records, memories and traces. It is only in the case of what is self-presenting (that I hope for rain or that I seem to me to have a headache) that the evidence for a proposition coincides with its truth-conditions. In all other cases, the two are logically independent; the one could be true while the other is false.[39]

The question 'Was it Caesar?' is not the same as the question:

'Do we have good evidence for thinking it was Caesar?' (or 'Have the criteria for saying that it was Caesar been fulfilled?'). This is true despite the fact that the most reasonable way of trying to find the answer to the first question is to try to answer the second.

And analogously for 'Will I be he?'

What I have said may recall this observation made by Leibniz: 'Suppose that some individual could suddenly become King of China on condition, however, of forgetting what he had been, as though being born again, would it not amount to the same practically, or as far as the effects could be perceived, as if the individual were annihilated, and a King of China were at the same instant created in his place? The individual would have no reason to desire this.' [40]

If I am being asked to consider the possibility that there is an *ens successivum* of which I happen to be the present constituent and which will subsequently be constituted by someone who will then be a King of China, then the fate of the later constituent may well be no special concern of mine. But what if Leibniz were not thus playing loose with 'is'?

In such a case, the proper reply to his question is suggested by the following observation in Bayle's *Dictionary*: 'The same atoms which compose water are in ice, in vapours, in clouds, in hail and snow; those which compose wheat are in the meal, in the bread, the blood, the flesh, the bones etc. Were they unhappy under the figure or form of water, and under that of ice, it would be the same numerical substance that would be unhappy in these two conditions; and consequently all the calamities which are to be dreaded, under the form of meal, concern the atoms which form corn; and nothing ought to concern itself so much about the state or lot of the meal, as the atoms which form the wheat, though they are not to suffer these calamities, under the form of wheat.' Bayle concludes that 'there are but two methods a man can employ to calm, in a rational manner, the fears of another life. One is, to promise himself the felicities of Paradise; the other, to be firmly persuaded that he shall be deprived of sensations of every kind.' [41]

CHAPTER IV

STATES OF AFFAIRS

Do you see, therefore, that truth is of propositions or thoughts – of possible ones, I mean – so that this at least is certain, that if someone thinks in a given way or its opposite, his thoughts will be true or false?

Leibniz [1]

1 Introduction

Let us turn, finally, to the ontology of states of affairs that is presupposed in the previous chapters.

States of affairs are here understood as abstract entities which exist necessarily and which are such that some but not all of them occur, take place or obtain. I will propose an ontology relating states of affairs to events and to what have traditionally been called 'propositions'. Events will be said to constitute one type of state of affairs and propositions another. I will defend this ontology by showing how it is capable of dealing with certain fundamental philosophical problems. And I will suggest, with respect to the alternative views, that either they are incapable of dealing with these problems or they are considerably more complex than the present view.

States of affairs, as they are considered here, are in no way dependent for their being upon the being of concrete, individual things. Even if there were no concrete, individual things, there would be indefinitely may states of affairs.[2] States of affairs, so conceived, resemble what have traditionally been called *propositions* in the following respect. Even though the author of *Waverley* was the author of *Marmion*, 'the author of *Waverley* being knighted' expresses a different state of affairs than does 'the author of *Marmion* being knighted' (the former state of affairs but not the latter could obtain in worlds in which there is no *Marmion*, and the latter but not the former could obtain in worlds in which there is no *Waverley*). And 'the proposition that the author of *Waverley* was knighted' expresses a proposition that is other than that expressed by 'the proposition that the author of *Marmion* was knighted' (the former proposition but not the latter implies that someone wrote *Waverley*, and the latter but not the former implies that someone wrote *Marmion*).

If the view to be defended here is correct, there is no need to assume that, *in addition* to states of affairs, there are such things as propositions and events.

The present view is thus to be contrasted with the view that events are to be included among the concrete things and individuals of the world. According to the latter view, which we will call the 'concrete event' view, there are such things as events but the class of events cannot be subdivided into those that occur and those that do not occur. If there were no concrete, individual things, then there would be no concrete events. The sentences that purport to describe concrete events are not like those that express states of affairs and propositions. 'Jones climbing Mount Monadnock' refers to the same concrete event as does 'Jones climbing the tallest mountain in southern New Hampshire' (but if Jones doesn't climb Mount Monadnock these expressions do not refer to an event at all). According to some, there are concrete events as well as states of affairs and propositions, and states of affairs are 'realised in' concrete events. And, as we will see, there are other possibilities. But the view here presupposed does not imply that there are such 'concrete events' in addition to states of affairs.

What are the facts to which any theory of events, propositions and states of affairs should be adequate? I will list thirteen true sentences, each containing a term ostensibly designating an event, proposition or state of affairs. I suggest that any adequate theory of events, propositions and states of affairs should be able to do one or the other of two things: (i) tell us what the terms in these sentences refer to; or (ii) show how to construe the sentences by using other terms and, if these other terms do not refer to properties, individual things, or times, then tell us what they do refer to. I believe that any theory adequate to these thirteen truths can also be made to accommodate whatever else we may know that seems to pertain to events, propositions or states of affairs.

(a) What Jones fears most is what Smith is trying to bring about,

(b) No proposition is both true and false,

(c) For all events, p, q and r, the probability of $p\&q$ in relation to r is the product of the probability of p in relation to r and the probability of q in relation to $p\&r$,

(d) There being round squares is impossible,

(e) One way of explaining the occurrence of an event *e* is to deduce *e* from a conjunction consisting of certain laws of nature and certain events which are known to have some prior probability,

(f) For all events *p* and *q*, if it is a law of nature (is physically necessary) that *p* occurs, and if *p* logically implies *q*, then it is a law of nature (is physically necessary) that *q* occurs.

(g) Someone walking is now occurring in Chicago,

(h) Truman being elected President occurred prior to Eisenhower being elected President,

(i) An incumbent President being re-elected has occurred more than seventeen times,

(j) The storm came into being on Tuesday and was all over by Thursday,

(k) Smith being ill contributed causally to Brown being re-elected,

(l) Smith perceived Jones to be robbed,

(m) The third occurrence of Jones being robbed contributed causally to his illness.

Considering this list objectively, one might say that the first six items – (a) through (f) – seem to commit us to states of affairs or propositions, and the final seven items – (g) through (m) – seem to commit us to concrete events. But, of course, from the fact that a true sentence *seems* to commit us to a certain type of thing it does not follow that there is in fact that type of thing. For perhaps what the sentence tells us can be re-expressed in such a way that it no longer even seems to commit us to the type of thing in question.

Consider, for example, the first type of fact to which we have referred. 'What Jones fears most is precisely what Smith is trying to bring about.' The sentence seems to tell us that there is a certain thing toward which Smith had one intentional attitude and toward which Jones had quite a different intentional attitude. Their common object, for example, could be Brown being elected mayor. They could have this common object even if Brown were not elected mayor. In that case, Jones's fears would have been unfounded and Smith's efforts unsuccessful. Brown being elected mayor, then, can *be* their common object even though it never occurs. The most natural view to take, therefore, with respect to this first type of fact, is to say that the common intentional object of Jones and Smith is a state of affairs – one that may or may not occur. And if we add to our supposition the fact that Brown will never be elected mayor, then our true sentence about Jones and Smith would seem to commit us to the existence of a certain state of affairs that will never occur. But knowing only that what Jones fears most is precisely what Smith is trying to bring about, we can say very little about the nature of their common concern.

From the fact that a true sentence *seems* to commit us to the existence of a certain object, it does not follow that there *is* in fact such an object. What we should say is rather this: If (i) there is a sentence which seems to commit us to the existence of a certain object, (ii) we know the sentence to be true, and (iii) we can find no way of explicating or paraphrasing the sentence which will make clear to us that the truth of the sentence is compatible with the nonexistence of such an object, then it is more reasonable to suppose that there is such an object than it is not to suppose that there is such an object. Given an adequate view of the nature of philosophy, it does not seem to me to be reasonable to deny this conditional. Now the example we have just considered satisfies conditions (i) and (ii) of the antecedent. I would say, therefore, that the issue to which the example gives rise turns on condition (ii). Can we paraphrase 'There is something that Jones long dreaded and that Smith tried very hard to bring about' in such a way that the result can be seen not to commit us to the existence of propositions or of states of affairs? I do not know of any such paraphrase.[3] (In considering any particular attempt to paraphrase the sentence in question, one should keep in mind that the sentence provides us with no clue as to what it is that Jones and Smith are concerned about. For all we know, it might be, say, the discovery of the Fountain of Youth or an attack by the abominable snowman.)

2 The Ontology of States of Affairs

We will say that the mark of a state of affairs is the fact that it is capable of being accepted:

D.IV.1 p is a state of affairs = Df It is possible that there is
           someone who accepts p.

Using 'considers' or 'entertains', in the way in which we have taken these expressions, we could also say that a state of affairs is whatever may be considered or entertained. Acceptance, as it is here understood, constitutes the subject matter of Appendix c ('The Objects of Belief and Endeavour').

Frege used the term 'thought' (*Gedanke*) as we are using 'state of affairs' and observed: 'The being of a thought may also be taken to lie in the possibility of different thinkers' grasping the thought as one and the same thought.' [4] (For the present, we will interpret many of the observations philosophers have made about *propositions* as being applicable generally to states of affairs. Subsequently, we will attempt to single out propositions as constituting a subspecies of states of affairs.)

The view is also suggested by the quotation from Leibniz with which we began this chapter: 'Do you see, therefore, that truth is of propositions or thoughts – of possible ones, I mean – so that this at least is certain, that if someone thinks in a given way or its opposite, his thoughts will be true or false?' Leibniz's expression 'possible thought' should be taken to mean the same as 'that which can be thought', or better, 'that which can be considered or entertained'. Commenting on this passage from Leibniz, Bernard Bolzano notes: 'The golden candlestick is a kind of candlestick, but the possible thought is not a kind of thought, but merely a kind of possibility. Therefore, if we wish to make the above expression more precise, we will have to say that, according to Leibniz, a proposition is "the possibility of a thought", or even more clearly, "it is something that *can* be thought or *can* constitute the content of a thought". There is indeed no doubt that this thinkability is a property of any proposition . . .' [5]

What would be a non-trivial criterion of identity for states of affairs? Since we are characterising states of affairs as possible intentional objects, as things which are such that they may be accepted, we can introduce the following strict concept of entailment:

D.IV.2 p entails q =Df p is necessarily such that (a) if it obtains then q obtains and (b) whoever accepts it accepts q.

And now we may affirm this non-trivial criterion of identity: if a state of affairs p is identical with a state of affairs q, then p entails q and q entails p.

Two undefined concepts are thus essential to our conception of states of affairs: that expressed by the intentional expression 'accepts' and that expressed by 'obtains' ('occurs' or 'takes place'). To clarify the conception still further, let us take note of certain very general principles.

We assume, first of all, that states of affairs, like properties or attributes exist necessarily:

(1)   For every p, if p is a state of affairs, then p exists necessarily.

Thus Whitehead said that all propositions, whether true or false, are 'eternal objects' and Husserl said that all states of affairs (*Sachverhalten*), including those that are impossible and absurd, are 'ideal unities' that neither come into being nor pass away.[6] To say of a state of affairs that it *exists* is not to say, of course, that it obtains or occurs.

We assume, secondly, that states of affairs are related to properties and relations in the following way:

(2)   For every property or relation G, there is a state of affairs p and there is a state of affairs q which are necessarily such that: p obtains if and only if G is exemplified and q obtains if and only if G is not exemplified.

This principle enables us to say that states of affairs are of two sorts: those that obtain (occur, or take place) and those that do not. It presupposes an extreme version of Platonism: there are attributes or properties, some of which are exemplified and some of which are not.

We assume that, for any two properties G and H, there is a property C which is necessarily such that a thing has C if and only if it has G and it has H. Hence there are properties which nothing can possibly have; an example is the property of *being both round and square*. And therefore there are states of affairs which cannot possibly obtain; an example is *there being round squares*. And there are also states of affairs which necessarily obtain; an example is *there being no round squares*. But all such states of affairs, whether or not they obtain and whether or not they can possibly obtain, exist necessarily.[7]

We will assume, thirdly, that every state of affairs is contradicted by some state of affairs:

(3)   For every p, if p is a state of affairs, then there is a state of affairs q which is necessarily such that it obtains if and only if p does not obtain.

Any two such states of affairs may be said to contradict each other. The concept of the *negation* of a state of affairs could be defined in terms of this relation.[8]

And we will assume, fourthly, that there are *conjunctive* states of affairs:

(4) For every state of affairs p and every state of affairs q, there is a state of affairs c which is necessarily such that, c obtains if and only if p obtains and q obtains.

Such a state of affairs c would be *a conjunction* of p and q.

Given the concepts of the negation of a state of affairs and of a conjunction of states of affairs, along with the general principles we have set forth, we may now interpret the formulae of the propositional calculus as being general principles about states of affairs.

3 Some Alternative Conceptions

The alternatives to the present conception are best distinguished by reference to the following list of ontological categories, or possible ontological categories:

(a) concrete events;
(b) states of affairs;
(c) propositions;
(d) facts.

One who held that each of these four categories is exemplified and that none is reducible to the others might distinguish them as follows: 'Concrete events, along with such concrete individual things as persons and physical bodies, comprise those things which are such that, although they exist, they need not have existed. States of affairs, on the other hand, are eternal objects some of which happen to be realised or manifested at particular places and times. Propositions are also eternal objects; but where states of affairs may be divided into those that obtain and those that do not obtain, propositions may be divided into that that are true and those that are false. Propositions, moreover, are either eternally true or eternally false. And facts are the things that make propositions true; if a proposition is true, it is true in virtue of a certain fact.'

But we need not say that there are, in the strict and proper sense, all four types of entity. For some of these categories may be reduced to others. Let us remind ourselves briefly of the principal possibilities.

It has been held that all four categories are reducible to concrete individual things. This is the 'reistic' view of Franz Brentano and Tadeuz Kotarbinski.[9]

It has been held that particular contingent events are reducible to sets of concrete individual things, properties and times. This is the 'property exemplification' account of events that has been set forth and defended in a series of articles by Jaegwon Kim.[10] According to this account, an event is a class that is constituted by (i) a concrete thing or things, (ii) a property or relation and (iii) a particular time. The event is said to *exist*, if and only if, at its constitutive time, its constitutive thing has its constitutive property – or its constitutive things stand in its constitutive relations.[11] Given this account, one may say, as Kim does, that events are identical provided their constitutive things, their constitutive properties or relations and their constitutive times are identical. Hence Jones climbing Mount Monadnock would be the same event as Mrs Jones's husband climbing the tallest mountain in the southern quarter of New Hampshire. Kim does not commit himself with respect to propositions and states of affairs, but in some of his writings he makes essential use of the concept of *a fact*.

It has also been held that there are concrete events and that it is possible to avoid commitment with respect to the entities in the other three categories listed above. This view has been suggested in a series of studies by Donald Davidson.[12]

There are several variants of the view that there are concrete events. Thus C. I. Lewis seems to have held that there are concrete events and also states of affairs.[13] Others who have said that there are both types of entity have gone on to say that states of affairs are *exemplified in* concrete events. If we call Kim's view the *property exemplification* view, we might call this the *event exemplification* view. It is sometimes put by saying that every concrete event is a case of indefinitely many 'generic events'.[14] (Consider this philosophical reasoning. 'Jones pulling the trigger was the same event as Jones killing Smith. One may object that, whereas his pulling the trigger was foreseen and predicted, his killing Smith was not. But actually what was foreseen and predicted was, not the event itself, but that it was to be a case of pulling the trigger, and what was not foreseen and predicted was that the event was also to be a case of someone killing someone.') I believe that this 'event exemplification' theory – that concrete events exemplify indefinitely many generic events – is also presupposed by those philosophers who formulate their theses in the 'under a description' terminology.[15] (Consider this philosophical reasoning: 'Jones pulling the trigger was the same event as Jones killing Smith. One may object that, whereas his pulling the trigger was foreseen and predicted, his killing Smith was not. But actually what was foreseen and predicted was only the event under one of its descriptions, that of "being

a case of someone pulling the trigger"; what was not foreseen
and predicted was the event under the description "being a case
of somebody killing somebody" '.) It has also been suggested that
states of affairs, or 'generic events', are exemplified in *times*.[16]

But I will suggest in what follows that concrete events, like
facts and propositions, may be reduced to states of affairs.[17] I
will not consider the other possible views polemically.

4 Propositions

In our list of pre-analytic data above, we cited thirteen different
types of fact. The first six items on the list would seem to require
a theory like our theory of states of affairs, for they are most
plausibly interpreted as pertaining to states of affairs or propositions. They are:

(a)   What Jones fears most is what Smith is trying to bring
      about,
(b)   No proposition is both true and false,
(c)   For all events, p, q and r, the probability of $p\&q$ in
      relation to r is the product of the probability of p in
      relation to r and the probability of q in relation to
      $p\&r$,
(d)   There being round squares is impossible,
(e)   One way of explaining the occurrence of an event e
      is to deduce e from a conjunction consisting of certain
      laws of nature and certain events which are known to
      have some prior probability,
(f)   For all events p and q, if it is a law of nature (is phy-
      sically necessary) that p occurs, and if p implies q, then
      it is a law of nature (is physically necessary) that q
      occurs.

Thus sentence (b) in our list of pre-analytic data is a truth
of logic ('no proposition is both true and false') and sentence
(c) is an elementary theorem of the theory of probability. These
are plausibly interpreted as referring to *propositions*.

If we take the term 'proposition' in what may now be said to
be its correct philosophical sense, we may say that this term, if
it refers to anything, refers to an abstract object existing in every
possible world.[18] Hence propositions, if there are such things,
are very much like states of affairs. Propositions, however, are
said to be true or false and not to occur or obtain. And states of
affairs – or some of them – are said to occur or obtain and not
to be true or false. Moreover, propositions are eternally true or
eternally false, but states of affairs, or some of them, are such

that they may occur or obtain at certain times and fail to occur or obtain at certain other times.

Yet it would seem that we are multiplying entities beyond necessity if we say that among the things that exist eternally in all possible worlds is *the state of affairs of Socrates being mortal* and also *the proposition that Socrates is mortal*. Can we reduce one to the other?

In defining the concept of a proposition, we will make use of the expression '*p* occurs at time *t*', which will be defined in D.IV.5 below. We might be tempted to say that a proposition is a state of affairs which is necessarily such that either it always occurs or it never occurs. But given what we will say about '*p* occurs at time *t*', it will be more accurate to say that a proposition is a state of affairs which is incapable of being such that it occurs at certain times and fails to occur at other times.

> D.IV.3   *p* is a proposition =Df *p* is a state of affairs, and it is impossible that there is a time *t* and a time *t'* such that *p* occurs at *t* and does not occur at *t'*.

A *true proposition* may now be defined as a proposition that occurs and a *false proposition* as one that does not occur. And *a fact* may be said to be a proposition that is true. (But we should note that in some of its uses the expression 'a fact' may be taken to refer to a proposition that is *known* to be true.)

Let us take note briefly of one possible objection to this reduction of propositions to states of affairs. We may put it as follows:

'(i) Your theory implies that, if a man believes that a storm is occurring, then that state of affairs which is the occurrence of a storm is the object of his belief. But (ii) the sentence "He believes that a storm is occurring" is natural and clearly grammatical, whereas " He believes the occurrence of a storm" is unnatural and not clearly grammatical. Hence (iii) if a man believes that a storm is occurring something other than the occurrence of a storm is the object of his belief.' [19]

The premises of the argument are certainly true. If we wish to say of a man that he believes that a storm is occurring, we do not *say* 'He believes the occurrence of a storm'. But we may say 'He *believes in* or *suspects*, or is *counting on*, or is *mindful of*, the occurrence of a storm'. And where we may say of a man that he fears, regrets, hopes or knows that a storm is occurring, we may also say, equally well, that he fears, regrets, hopes for or is cognisant of the occurrence of a storm. Such points of usage may throw light upon various intentional attitudes. But surely they give us no reason to suppose that 'the occurrence of a storm' and 'that a storm is occurring' refer to different things. The argument is simply a *non sequitur*.

Given that there are states of affairs, and given our reduction of propositions to states of affairs, we can interpret the first six truths on our list of pre-analytic data as pertaining to states of affairs. The first is a truth about propositional attitudes; the second a truth of logic; the third a truth about the theory of probability; the fourth a truth of logic or metaphysics; the fifth a truth about the theory of explanation; and the sixth a truth about laws of nature or physical necessity.

But we will note in passing the following objection to our suggestion that states of affairs constitute the objects of the theory of explanation: 'Presumably the tallest man marrying the shortest woman is the same state of affairs as the shortest woman marrying the tallest man. But to explain why the tallest man married the shortest woman need not be to explain why the shortest woman married the tallest man. How can this be?' [20] An answer to this objection will be given at the end of Section 9 below.

If the first six truths on our list of pre-analytic data are most plausibly interpreted as pertaining to *propositions,* then the seven truths that follow – namely, (g) through (m) – would seem to pertain to *events.* But I suggest that events, like propositions, may be reduced to states of affairs.

5 The Times and Places of States of Affairs

Of the final seven items on our list of pre-analytic data, the first two are these:

(g)   Someone walking is now occurring in Chicago,
(h)   Truman being elected President occurred prior to Eisenhower being elected President.

Can we construe these truths as truths about states of affairs?

States of affairs, we have said, are abstract and eternal objects. How, then, can they be so intimately connected with places and times?

Let us first remind ourselves that states of affairs may be said to entail, not only states of affairs, but also relations and properties. Thus we made use of this definition in Chapter I:

D.I.3 p entails the property of being F $=$Df p is necessarily such that (i) if it obtains the something has the property of being F and (ii) whoever accepts p believes that something is F.

We next introduce the concept of the *concretisation* of a state of affairs.

Some of the properties entailed by a state of affairs are restricted to contingent things – to things which are such that they exist but do not necessarily exist. Thus *Brutus killing Caesar* entails the following properties among others: killing someone; being killed by someone; being identical with Brutus; being identical with Caesar. Each of these properties is such that it can be instantiated only by contingent things. Now every such property that is entailed by *Brutus killing Caesar* is instantiated by members of the class consisting just of Brutus and Caesar.[21] Some are instantiated by both and some just by Brutus and some just by Caesar. But no proper subset of the class consisting of Brutus and Caesar is such that its members instantiate all such properties entailed by *Brutus killing Caesar*.[22] We may define concretisation as follows:

> D.IV.4   *e* is concretised by A at *t* =Df *e* occurs; for every property P, if *e* entails P, and if P is had only by contingent things, then some member of A has P at *t*; and there is no proper subset S of A which is such that, for every such P, some member of S has P.[23]

Now we may say that that state of affairs which is *Brutus killing Caesar* was concretised in 44 BC by the set consisting just of Brutus and Caesar.

Given this concept of concretisation, we may now say what it is for a state of affairs to occur at a given time and at a given place:

> D.IV.5   *e* occurs at time *t* =Df There is a set A such that *e* is concretised by A at time *t*.

> D.IV.6   *e* occurs at place P =Df There is a set A and a time *t* such that *e* is concretised by A at *t*, and all the members of A are at place P at *t*.

Our definition may now be applied in a straightforward way to item (g) on our list of pre-analytic data: 'Someone walking is now occurring in Chicago.'

Item (h) on our list – 'Truman being elected President occurred prior to Eisenhower being elected President' – becomes 'There are a time *t* and a time *t'* such that Truman being elected President occurred at *t*, Eisenhower being elected occurred at *t'*, and *t* is prior to *t'*.'

Given this way of looking at the times and places of states of

affairs, we cannot say, of every state of affairs, that if it occurs
then it occurs at a certain place (but presumably we can say, of
every state of affairs, that if it occurs, then it occurs at a certain
time or times). There being no unicorns occurs, but we cannot,
in our account, specify any place within which it occurs – for it
is a state of affairs that could occur in a universe in which there
were no concrete things. (Of course, we could, if we chose, give
a meaning to 'There being no unicorns occurs at place P'. For
example, we could define it as saying 'P is a place and there
being unicorns does not occur'. This would allow us to say that
there being no unicorns occurs everywhere.)

By reference to the places and times at which states of affairs
occur, we could go on to consider such concepts as the spatial
and temporal *extent* of a state of affairs, the spatial and temporal
parts of a state of affairs, and even the *motion* of a state of affairs.
(If there is a certain disorder which occurs in a man's foot and
not in his ankle, then occurs in the upper part of his foot and
the lower part of his ankle but not in the lower part of his foot
or in the upper part of his ankle, and then occurs in his ankle
but not in his foot, we could say that the disorder 'has moved'
from his foot to his ankle.) To fix these concepts precisely, we
would need to consider certain problems about space, time,
continuity and motion which are not relevant to our present
concerns.

6 Events

I have said that *events*, like propositions, constitute a subspecies
of states of affairs.

A possible definition of '*p* is an event' would now be this:
'*p* is a state of affairs which is not a proposition and which is
concretised at some place and time'. This definition would enable
us to restrict events to those states of affairs which occur and
which would not occur if there were no individual things. But
the definition would be too broad.

It would require us to say, not only that 'The Archduke
Ferdinand being shot' expresses an event, but also that 'The
Archduke Ferdinand being such that he will be shot in a year'
expresses an event. Then we will have to say that, if the occurrence of the first event contributed causally to World War I
in 1914, then the occurrence of the second event contributed
causally to World War I in 1913. But if we were to list the events
of 1913 that led to World War I, we should not include among
them that state of affairs which is the Archduke Ferdinand being
such that he would be shot within a year. Our theory of events,

then, should not commit us to saying that such a state of affairs is an event.

Let us recall the distinction made in the previous chapter between those properties (and relations) which are rooted outside the present and those which are not. Thus we said that some properties are 'rooted outside times at which they are had':

D.III.6   G is rooted outside times at which it is had $=$Df Necessarily, for any x and for any period of time t, x has the property G throughout t only if x exists at some time before or after t.

The following properties are all rooted outside times at which they are had: being such that it will move; being such that it did move; being such that he is taking his second walk of the day; being such that she is taking the first of her two walks; being such that he will be shot in a year.

We noted that some properties may but need not be rooted outside times at which they are had:

D.III.7   G may be rooted outside times at which it is had $=$Df G is equivalent to a disjunction of two properties, one of which is, and the other of which is not, rooted outside times at which it is had.

Examples of properties that may but need not be rooted outside times at which they are had are: being such that either it is walking (s) or did walk (Q); being such that either it is walking (s) or will walk (Q); or being such that it either is, was, or will be walking.

And finally, we said, some properties are *not* such that they may be rooted outside times at which they are had.

How shall we characterise events?

We will restrict events to those states of affairs which occur at certain places and times. Hence two and two being four, two and two not being four, there being unicorns, and there being no unicorns are all such that they are not events.

Events will not be included among those states of affairs which are necessarily such that either they always occur or they never occur. Hence they will not be propositions.

And events will entail properties that may not be rooted outside the times at which they are had.

Can we now say that *John being such that he will walk* is not an event? Not quite yet; for it entails some properties that must be rooted in the present. Examples are the property of being self-identical and the property of being an individual thing. But these properties are essential to John – and indeed to every individual thing. Let us say that an event must entail certain non-essential properties that may not be rooted outside the present.

And so we will characterise events this way:

D.IV.7 p is an event $=Df$ p is a state of affairs which is such that: (i) it occurs; (ii) it is not a proposition; and (iii) it entails a property G which is such that (a) only individual things can exemplify G, (b) it is possible that no individual things exemplify G, and (c) G is not such that it may be rooted outside the times at which it is had.

If we may assume that all individual things have spatio-temporal location, then we may deduce that every event is such that it occurs at some place and some time. And so we may say that events, like propositions, constitute subspecies of the genus states of affairs.

This definition of event enables us to deal with a question that was left unanswered in Chapter II: 'If a sufficient causal condition c of a certain event e is such that c occurs at 10 a.m., then did there occur at 9 a.m. another sufficient causal condition of e (the world being such that c will occur in an hour) and does there occur throughout eternity a sufficient causal condition of e (c occurring at 10 a.m.)?' We said that a sufficient causal condition is an *event*; and now we can say that 'the world is such that c will occur in an hour' and 'c occurs at 10 a.m.' do not refer to events. Hence, from the fact that a sufficient causal condition of e occurred at 10 a.m., it does not follow that there has occurred throughout eternity a sufficient causal condition of e.

7 Recurrence

Some states of affairs don't occur at all; some occur exactly once; and some occur more than once and thus may be said to *recur*. A state of affairs of the latter sort is the one referred to in item (i) on our list of pre-analytic data: 'An incumbent President being re-elected has occurred more than seventeen times'.

Recurrence, it may be noted, poses certain difficulties for what we have called the concrete event theory, for this theory, at least as it is commonly set forth, does not allow for the literal recurrence of events. The fact of recurrence may constitute one reason for saying that, if there are concrete events, then there are 'generic events' (very much like states of affairs).

We may now characterise recurrence by reference to concretisation:

D.IV.8   A is such that at t it has concretised p exactly n times =Df There are n periods of time such that: no two of them are continuous with each other; none is later than t; A concretises p during each; and A does not concretise p at any other time within or prior to t.

D.IV.9 p is such that at t it has been concretised exactly n times =Df Consider each set that concretises p at t or prior to t; for each such set take that number which is the number of times such that the set at t has concretised p exactly that number of times; the sum of all such numbers is n.

Item (i) on our list of pre-analytic data – 'An incumbent President being re-elected has occurred more than seventeen times' – now becomes: 'There is a number n such that n is greater than seventeen and an incumbent President being re-elected has been concretised n times.' [24]

We are now in a position to answer an objection to our proposal that events may be reduced to states of affairs. The objection may be put in the following form: '(i) The author of *Waverley* was identical with the author of *Marmion*. (ii) That state of affairs which is the author of *Waverley* being knighted is other than that state of affairs which is the author of *Marmion* being knighted. But (iii) at the place and time the author of *Waverley* was knighted only *one* knighting occurred. Hence (iv) the knighting of the author of *Waverley* was identical with the knighting of the author of *Marmion*. And therefore (v) the knighting of the author of *Waverley*, i.e. the knighting of the author of *Marmion*, is not a state of affairs.' [25]

We may note that (iv) does not follow from (iii). For (iii) – 'at the place and time the author of *Waverley* was knighted only *one* knighting occurred' – may be construed as telling us that that state of affairs which is someone being knighted was concretised just once at that place and time.

Suppose Socrates walks for a while, then sits down to rest, and then walks again. Then Socrates walking will be such that there is a certain time during which it occurs, a certain later time during which it does not occur, and a certain still later time at which it occurs once again. St Thomas finds the following difficulty in this assumption: '. . . when a walking man pauses, that walking ceases. But when he begins to walk again, then there will be walking again. Therefore, if it be said that the walking is one and the same, then one and the same thing both is and is corrupted many times. But this is impossible.' [26]

We need not accept St Thomas's statement that, if the walking is one and the same on the two occasions, 'then one and the same thing both is and is corrupted many times'. For the state of affairs which is Socrates walking doesn't come into being when he begins to walk and doesn't cease to be when he ceases to walk. Rather, we have said, it is an abstract object that exists throughout eternity. And this is entirely consistent with saying that it occurs at certain times and places and fails to occur at other times and places. But this conclusion may seem to conflict with our item (j).

8 Events as Coming into Being and Passing Away

Item (j) is this: 'A storm came into being on Tuesday and was all over by Thursday.'

If states of affairs are eternal objects, then they do not come into being or pass away. Hence (j) cannot be construed as telling us that a certain state of affairs came into being on Tuesday and passed away by Thursday. What, then, does it tell us?

Let us first note that the states of affairs we have been discussing up to now are relatively simple. They are designated by such sentential gerundives as 'Jones being ill' and 'the President being elected'. The terms within these gerundives ('Jones' and 'the President') designate concrete individual things and not states of affairs or events. But the term 'storm' is not a sentential gerundive. If we are to make it apparent that sentences about storms can be construed as sentences about states of affairs, then we should show how they might be re-expressed in sentences containing sentential gerundives – where these gerundives do not themselves contain terms purporting to designate events or states of affairs. Replacing 'storm' by 'there being a storm' will not help, for the latter expression contains the term 'storm' which purports to designate an event or state of affairs.

What is a storm? Keeping our meteorology somewhat primitive, we could say that a storm is either a storm of precipitation or a wind storm. A storm of precipitation would be rain or snow or hail falling from the clouds and a wind storm would be things being blown about. (Perhaps we should qualify the latter, requiring that the things be above a certain specified size and weight and that the area be greater than a certain specified volume. Perhaps we should specify, too, that the things be blown about as a result of certain natural causes. But these are details of meteorology and do not affect any principle involved in our present discussion.) Given this simple meteorology we could define 'a storm' as 'rain, snow or hail falling from clouds or things being blown about'.

What, now, of item (j): 'A storm came into being on Tuesday and was all over by Thursday'? This would become: 'There was a time on Tuesday or immediately before Tuesday when a storm did not occur; there was a time after that on Tuesday when it did occur; and then it occurred without interruption until some time before Thursday.'

Note that, if we do say that events come into being and pass away, we must find a solution to the following philosophical puzzle: 'When did the performance of the symphony come into being? Not with the playing of the first notes, for the performance of the symphony didn't exist *then*. Not with the playing of the final note, for in that case, unless the performance existed only as long as the final note existed, it existed before it came into being. Somewhere, then, towards the end of the second movement?' [27]

9 De Re *Explanation*

That state of affairs which is the President being in Washington may be said to imply, with respect to Mr Ford, that he is Washington. Let us recall, once again, our definition of what it means to say of a state of affairs that it implies something with respect to a thing.

> D.I.6 p implies x to have the property of being F $=$Df
> There is a property G such that (i) G is an individual concept, (ii) p entails the conjunction of G and the property of being F, and (iii) x has G.

(An individual concept, we had said, is a property which can be exemplified but only by one thing at a time.)

Philosophers sometimes use, without defining it, the expression 'constituent of a proposition'. We could say that a *constituent of a state of affairs p* is anything which is such that p implies it to have a certain property. Thus Mr Ford is a constituent of the President being in Washington. (We should note that, given our definition, we cannot say that particular men are constituents of all men being mortal, for this state of affairs does not imply any particular man to be mortal.)

Let us now consider one of the objections set forth at the end of Section 4 above. The objection was: 'Presumably the tallest man marrying the shortest woman is the same state of affairs as the shortest woman marrying the tallest man. But to explain why the tallest man married the shortest woman need not be to explain why the shortest woman married the tallest man. How can this be?'

We should distinguish: (i) explaining that state of affairs which is the tallest man marrying the shortest woman (and which is the same as that state of affairs which is the shortest woman marrying the tallest man); (ii) explaining, with respect to the tallest man, why he married the shortest woman; and (iii) explaining, with respect to the shortest woman, why she married the tallest man.

We could say that (i) would be an instance of *de dicto* explanation and (ii) and (iii) would be instances of *de re* explanation. Let us assume that we have an adequate account of *de dicto* explanation – of what it is for one proposition to explain another proposition. How we are to understand the concept of *de re* explanation which is involved in (ii) and (iii) above? I suggest we can understand it this way:

> D.IV.10 p explains, with respect to x, why it has the property of being F $=$ Df There is a q which implies x to have the property of being F, and p explains q.

Suppose that q is the proposition expressed by 'the tallest man undertook to marry the shortest woman and succeeded'. And suppose that p is the proposition expressed by 'The tallest man wanted to marry a wealthy woman; the shortest woman was available to him for marriage; he believed her wealthy . . .' Let us imagine that p constitutes an adequate *de dicto* explanation of q. We may now say, given our definition of *de re* explanation, that p explains with respect to the tallest man why he has the property of marrying the shortest woman.

A proposition which explains, with respect to the tallest man, why he married the shortest woman, will be of this sort: for some property that the shortest woman has, the proposition will explain, with respect to the tallest man, why he married someone having *that* property – but the property need not be that of being the shortest woman. And a proposition which explains, with respect to the shortest woman, why she married the tallest man, will be of this sort: for some property that the tallest man has, the proposition will explain, with respect to the shortest woman, why she married someone having *that* property – but that property need not be the property of being the tallest man. Hence a proposition which explains, with respect to the tallest man, why he has the property of marrying the shortest woman, need not be one which explains, with respect to the shortest woman, why she has the property of being married to the tallest man.

This way of looking at the matter will keep us from being entangled in still other snares. Consider a proposition *p* which explains why it is that the tallest man, who happens to have been married twice before, married the shortest woman. One need not expect *p* to throw light upon the earlier marriages of the tallest man, for *p* need not explain that state of affairs expressed by 'the tallest man, who happens to have been married twice before, married the shortest woman'. Rather *p* will be a proposition of this sort: there is an *x* such that (a) *x* is the tallest man, (b) *p* explains, with respect to *x*, why *x* married the shortest woman and (c) *x* had been married twice prior to marrying the shortest woman.

10 *Cause and Effect:* De Dicto *and* De Re

We have noted that truths about physical necessity or laws of nature (see item (f)) are plausibly construed as pertaining to states of affairs. We may say the same thing, therefore, of truths about *necessary causal conditions* and *sufficient causal conditions,* for the latter two concepts are readily explicated by reference to laws of nature, times and states of affairs.[28] We are now concerned with the concept of *causal contribution* as this is to be understood in item (k): 'Smith being ill contributed causally to Brown being re-elected.'

Our present problem is not that of analysing the concept of causal contribution. It is, rather, to show that truths about causal contribution, such as (k), may be construed as truths about states of affairs. We will permit ourselves the undefined expression 'at *t p* contributes causally to *q*', which may be taken to imply that *p* occurs at *t* and that *q* occurs at *t* or some time after *t*.

Item (k) – 'Smith being ill contributed causally to Brown being re-elected' – tells us more than that that state of affairs which is Smith being ill contributed causally to that state of affairs which is Brown being re-elected. The terms 'Smith' and 'Brown' in (k) are referentially transparent and thus may be replaced by any co-designative terms. Hence (k) in conjunction with 'Smith is the town grocer and Brown is the town plumber' will imply: 'The town grocer being ill contributed to the town plumber being re-elected.'

Looking back, once again, to D.I.6 (our definition of 'p implies x to have the property of being F'), we may note that that state of affairs which is Smith being ill implies Smith to have the property of being ill, and that that state of affairs which is Brown being re-elected implies Brown to have the property of being re-elected.

Given the concept of *de dicto* causal contribution, i.e. the concept of one state of affairs contributing causally to another state of affairs, we may now add this schematic definition of causal contribution *de re*:

> D.IV.11 x being F contributes causally at t to y being G
> = Df Consider all those states of affairs which are such that they occur, they imply x to be F at t, and they do not imply y to be G; each such state of affairs contributes causally to a state of affairs which implies y to be G.

Thus (k) becomes: 'Consider all those states of affairs which are such that they occur, they imply Smith to be ill, and they do not imply Brown to be re-elected; each such state of affairs contributes causally to a state of affairs which implies Brown to be re-elected.' The terms 'Smith' and 'Brown' in this statement may be replaced by any co-designative terms.[29]

One may object: 'Suppose Smith takes cyanide and dies in consequence. And suppose Jones believed truly that Smith would take cyanide. Your definition has the absurd consequence that Jones having this true belief contributed causally to the death of Smith. To see this assume that x is Jones, y is Smith, 'being F' stands for the property of truly believing that Smith takes cyanide and 'being G' stands for the property of dying.'

The reply is that it is *not* absurd to say that the state of affairs expressed by 'Jones believes truly that Smith takes cyanide' causally contributes to the death of Jones. For to say that Jones believes truly that Smith takes cyanide is to say of *Smith taking cyanide* that it obtains and is accepted by Jones.[30] In other words, 'Jones believes truly that Smith took cyanide' tells us that Smith took cyanide and that Jones believed that he did. But if that state of affairs which is Smith taking cyanide contributed causally to Smith's death, then so did that wider state of affairs which is Smith taking cyanide and Jones believing that he did. For if p contributes causally to q, and r is an event, then p and r contributes causally to q.

11 Perception

Perception may be viewed as a propositional attitude and hence as taking states of affairs as its intentional object.[31] Perception may also be directed upon particular concreta. Item (l) on our list – 'Smith perceived Jones to be robbed' – would seem to describe a case wherein perception is directed upon a concretum. For we may interpret it in such a way that it implies 'Smith perceived Jones'. If we do take (l) in this way it would seem to be referentially transparent. Thus the conjunction of 'Jones is the man on the beach' and 'Smith perceived Jones to be robbed' implies 'Smith perceived the man on the beach to be robbed'.

If we are inclined to accept the concrete event theory, we may say: 'The object of the perception described in (l) is more than just Jones and the other individual things involved; it is that thing which is *Jones* being robbed. Because of the referential transparency of (l), we see that the perception in question involves as its object something other than Jones and states of affairs. It is directed upon a concrete event.'

But let us add this schematic definition:

> D.IV.12 s perceives x to have the property of being F = Df There is a state of affairs p which is such that: s perceives p; and p implies x to have the property of being F.

If we construe 'Smith perceived Jones to be robbed' in this way, then we can say that the perception with which it is concerned involves no objects other than individual things and states of affairs. And we may take it to imply 'Smith perceives Jones', if we construe the latter expression this way:

> D.IV.13 s perceives x = Df There is a property such that s perceives x to have that property.

(If what we have said in Chapter I is correct, the property is likely to be one that relates x uniquely to s.)

12 Particular Occurrences

The last item on our list is (m): 'The third occurrence of Jones being robbed contributed causally to his illness.'

In analysing this, we appeal to the concepts defined in D.IV.9 ('p is such that at t it has been concretised exactly n times') and in D.IV.11 ('x being F contributes causally to y being G') along with the concept of causal contribution as a relation that holds between states of affairs. We may interpret (m) in this way:

'There is a time t such that: Jones being robbed occurs at t; Jones being robbed is such that at t it has been concretised exactly three times; and Jones being robbed contributes causally at t to Jones being ill.'

There are other truths which, like (m), ostensibly pertain to the particular occurrences of states of affairs. Some of these combine the features of (k) and (m); for example, 'Smith perceived the third occurrence of Jones being robbed'. But, so far as I have been able to see, each of these is such that it can be construed as pertaining just to individual things, properties and states of affairs.

I believe, then, that the view of states of affairs here presupposed is adequate to the pre-analytic data here set forth.[32] I know of no other philosophical theory which is, or even claims to be, adequate to all these data.

13 Individual Things

If what I have said is correct, then there is no need for us to suppose that the class of contingent things contains anything other than *entia realia* or concrete, individual things. Therefore we may say:

> D.IV.14 x is an individual thing $=$ Df There exists a y such that y is identical with x and it is possible that there does not exist a y such that y is identical with x.

What now of persons? States of affairs, we have said, are things which are such that it is possible that there is something which accepts them. They are possible *objects* of acceptance. It is tempting, therefore, to define persons as possible *subjects* of acceptance – as individual things which are such that it is possible that they accept something. But it is more accurate to the traditional conception of a person to replace 'acceptance' by 'endeavour': a person is an individual thing which is capable of intentional action or endeavour – in short, a possible agent.

What sense of 'possible', then? Shall we say that a person is an individual thing which is such that it is *logically possible* that it undertakes something? We may say, of a stone, that it is logically possible that it undertakes something, but we may not say of a stone that it is a person. Shall we say, then, that a person is an individual thing which is such that it is *physically possible* that it undertakes something? We would be saying, in this case, that a person is an individual thing of this sort: it is not contrary to the laws of nature that it perform an intentional act.

This would mean that, in those possible worlds in which there are no laws of nature, all individual things, including stones, would be persons. Let us add, then, that persons are *necessarily* such that it is not contrary to the laws of nature that they perform intentional acts.

Thus we now have:

  D.IV.15 *x* is a person = Df *x* is an individual thing which is necessarily such that it is physically possible that there is something which it undertakes to bring about.

It should be noted that we are not defining persons as 'potential' agents. For if we take 'potential' in its ordinary sense, then we may say that our potentialities are variable and dependent upon our circumstances at any particular time. But physical possibility, as that which is not precluded by the laws of nature, is invariable. Our definition has the consequence that, if an individual thing *x* is a person, then, in every possible world in which *x* exists, *x* is a person from the moment it comes into being until the moment it passes away.[33] The definition, then, would seem to be equivalent in intent to that proposed by Boethius: A person is an individual substance of a rational nature.

APPENDIX A

THE DOCTRINE OF TEMPORAL PARTS

1 Temporal Parts

The doctrine of temporal parts is accepted by a number of distinguished theologians, logicians and philosophers of science. Since it may appear to conflict with what I have said in Chapter III about identity through time, I will consider it briefly.

Jonathan Edwards set forth the doctrine in his *Doctrine of Original Sin Defended* (1758). He was there concerned with the question whether it is just to impute to you and me the sins that were committed by Adam. And he appealed to temporal parts to show that it is *as* just to attribute Adam's sins to you and me now as it is to attribute any other past sins to you and me now.

He based his view upon a general theological thesis: God not only created the world *ex nihilo*, he also constantly preserves or upholds the things he creates, for without God's continued preservation of the world, all created things would fall into nothingness. 'God's upholding created substance, or causing its existence in each successive moment, is altogether equivalent to an immediate *production out of nothing*, at each moment.'[1] In preserving the table in its being, God cannot make use of what existed at any prior moment. The table is not there waiting to be upheld or preserved, for if it were, then God would not *need* to uphold or preserve it.

Edwards compares the persistence of created substances with that of a reflection or image on the surface of a mirror. 'The image that exists this moment, is not at all *derived* from the image which existed the last preceding moment . . . If the succession of new *rays* be intercepted, by something interposed between the object and the glass, the image immediately ceases; the *past existence* of the image has no influence to uphold it, so much as for one moment. Which shows that the image is altogether completely remade every moment; and strictly speaking, is in no part numerically the same with that which existed in the moment preceding. And truly so the matter must be with the *bodies* themselves, as well as their images. They also cannot be the same with an absolute identity, but must be wholly renewed every moment . . .' Edwards summarises his doctrine of preservation this way: 'If the existence of created *substance*, in each successive moment, be wholly the effect of God's immediate power, in *that* moment, without any dependence on prior existence, as much as the first creation out of *nothing*, then what exists at this moment, by this power, is a *new effect*, and simply and absolutely considered, not the same with any past existence . . .'

This conception of persisting physical things, though not its theological basis, is also defended by a number of contemporary philosophers. It may be found, for example, in the axiom system concerning things and their parts that is developed in Carnap's *Introduction to Symbolic Logic*.[2] Carnap's system is derived from the systems developed by J. H. Woodger and Alfred Tarski, in Woodger's *The Axiomatic Method in Biology*.[3] These authors say that, for every moment at which a thing exists there is a set of momentary parts of the thing; none of these parts exists at any other moment; and the thing itself is the sum of its momentary parts.[4]

The thing that constitutes you now, according to this view, is diverse from the things that have constituted you at any other moment, just as you are diverse from every other person who exists now. But God, according to Jonathan Edwards, can contemplate a collection of objects existing at different times and 'treat them as one'. He can take a collection of various individuals existing at different times and think of them as all constituting a single individual. Edwards thus appeals to a doctrine of truth by divine convention; he says that God 'makes *truth* in affairs of this nature'. God could regard temporally scattered individuals – you this year, me last year, and the Vice-President the year before that – as comprising a single individual. And then he could justly punish you this year and me last year for the sins that the Vice-President committed the year before that. And so, Edwards concludes, 'no solid reason can be given, why God . . . may not establish a constitution whereby the natural posterity of Adam . . . should be treated as *one* with him, for the derivation, either of righteousness, and communion in rewards, or of the loss of righteousness, and consequent corruption and guilt'.[5]

Suppose that today I hope for rain and tomorrow I hope for snow instead. If Edwards's doctrine is correct, the situation would seem to involve at least *three* different individual things: today's temporal part of me, tomorrow's temporal part of me and the thing of which these two things *are* temporal parts.[6] Today's temporal part of me will be other than yesterday's and each will be other than any thing of which *they* are proper parts. Which is the thing that hopes for rain – today's temporal part of me, or the thing of which it is a part, or both? Can we say of the temporal parts – of the temporally dimensionless slices – that they are *entia per se*? If we can, can we say of the whole of which they are slices that it is *also* an *ens per se*?

If there were good reasons to accept the doctrine of temporal parts, we would have to deal with these difficult questions. But why should we accept it? I will consider two different reasons that have been offered on behalf of the doctrine. I believe we will find that, even when considered together, they do not seem to lend any significant presumption to the doctrine. And then I will ask whether the doctrine might throw light on our problems involving identity through time.[7]

2   The Argument from Spatial Analogy

The first of two arguments for the doctrine of temporal parts appeals to an analogy between space and time. One version of it might be put as follows. '(i) Whatever may be said about spatial continuity and identity may also be said, *mutatis mutandis,* about temporal continuity and identity. But (ii) every object extending undivided or unscattered through any portion of space during any given time has, for each subportion of that space, a set of *spatial parts* which exist during that time only in that subportion of space, and the only parts that the object then has are within that portion of space. (More exactly: every object extending undivided or unscattered through any portion of space during any given time has, for each subportion of that space, a set s of spatial parts which is such that all the members of s are in that subportion of space at that time and any part of the object in that space at that time is a member of s.) Therefore (iii) every object persisting uninterruptedly through any period of time within a given place has, for each subperiod of that time, a set of *temporal* parts which exist within that place and only during that period of time.'

Is the first premise in this argument true? I would say that it is not. For there is a fundamental *disanalogy* between space and time.

The disanalogy may be suggested by saying simply: 'One and the same thing cannot be in two different places at one and the same time. But one and the same thing can be at two different times in one and the same place.' Let us put the point of disanalogy, however, somewhat more precisely.

When we say 'a thing cannot be in two different places at one and the same time', we mean that it is not possible for *all* the parts of the thing to be in one of the places at that one time and *also* to be in the other of the places at that same time. It *is* possible, of course, for *some* part of the thing to be in one place at a certain time and *another* part of the thing to be in another place at that time. And to remove a possible ambiguity in the expression 'all the parts of a thing', let us spell it out as 'all the parts that the thing ever will have had'.

Instead of saying simply 'a thing cannot be in two different places at one and the same time' let us say this: 'It is *not* possible for there to be a thing which is such that all the parts it ever will have had are in one place at one time and also in another place at that same time.' And instead of saying 'a thing can be at two different times in one and the same place', let us say this: 'It *is* possible for there to be a thing which is such that all the parts it ever will have had are in one place at one time and also in that same place at another time.'

It seems to me to be clear that each of these two theses is true and therefore that there is a fundamental disanalogy between space and time. And so I would reject the first premise of the argument above. (One may, of course, use the doctrine of temporal parts in order to *defend* the view that there is no such disanalogy. One may use it, in particular, to criticise the second of the two theses I set forth above – the thesis according to which it is possible for there to be a thing which is such that all the parts it ever will have had are in one place at one time and also in that same place at another time. But if we were to defend (i) in the argument above by appeal to (iii), then our reasoning would be circular.)

3 *Phillip Drunk and Phillip Sober*

A second argument for the doctrine of temporal parts is suggested by the following quotation from C. S. Peirce: 'Phillip is drunk and Phillip is sober would be absurd, did not time make the Phillip of this morning another Phillip than the Phillip of last night.' [8]

Thus one might construct a philosophical puzzle: '(i) For any x and y, if x is identical with y, then whatever can be truly said of x can also be truly said of y. But (ii) the Phillip of this morning is identical with the Phillip of last night. Now (iii) the Phillip of this morning was sober. And therefore (iv) the Phillip of this morning was not drunk. But (v) the Phillip of last night was drunk. And therefore (vi) something can truly be said of the Phillip of last night that cannot be truly said of the Phillip of this morning. How can this be?' The doctrine of temporal parts might now be invoked as a way of solving the puzzle: 'The second premise is false. The Phillip of this morning and the Phillip of last night are *different* temporal parts of one and the same thing and therefore the thing that was drunk is not identical with the thing that was sober.'

But there is another way of dealing with the puzzle. If 'The Phillip of this morning was sober' is something we know to be true, then it tells us no more, and no less, than that Phillip was sober this morning. And if 'The Phillip of last night was drunk' is something we know to be true, then it tells us no more, and no less, than that Phillip was drunk last night. Consider now step (iv) of our puzzle: 'The Phillip of this morning was not drunk.' This statement may be taken either as saying 'Phillip was not drunk last night' or as saying 'Phillip was not drunk this morning'. If it is taken the first way, as saying 'Phillip was not drunk last night', then it does not follow from the premises that precede it. But if it is taken the second way, as saying 'Phillip was not drunk this morning', then we cannot derive the conclusion of the puzzle. That is to say, we cannot conclude, as we do in (vi), that something can truly be said of 'the Phillip of last night', i.e. Phillip, that cannot also be truly said of 'the Phillip of this morning'.

We spoke earlier of 'playing loose with the "is" of identity'. We could speak here of 'playing loose with the "isn't" of diversity'. This is exemplified in: 'Since Phillip differed last night from what he was this morning, the Phillip of last night is other than the Phillip of this morning.' Or, if we need an example that is not concerned with the point at issue: 'Since Phillip is considerate toward his friends and inconsiderate toward his employees, Phillip the friend is other than Phillip the employer.'

4 Does the Doctrine Help Us?

One consideration that seems to have led many philosophers to accept the doctrine of temporal parts is this: the doctrine enables us to deal satisfactorily with the problem of the Ship of Theseus and with other such puzzles about identity through time.

This point of view has been defended, in many different writings, by W. V. Quine.[9] He illustrates the doctrine in application to Heraclitus's puzzlement about whether or not one can bathe in the same river twice. Let us consider this application and ask whether in fact it *does* throw light upon Heraclitus's problem. What may be said about the river may also be said, of course, about the Ship of Theseus and the other objects of our initial puzzlement.

Quine suggests that the temporal parts of individual things

are like the temporal parts of the careers, histories or biographies of those things: they are *events* or *processes*.[10] He does not hesitate to say, therefore, that the temporal parts of a thing are 'stages' of the thing. He writes: 'a physical thing – whether a river or a human body or a stone – is at any one moment a sum of simultaneous momentary states of spatially scattered atoms or other small physical constituents. Now just as the thing at a moment is a sum of these spatially small parts, so we may think of the thing over a period as a sum of the temporally small parts which are its successive states.' [11] A river is thus a *process* through time, a sum of momentary 'river stages'. Quine now says that this way of looking at the matter provides the solution to Heraclitus's problem. 'The truth is that you *can* bathe in the same *river* twice, but not in the same river stage.' [12]

We should note, however, that this way of looking at the matter, if it is thus to yield a solution to Heraclitus's problem, would seem to *presuppose* the concept of the persistence of an individual thing through time – the concept of one and the same individual existing at different times. Even if it is true that all rivers are sums of river stages, it is not true that all sums of river stages are rivers. Indeed a sum of river stages occupying a continuous period of time need not be a river. Thus the Merrimack, from 9 to 10 a.m., Eastern Standard Time, the Housatonic from 10 to 11, and the Blackstone from 11 to 12, would be such a sum of river stages, occupying a three-hour period. But this particular sum, if there is such an entity, does not constitute a river.

What more is required for a sum of river stages to yield a river? Five possible answers suggest themselves. (i) We could say, of course, that river stages *a*, *b* and *c*, occurring or existing at different times, are stages of the same river if and only if there is an *x* such that *x* is a river and such that *a*, *b* and *c* are all stages of *x*. This answer obviously presupposes the concept of *a river* persisting through the time in question. (ii) We could say that *a*, *b* and *c* are all to be found in the same river bed, or between the same river banks.[13] But this would be to presuppose that the *river bed*, or the pair of *river banks*, persists through the time in question.

To be sure, we do not need to presuppose the concept of a persisting *physical thing* in order to say what sums of river stages make up rivers and what sums of river stages do not. Thus (iii) we might be able to define a persisting river in terms of its stages and their accessibility to the observation of some person or persons. But this would be to presuppose the concept of a person persisting through time. Or (iv), given the concept of a *place* persisting through time, we could say that a sum of river stages makes up a river provided its elements all occupy the same place. But this would presuppose an absolute theory of space, for we could not then expect to define the persistence of a place through time in terms of the persistence of the various physical things that might be said to occupy it.

Or, finally, (v) we could introduce a technical term – 'cofluvial' for example – and say that *a*, *b* and *c* are stages of the same river if and only if they are *cofluvial* with each other.[14]

Whatever there is to recommend this doctrine, it can hardly be that it throws light upon Heraclitus's problem: 'How do I step into the same river twice?' For the answer would be: 'By stepping at different times into things that are cofluvial.' And if we then ask what it is for things to be cofluvial, the answer, if there is one, could only be: 'Things are cofluvial provided they are parts of the same river.'[15]

APPENDIX B

MEREOLOGICAL ESSENTIALISM

1 The Principle of Mereological Essentialism

I shall consider a philosophical puzzle pertaining to the concepts of whole and part. The proper solution, I believe, will throw light upon some of the most important questions of metaphysics. It will illustrate in a straightforward way the view of philosophy set forth in the Introduction. And it will clarify and confirm the doctrine, set forth in Chapter III, according to which such familiar things as ships, trees, houses, chairs and cars may be said, only in a loose and popular sense, to persist through time.

The puzzle pertains to what I shall call the principle of mereological essentialism. The principle may be formulated by saying that, for any whole x, if x has y as one of its parts then y is part of x in every possible world in which x exists. The principle may also be put by saying that every whole has the parts that it has necessarily, or by saying that if y is part of x then the property of having y as one of its parts is essential to x. If the principle is true, then if y is ever part of x, y will be part of x as long as x exists.

Abelard held that 'no thing has more or less parts at one time than at another'.[1] Leibniz said 'we cannot say, speaking according to the great truth of things, that the same whole is preserved when a part is lost'.[2] And G. E. Moore gave us this example:

Let us take as an example the relational property which we assert to belong to a visual sense-datum when we say of it that it has another visual sense-datum as a spatial part: the assertion, for instance, with regard to a colored patch half of which is red and half yellow: 'This whole patch contains this patch' (where 'this patch' is a proper name for the red half). It is here, I think, quite plain that, in a perfectly clear and intelligible sense, we can say that any whole, which had not contained that red patch, could not have been identical with the whole in question: that from the proposition with regard to any term whatever that it does not contain that particular patch it *follows* that that term is other than the whole in question – though *not* necessarily that it is qualitatively different from it. That particular whole could not have existed without having that particular patch for a part. But . . . it seems quite clear that, though the whole could not have existed without having the red patch for a part, the red patch might perfectly well have existed without being part of that particular whole.[3]

Instead of considering such things as sense-data and visual patches, let us consider physical things. Let us picture to ourselves a very simple table, improvised from a stump and a board. Now one might have constructed a very similar table by using the same stump and a different board, or by using the same board and a different stump. But the only way of constructing precisely *that* table is to use that particular stump and that particular board. It would seem, therefore, that that particular table is *necessarily* made up of that particular stump and that particular board.

But to say of the table that it is necessarily made up of the stump and board is not to say of the stump and the board that *they* are such that they are necessarily parts of the table. And it is not to say that the stump is necessarily joined with the board. God could have created the stump without creating the board; he could have created the board without creating the stump; and he could have created the stump and the board without creating the table. But he could not have created *that* particular table without using the stump and the board.

Let us be clear about the view that is here set forth. It is no spurious essentialism. (That is to say, it is not the kind of essentialism that is arrived at in such arguments as these: 'Szigeti was a violinist; necessarily all violinists are musicians; therefore Szigeti was necessarily a musician'; and 'The word "Homer", as we use it, connotes or intends the property of being a person who wrote the *Iliad* and the *Odyssey*; therefore Homer, if he existed, was such that he necessarily wrote the *Iliad* and the *Odyssey*'.) We are saying, in application to our example of the table, that there exist an x, a y and a z such that: x is identical with this table, y is identical with this stump, z is identical with this board, and x is such that, in every possible world in which x exists, it is made up of y and z. Our statement says nothing whatever about the way in which human beings may happen to conceive or to look upon such things as this table. And, *a fortiori*, it says nothing whatever about the way in which we may happen to describe this table or use the language we do. Its subject matter is no more nor less than this table, the parts of this table, and the possible worlds in which this table exists.

Considered in the abstract and considered in application to such simple examples as these, the principle of mereological essentialism may seem to be obvious. Indeed, I would say that it ought to seem to be obvious. Yet the principle appears to conflict with certain other truths which, perhaps from a somewhat different point of view, would *also* seem to be obvious. I will indicate these other truths by formulating two objections to the principle of mereological essentialism.

(A) '(i) My car had parts last week that it does not have this week and it will have parts next week that it never had before. But (ii) the principle of mereological essentialism implies that, if anything is ever a part of any whole, then that thing is a part of that whole as long as the whole exists. And therefore (iii) the principle of mereological essentialism is false.'

(B) '(i) I could have bought different tyres for my car. (ii) If I had bought different tyres for my car, then it would have had different parts from those it has now. Therefore (iii) my car could have had different parts from those it has now. Hence (iv) my car is such that, in some possible worlds, it has parts it does not have in this one. But (v) the principle of mereological essentialism implies that in every world in which my car exists it has exactly the same parts it has in this one. And therefore (vi) the principle of mereological essentialism is false.'

Philosophers who are interested in the ways in which people ordinarily talk may wish to multiply examples at this point. But I believe that our two examples are enough.

I would say, then, that we have here a typical philosophical puzzle – an apparent conflict of intuitions.

2 Mereological Inessentialism
Before we try to solve the puzzle and to reply to the two objections we have just formulated, let us consider the antithesis of extreme mereological essentialism. This would be what we might call complete, unbridled mereological *inessentialism*.

Complete, unbridled mereological inessentialism would seem to be manifestly absurd. This would be the view that, for any whole *w*, *w* could be made up of any two things whatever. For, given such a view, one could say, of *this table*, that it could have been made up of the number thirty-six and the property blue.

Perhaps it will be conceded that the set of things which are capable of being parts of this table must be restricted in at least a general way – say, to things of the same ontological category as the table. Suppose, then, one says that, for any two physical objects, this table could have been made up of those two objects.

If the view is true, then *this table,* this physical thing that is before us now, is such that it could have been made up of my left foot and the Grand Central Station. Or, to be more exact, if extreme mereological inessentialism is true, then this table, my left foot and the Grand Central Station are three things which are such that there is a possible world in which the first is made up of the second and third – in which *this table* is made up of what, in this world, are my left foot and the Grand Central Station.

Indeed, there would be indefinitely many such possible worlds. In trying to imagine this table being made up of my foot and the station, perhaps we thought of my foot and the station as they now are, with all the particular parts that they now happen to have. But if extreme mereological inessentialism is true, then the foot and the station could have had parts entirely other than those that they have in fact. The foot could have been made up of Mt Monadnock and Mr Robinson's violin and the station could have been made up of a certain horse and a certain fish. So, of the indefinitely many possible worlds in which this table is made up of the foot and the station, some of those will be such that in them the foot is made up of the mountain and the violin while the station is made up of the horse and the fish, but others will be such that in them the station is made up of the horse and the violin while the foot is made up of the mountain and the fish.

It is difficult to imagine how even God could tell these worlds apart. Which are the ones in which the violin is made up of the horse and the station and which are the ones in which the mountain is made up of the fish and the foot? Note that, if we are thus mereological inessentialists, we would have to say, of the mountain and the violin and the horse and the fish, that *they* could have been made up of other things, too. Hence, of those worlds in which the foot is made up of the mountain and the fish, there will be those in which the fish is made up of the violin and the station . . .

But we need not formulate such extreme examples. Consider just two tables, *x* and *y,* and suppose, what from one point of view would seem to be reasonable, that these tables are such that they could survive replacement of any of their smaller parts. We consider, then, the consequences of exchanging certain of their smaller parts; then there will be a world possible in respect to this one in which *x* has one of the parts that *y* has in this world and y has one of the parts that x has in this world; then there will be a world possible in respect to *that* world, and therefore also in respect to this one, in which x and y will have exchanged still other smaller parts. We can imagine the process continued in such a way that it will remind us of the ancient problems of the Ship of Theseus and the Carriage. There will be a possible world which is like this one except for the fact that in that one x has the parts that y has in this one and y has the parts that x has in this one. We have only to reflect a moment to see that there will be indefinitely many such possible worlds. Thus of those possible worlds w, which are such that the thing u which is one of the legs of x in this world is the corresponding leg of y in w and the thing v which is one of the legs of y in this world is the corresponding leg of x in w, there will be those worlds w' which are such that the things that are parts of u in this world will be parts of v in w' and there will be those worlds w" which are such that the things that are parts of v in this world will be parts of u in w", and so on, *ad infinitum*.

3 Other Possibilities

The principle of mereological essentialism that I have advocated may be put this way:

(A) For every x and y, if x is ever part of y, then y is necessarily such that x is part of y at any time that y exists.

We have contrasted this view with 'extreme mereological inessentialism':

(B) There is no x and no y such that y is necessarily such that it ever has x as a part.

The word 'part' is here to be taken in the sense of 'proper part'.

Is there a way of getting between extreme mereological essentialism and extreme mereological inessentialism? Could we specify, for example, that certain parts are essential to their wholes and others not? At first thought, this may seem easy. 'Just tell me what whole you are talking about,' one may say, 'and I'll tell you what parts are essential to it. Are you talking about cyclists, for example? Necessarily all cyclists have feet; therefore all cyclists are necessarily such that they have feet, and so among the parts that are essential to cyclists are their feet. Or are you talking about cars? Necessarily all cars have engines, but some cars don't have radios; therefore cars necessarily have engines but do not necessarily have radios, and so engines but not radios are among the parts that are essential to cars.' The statements coming after the 'therefore's' do not, of course, follow from those that precede them; and the statements coming after the 'and so's' do not follow from those that precede them.[4]

Alvin Plantinga has suggested two possible ways of going between the extremes of (A) and (B) above.[5] The first is a principle which may be put this way:

(c)   For every x and y, if x is ever a part of y, then y is necessarily such that x is part of it at some time or other.

This principle, like principle (A) above, seems to conflict with common sense. Thus it seems to tell us, with respect to each of the parts that my car ever will have had, that the car had to have precisely that part at *some* time or other; it had to have precisely the tyres it now does have, though it might instead have had some of them earlier or some of them later; and if it hadn't ever had this particular radio, then it would never have existed at all.[6]

Plantinga formulates another principle which might also be taken as an alternative to the extremes of mereological essentialism and inessentialism. We may put it this way:

(D)   For every x, y, and t, if x has y as a part at t, then x necessarily has y as a part at t.

This principle, too, seems to conflict with common sense. For it seems to tell us, with respect to each thing, that the time of the thing's existence is essential to it. This table couldn't have come into being at any time other than that precise moment at which it did come into being. And if it is going to cease to be, say, three years from now, then it is necessarily such that it is going to cease to be three years from now. Its history couldn't be a moment longer or a moment shorter than what it is going to be in fact.

It would seem, then, that these ways of going between the means of extreme mereological essentialism and extreme mereological inessentialism are not entirely satisfactory. Each possibility seems to conflict with our common sense.

There are still other possibilities.[7] But I propose that, instead of trying to spell out the alternatives, we look further into what is actually implied by the principle of mereological essentialism. There is in its favour: a certain intuitive plausibility; the support of an impressive philosophical tradition; and the fact that it enables us to deal with what otherwise seems to be insoluble philosophical puzzles. I will formulate within the terms of a more general mereological system and then show that, although it seems to conflict with common sense, it does not do so in fact.

4 Principles of Mereology

Let us begin by introducing some mereological definitions and axioms, taking as undefined 'x is part of y' where 'part' is understood in the sense sometimes expressed by 'proper part'. Now it is possible that the term 'part' is taken in one way in our formulation of the principle of mereological essentialism and in another way in our formulation of the objections to it. In the principles that follow, we will use the term 's-part' instead of 'part'. Use of 's-part' will indicate that we are speaking strictly and philosophically. Later we will introduce 'L-part' for the ordinary, or loose and popular, sense of the term. Then we may formulate, without ambiguity, certain questions about the relation of 'L-part' or 'part' in its ordinary, or loose and popular, sense, and 's-part' or 'part' in its strict and philosophical sense.

Of the four axioms and the three definitions that follow, the first two in each group were set forth, though in a somewhat different terminology, by Whitehead in *The Organisation of Thought*.[8]

(A1)   If x is an s-part of y and y is an s-part of z, then x is an s-part of z.

(A2)   If x is an s-part of y, then y is not an s-part of x.

(A3)   If x is an s-part of y, then y is such that in every possible world in which y exists x is an s-part of y.

(A4)   For every x and y, if x is other than y, then it is possible that x exists and y exists and that there is no z such that x is an s-part of z and y is an s-part of z.

In taking (A3) as an axiom, we are suggesting that the principle of mereological essentialism is a basic tenet of the theory of part and whole.

Axiom (A4) tells us, with respect to any two things, that they may coexist without being parts of any third thing. It implies that if something x is a strict proper part of something y, then there is a possible world in which x exists and in which x is not a proper part of y. And this fact, in conjunction with the principle of mereological essentialism, implies that every compound thing is contingent, i.e. such that there is a possible world in which it does not exist.

We now add two definitions.

> D.B.1 x is discrete from y = Df (i) x is other than y, (ii) there is no z such that z is an s-part of x and z is an s-part of y, and (iii) x is not an s-part of y and y is not an s-part of x.

> D.B.2 w is strictly made up of x and y = Df (i) x is an s-part of w, (ii) y is an s-part of w, (iii) x is discrete from y, and (iv) no s-part of w is discrete both from x and from y.

One might suppose that the definition of 'x is discrete from y' is needlessly complex. Thus Whitehead, who had set forth axioms equivalent to (A1) and (A2), said that two things are discrete (his word was 'separated') if nothing is part of both. But Whitehead had also affirmed an axiom ruling out the possibility of monadism, i.e. the doctrine that there are individual things having no proper parts. (He said, in effect, that if x is a part of y, then there is a z such that z is part of x.) But if we allow for the possibility of monads our definition of 'discrete' must be more complex than the definition proposed by Whitehead. It will not be enough to say merely that if x is discrete from y, then there is no z such that z is part of x and z is part of y.

We must add, first of all, that if x is discrete from y, then x is other than y. For if there are monads then, given the original Whiteheadian definition, we would have to say that every monad is discrete from itself. For having no (proper) parts, each monad x is such that there is no y such that y is part of x and y is part of x.

But we must also add, secondly, that if x is discrete from y, then x is not part of y and y is not part of x. Consider two objects x and y, which make up a third object, w, and suppose that a certain monad m is a proper part of x. The monad m, given the Whiteheadian definition of 'discrete', would be discrete both from x and from y (for having no parts it shares no part either with x or with y). And given the first modification above of the Whiteheadian definition, m would still be discrete both from x and from y, for it is other than x and other than y. But this would mean that w, contrary to our assumption, is not made up of x and y.[9] For given D.B.2, our definition of 'w is strictly made up of x and y', if w is made up of x and y, then *no* part of w is discrete both from x and from y.

It is useful also to single out the relation expressed by 'x is joined with y' where this may be taken to imply that neither one of the two things, x and y, is a part of the other. Let us say:

> D.B.3 x is strictly joined with y =Df There is a w such that
> w is strictly made up of x and y.

We could say that, if a thing x is thus strictly joined with a thing y, then x is *an appendage* of y. This would enable us to say that, although a whole cannot survive the loss of any of its parts, it could survive the loss of any of its appendages.[10]

How are we to decide whether one individual thing x is joined with another individual thing y? In other words, what are the *criteria* of joining? We might say that two things are *strictly joined* if no third individual falls between them; then we could say that two things are *joined* if part of the one is strictly joined with part of the other. This would allow us to say that scattered subatomic particles may be parts of an individual thing. But we would not need to say that a suite of furniture separated by various objects is itself an individual thing. Axiom (A4) and these criteria allow us to say that *some* things that are not in direct or indirect physical contact may be parts of the same individual thing, but they do not require us to say that *any* two separated things are parts of one individual thing.

5 Mereological Change
What I have said implies that, if anything y is ever a part, in the strict and philosophical sense, of anything x, then y is a part of x at any time that x exists. Does this mean that there cannot be any mereological change?

If what I have said is correct, at least *four* types of mereological change are possible. The first two are coming into being and passing away; for wholes do come into being and pass away. (Unlike some philosophers, I am not reluctant to say that coming into being and passing away involve a kind of change in their subjects.) And the second two types of mereological change are joining and disjoining. Objects may be joined together to form a whole that hadn't previously existed. And objects may be disjoined from each other and, unlike the whole that they had formed, survive the change.[11]

Or, if we use 'appendage' in the way suggested at the end of the previous section, we may say that objects may be altered mereologically by taking on or losing appendages.)

We may take note, in passing, of this interesting metaphysical question: can there be any change without there being mereological change? Of course, everything changes if anything changes, but can anything change if nothing undergoes mereological change? I suggest that the answer to this is 'Yes'. It is *possible*, surely, for me to think now of this and now of that without it being the case that I or any other thing undergoes any mereological change.

We are now in a position to reply to the two objections we had formulated earlier.

(A) '(i) My car had parts last week that it does not have this week and it will have parts next week that it has never had before. But (ii) the principle of mereological essentialism implies that, if anything is ever a part of any whole, then that thing is a part of that whole as long as the whole exists. And therefore (iii) the principle of mereological essentialism is false.'

In reply to this objection we may observe that the term 'part' is used in one way in the first premise and in another way in the second and hence that the conclusion rests upon an equivocation. But if the reply is to be taken seriously, we must state what the two uses of the term 'part' are and how they are related to each other.

In formulating the principle of mereological essentialism, we used the expression 's-part', suggesting that this might be read as 'part in the strict and philosophical sense'. (Perhaps the reader would prefer to read it as 'part in the philosopher's sense'.) We proposed three axioms in the attempt to explicate 's-part'. This is the sense in which 'part' should be taken in premise (ii) of the above objection.

What of premise (i)? Here, I suggest, 'part' must be taken in the loose and popular sense. (Perhaps the reader would prefer to say: 'Here "part" must be taken in its ordinary sense.') When we take 'part' in its loose and popular sense, then we must interpret it in such a way that it is applicable, not only to genuine wholes, but also to those things I have called *entia successiva*. I suggested in Chapter III that an *ens successivum* is a thing which is such that, at any moment of its existence, something other than itself serves as its stand in and does duty for it. And I tried to show that all such entities are reducible to the genuine wholes that may be thus said to serve as their constituents. Let us now apply this conclusion to our present problem.

To say, for example, that a certain tyre is now a part of my car is to say that what now constitutes that tyre is a part, in the strict and philosophical sense, of what now constitutes my car. And to say of a certain other tyre that it was a part of my car yesterday is to say that something that constituted that tyre yesterday was a part of something that constituted my car yesterday. Let us use 'L-part' for this ordinary, loose and popular sense of 'part'. We may now characterise this concept as follows in terms of the vocabulary here introduced:

> D.B.4 x has y as an L-part at t =Df x is an *ens successivum*; and either y or something that constitutes y at t is an s-part of something that constitutes x at t.

The disjunctive phrase 'either y or something that constitutes y' is to provide for the possibility that an L-part of an *ens successivum* may itself be either another *ens successivum* or a genuine individual.

Taking 'part' in this ordinary, or loose and popular, sense, we may now say of a successive thing, such as my car, that it may have one L-part at one time and another L-part at another time. And saying this will be quite consistent with saying, as our principle of mereological essentialism requires us to say, that in a strict and philosophical sense if a thing y is ever an s-part of a thing x then that thing y is an s-part of x at any time that x exists.

The second objection was this:

(B) '(i) I could have bought different tyres for my car. (ii) If I had bought different tyres for my car, then it would have had different parts from those it now has. Therefore (iii) my car could have had different parts from those it has now. Hence (iv) my car is such that, in some possible worlds, it has parts it does not have in this one. But (v) the principle of mereological essentialism implies that in every world in which my car exists it has exactly the same parts it has in this one. And therefore (vi) the principle of mereological essentialism is false.'

Here, too, we may observe that the term 'part' is used equivocally – in the loose and popular sense in premises (ii) and (iii) and in the strict and philosophical sense in premise (v). But now we must show how the 'could have' of premises (ii) and (iii) is to be explicated in the strict and philosophical vocabulary. And when we have done that, we may consider the status of premise (iv) – the premise according to which my car is such that in some possible worlds it has parts it does not have in this one.

The statement, 'My car could now have a certain thing as one of its L-parts', even when thus restricted to its ordinary or loose and popular sense, has a certain ambiguity. On the one hand, it could be taken somewhat narrowly to mean the same as (i) 'My car could have o as one of its L-parts and *remain a car* while having o as an L-part'. On the other hand, it could be taken more broadly to mean the same as (ii) 'My car could become a thing that has o as a part', where there is no implication that the thing which is my car remains *a car* after it has taken on o as a part. Let us define 'x could have y as a part at t' in this second, broader sense. For given this broader sense of 'could', one can then readily express in terms of it what is intended by the more narrow sense of 'could' (as in our example, 'x is a car and x could be at t a car having o as a L-part').

If something w is strictly made up of two things x and y, then x is strictly joined with y (see D.B.2 and D.B.3). Our principles imply that, in such a case, w is necessarily such that it has x as a part, in the strict and philosophical sense of the term 'part'. But they do not imply that x is necessarily such that it is a part of w. And they do not imply that x is necessarily such that it is joined with y. Returning to our very simple table which, we supposed, was strictly made up of a stump and a board, we may recall that, although the table is necessarily such that it has the stump as a part, in the strict and philosophical sense of the term 'part', the stump is not necessarily such that it is a part of the table and it is not necessarily such that it is joined to the board.

To say, then in the loose and popular sense, that my car could now be a thing having a certain tyre will be to say that some-thing that now constitutes a part of my car could be joined with something that now constitutes the tyre.

Let us say, then:

> D.B.5 x could have y as an L-part at t $=$ Df There are a w and a v such that (i) w is an s-part of something that constitutes x at t, (ii) either x is identical with y or there is a time at which v constitutes y, and (iii) there is a possible world in which w is strictly joined with v.

If we say, then, in this loose and popular sense, that my car could have a certain tyre as one of its parts, we are *not* saying that there is a possible world in which that car does have that tyre as one of its parts. We are saying, rather, that something that constitutes a part of my car and something that constitutes the tyre are such that there is a possible world in which *they* are joined together.

And so now we see that the fourth proposition in our objection does not follow from the second and third. From that fact that my car *could*, in this loose and popular sense, have a certain tyre as a part, it does not follow that my car is such that in some possible world it *does* have that tyre as a part.

If, for any reason, we should persuade ourselves that this table could have been made up of my left foot and the Grand Central Station, we need not be led to the infinity of indiscernible possible worlds discussed earlier. We need not suppose that, of the worlds in which this table is made up of the foot and the station, some are such that the foot is made up of the mountain and the horse, and others are such that it is made up of the violin and the fish. For we may say what we like about the possible make-up of the table, the foot and the station, without committing ourselves to the thesis that any of these things exists in any possible world other than this one.

The theory of possibility does not require us to say, of any of these successive or common sense objects – the car, the table, the station, the mountain, the horse, the foot, the violin and the fish – that they exist in any other possible worlds. But it does require us to say, of the strict and philosophical wholes that constitute these common sense objects, that *they* exist in other possible worlds.

What we can truly say about the unrealised possibilities of *entia succesiva* may be reformulated more precisely in terms of the unrealised possibilities of genuine individuals. We do not need to suppose, therefore, that there are some possible worlds which are indiscernible except for the fact that some *entia succesiva* are constituted by one set of genuine individuals in one of them and by another set in another. And so what we say is entirely compatible with the principle of mereological essentialism: if *x* has *y* as one of its parts, in the strict and philosophical sense of the term 'part', then in every possible world in which *x* exists, *x* has *y* as one of its parts.

6 *The Problem of Increase*

Our suggestions may be confirmed independently by noting how they may be applied to still another metaphysical problem.

The problem has been called 'the Paradox of Increase'. It is suggested by a question that Aristotle raises when he discusses growth and nourishment: 'One might also raise this difficulty: What is it which grows? Is it that to which something is added?'[12] Let us consider this version of the problem:

'It is impossible for anything to increase by the addition of parts, since when further parts are adjoined to a thing, neither that to which the parts are adjoined, nor the adjoined parts themselves, increase in the sense that they have more parts than they had before . . . What then can be made of the way in which both ordinary usage and logic appear to countenance increase?'[13]

We think we can make things bigger just by adding parts to things. But what *are* the things that we then make bigger? Suppose we have a certain thing A and then attach to it a certain other thing B. We then have a bigger object than we had before (assuming that neither A nor B shrunk or contracted during the process).

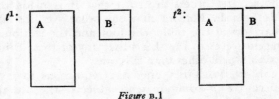

Figure B.1

At the earlier time, t^1, A and B were separated; at the later time, t^2, they are conjoined. But what object *became* bigger? It was neither A nor B, for *these* things remained the same size they were before. And it was not AB for AB did not exist until A was joined with B. That is to say, AB did not have two different sizes, a smaller one at one time and a larger one at another.

We can say that none of the genuine wholes involved in the situation became any bigger – for wholes do not get any bigger or any smaller unless they simply expand or contract. But if none of the genuine objects got any bigger, how are we to interpret the proposition that *something* got bigger? We may interpret it according to the theory of *entia successiva* that we have set forth here. The proposition that something got bigger is ostensibly about an *ens successivum*, but it may be reduced to a proposition about the things that are said to make it up. It tells us simply that what constituted the thing at the later times is larger than what constituted it at the earlier time. In other words:

D.B.6 x is larger at t^2 that it is at t^1 =Df There exists a y and there exists a z such that (i) y constitutes x at t^1, (ii) z constitutes x at t^2, and (iii) z is larger than y.

The *ens successivum* was first constituted by A and subsequently by AB; AB was larger than A; therefore the *ens successivum* may be said to have increased in size.

APPENDIX C

THE OBJECTS OF BELIEF AND ENDEAVOUR

1 Introduction

States of affairs have here been viewed intentionally. The mark of a state of affairs, I have said, is that it is something capable of being accepted. And I have said that if one state of affairs entails another, then the one is necessarily such that whoever accepts it also accepts the other. We now consider such acceptance in more detail and note how it is analogous to endeavour.

I first consider *de dicto* belief and endeavour – that belief and endeavour which may be said, in a straightforward sense, to be directed upon states of affairs. I then consider what has been called '*de re* belief' and what could be called '*de re* endeavour'. Such belief and endeavour may be directed upon things other than states of affairs, for one may have beliefs and projects that are directed upon individual things. But all such beliefs and projects are *also* directed upon states of affairs. I will attempt to show that *de re* belief and endeavour constitute subspecies of *de dicto* belief and endeavour.[1]

2 De Dicto *Belief and Endeavour*

I will first make a distinction between object and content. For philosophers often confuse object with content and they often confuse content with object. This confusion has led to a misconception of the role of states of affairs as objects of belief.

So that I may make the points I have in mind with as little circumlocution as possible, I propose we restrict the locution

s believes that *p*

(where '*p*' may be replaced by any English sentence) to what we may call its ordinary *de dicto* sense.

This will mean, for one thing, that we cannot existentially generalise over any term within the sentence in the place of '*p*'. Thus if our *de dicto* belief sentence is

Jones believes that the tallest man is wise

we cannot take it to entail

There is an x such that Jones believes that x is wise.

Nor can we replace any term within the sentence occupying the place of 'p' by any other term having the same extension. Hence, even if we know both that (1) the tallest man is the fastest runner and that (2) Jones believes that the tallest man is wise, we cannot, on the basis of this information, draw the inference to

Jones believes that the fastest runner is wise.

Another way of characterising this *de dicto* use of 'Jones believes that the tallest man is wise' is to say this: if we know that the sentence is true, in this *de dicto* use, then we may say of Jones that, if he is asked 'Is the tallest man wise?', if he understands the question, and if he intends to reply honestly and correctly, then he will endeavour to reply in the affirmative.

In suggesting that we restrict the locution 's believes that p' to this *de dicto* sense, I am *not* suggesting that the locution is in fact so restricted in ordinary English. (Sometimes it would seem to be so restricted but at other times it is not.)

If we are sensitive to what seem to be the ontological implications of belief, the ontological implications of the fact that people believe things, we will realise that

(1)   Jones believes that the tallest man is wise

implies that

(2)   There is something that Jones believes.

If we do not see this at once, perhaps it will help us if we consider such facts as the following. If we know, not only that (1) is true, but also that Smith believes that the tallest man is wise, then we may infer that there is something that both Jones and Smith believe. But if there is something that both Jones and Smith believe, then there is an answer to the question: and what is that something? (Or there is an answer to the question: what is one thing that they both believe?) In the case of our example the answer would be: that the tallest man is wise.

We may obviously infer (2) above from 'There is something that both Jones and Smith believe'. But the truth of (2) is hardly dependent upon the fact that Smith happens to believe the same thing Jones does. It would seem, therefore, that once we are clear about what is implied by (1), when (1) is taken in the way we have suggested, then we should see that (1) implies (2).[2]

Given, then, that (1) does imply (2), it is useful for philo-sophical purposes to make (1) more explicit. The logical structure of (1) is somewhat more adequately exposed if we rewrite it as

(3) Jones accepts the proposition that the tallest man is wise.

Statement (3) expresses a straightforward dyadic relation between Jones and a certain proposition, enabling us to infer 'There exist an x and a y such that x accepts y'.

Thus our sentence (3) is an instance of this general schema:

s accepts the proposition that p.

I propose we take this locution as the paradigmatic expression of belief *de dicto* and introduce the more ordinary locution, instanced by (1), as an abbreviation. Thus we will have

D.C.1   s believes that p =Df s accepts the proposition that p.

The definition is schematic; we may replace 'p' by any English sentence.

Referring now to our general schema, 's accepts the proposition that p', I will say that the part after the word 'accepts' (viz., 'the proposition that p') *designates the ontological object* of the belief, and that the part after the word 'that' (viz., the sentence occupying the place of 'p') *express the content* of the belief. Instead of thus using the word 'content', we could also say that the part after the word 'that' tells us *what* it is that the man believes.

There is an important sense, which I will try to make clear. in which the *ontological objects* of belief, and of other psycho-logical attitudes, may yet be such as not to enter into the *content* of these attitudes. And there is an important sense in which the objects that do seem to be a part of the *contents* of these attitudes may yet not be the *ontological objects* of these attitudes. But philosophers often confuse object with content and they often confuse content with object.

I have said that what follows the word 'that', in the locution 's accepts the proposition that p', tells us *what* it is that the man believes. To understand the point of the expression '*what* it is that the man believes', let us suppose that the following statement is true:

(4)   The proposition that the tallest man is wise is identical with the proposition that is expressed on the top of page 17 of B.

(We may imagine that 'B' is a definite description of a certain book.) Statement (4) illustrates different ways of designating one and the same proposition. The first description – 'the proposition that the tallest man is wise' – could be said to give us the *essence* of the proposition in question; for that proposition, and only that proposition, is such that it *necessarily* has all and only those properties that are implied by saying that it is the proposition that the tallest man is wise. But the second description in statement (4) – 'the proposition that is expressed on the top of page 17 of B' – does not, in the same sense, tell us *what t*he proposition in question is. It does pick out the proposition from among all other objects, but it does so only by citing certain accidental features of that proposition, certain things that happen to be true of it in the world but which are not true of it in every possible world.

Let us say that the first expression ('the proposition that the tallest man is wise') gives us an *essential description* of a certain proposition and that, given our assumption that (4) is true, the second expression ('the proposition expressed on the top of page 17 of B') gives us an *accidental description* of that same proposition.

The distinction is important for it enables us to put clearly what we might put somewhat more obscurely as follows: 'A proposition may be the *object* of a man's belief even though the man does not thereby believe anything about that proposition. And a man may believe something *about* a certain proposition even though that proposition is not the *object* of his belief.'

To put this more clearly, I will attempt to illustrate and describe two fallacies which one readily commits when one considers philosophical questions about believing.

I will call the first fallacy 'the fallacy of inferring the content of belief from an accidental description of the object of belief'. (An alternative label, perhaps somewhat less misleading, would be: 'the fallacy of taking an accidental description of the object of belief to be an essential description of the content of belief'.) To illustrate the fallacy, let us continue to suppose that (1), (2), (3) and (4) are true. From (3) and (4) we may deduce

(5)   Jones accepts the proposition that is expressed on the top of page 17 of B.

We commit 'the fallacy of inferring the content of belief from an accidental description of the object of belief', if we take (4) and (5) to imply

(6) Jones believes that the proposition that is expressed on the top of page 17 of B is true.

If one understands our undefined expression '*x* accepts *y*' in the sense that is here intended, then one can readily imagine conditions in which (1) and (4) and therefore also (5) are true and in which (6) is false. Suppose, for example, that (1), (4) and (5) are true and that Jones does not have the concepts requisite for understanding what is meant by the English sentence 'the proposition expressed on the top of page 17 of B is true'; possibly he lacks the concept of *page,* or of *truth,* or of a *proposition.* In such a situation (6) will be false.

How, then, shall we characterise 'the fallacy of inferring the content of belief from an accidental description of the object of belief'? One commits this fallacy if one argues in the following way:

The premises of the argument tell us that there is a certain proposition *x* which is the ontological object of a man's belief and they characterise *x* by means of an accidental definite description but not by means of an essential definite description. And the conclusion of the argument contains an essential description of the object of belief and thus tells us *what* the proposition is that the man believes.

And so, as we have noted, to describe the fallacy we don't really need to introduce the term 'the content of the man's belief'. This is just as well, for we can readily imagine a philosopher reacting this way: 'You say the man's belief has an ontological object and that it *also* has a content? What does he believe, then – the object, or the content, or something made up of both?'

I have said that there is also a second fallacy which one readily commits when one considers philosophical questions about believing. This fallacy is, in a certain sense, the converse of 'the fallacy of inferring the content of belief from an accidental description of the object of belief'. I shall call it 'the fallacy of inferring the object of belief from a partial description of the content of belief'. (An alternative label would be: 'the fallacy of inferring the object of belief from a partial description of *what* is believed'.)

To illustrate 'the fallacy of inferring the object of belief from a partial description of the content of belief', we have only to revise the assumption of our former example. For one commits this fallacy if one takes (6) and (4) to imply (1). Let us imagine, then, that (6) and (4) are true. As before, the proposition on the top of page 17 of B is the proposition that the tallest man is wise. And now we picture a situation in which (6) is true – a situation in which Jones can be said to believe, *de dicto*, that the proposition on the top of page 17 of B is true. Perhaps Jones has been persuaded that B is composed of holy scriptures or that it is the work of some other completely reliable authority, and he has been persuaded further that there is one and only one sentence on the top of page 17 and that this sentence expresses a proposition. But Jones has not seen the book and does not know *what* this proposition is; hence he has no idea that (4) is true. In this case (6) will be true; Jones will believe that the proposition expressed on page 17 of B is true. But this situation is quite compatible with the negation of (1); that is to say, it is quite compatible with saying that Jones does not believe that the tallest man is wise. Perhaps Jones doesn't think that there *is* a tallest man, or perhaps he thinks that being tall is incompatible with being wise.

How, then, shall we characterise 'the fallacy of inferring the object of belief from a partial description of the content of belief'? I suggest that one commits this fallacy if one argues in the following way:

The premise of the argument tells us *what* it is that a man believes and a proper part of this characterisation is a reference to a certain proposition x. But the premise does not tell us that x is *what* the man believes. (That is to say, the premise could be put in this form: 's accepts the proposition that *p*.' In the sentence occupying the place of '*p*' there occurs an accidental description of a proposition x, but x is not implied by the proposition designated by the sentence in the place of '*p*'.) And the conclusion of the argument tells us that the man accepts x.

Analogous points may be made about endeavour. To make them, we have only to replace the two expressions 's believes that *p*' and 's accepts the proposition that *p*', respectively, by 's acts with the intention of bringing it about that *p*' and 's undertakes to bring about the state of affairs that *p*'. Thus we would have this definition:

D.C.2   s acts with the intention of bringing it about that *p*
          =Df s undertakes to bring about the state of affairs
          that *p*.

(Perhaps there is a certain awkwardness in the locution 's undertakes to bring about the state of affairs that the Vice-President is elected President'. The awkwardness could be removed by replacing 'bring about' by 'make true' and replacing 'state of affairs' by 'proposition'. But if what we have said about states of affairs and propositions is correct, then the locution used here is the more accurate.)

The statements (1) through (6) above could now be adapted to endeavour. And we could distinguish 'the fallacy of inferring the content of endeavour from an accidental description of the object of endeavour' and 'the fallacy of inferring the object of endeavour from a partial description of the content of endeavour'.

3 De Re *Belief and Endeavour*

I will now make analogous points about what has been called *de re* belief.

If we remain sensitive to what seem to be the ontological implications of belief, we will realise that

(1) The tallest man is believed by Jones to be wise

implies

(2) There is something that Jones attributes to the tallest man.

(In the place of 'attributes to the tallest man', we might say 'believes of the tallest man'.) If one does not see immediately that (1) implies (2), one has only to note that, if (2) is true, and if the tallest man is also believed by Smith to be wise, then we could say that there is something that both Jones and Smith attribute to the tallest man. The logical structure of (1), then, is somewhat more adequately expressed if we rewrite it as

(3) Jones attributes the property of being wise to the tallest man.

Our sentence is thus an instance of this general schema:

s attributes to x the property of being F

where the letter 'F' is replaceable by any predicate-expression (e.g. 'wise' or 'such that he is wise' or 'such that he is wise and all men are mortal').

I propose we take this locution as the paradigmatic expression of belief *de re* and introduce the more ordinary locution, instanced by (1), as an abbreviation. Thus we will have

> D.C.3   *x* is believed by S to be F $=$ D*f* S attributes the property of being F to *x*.

Let us say, of any sentence fulfilling the schema 's attributes the property of being F to *x*', that the expression in the place of 'the property of being F' designates the *property attributed*. (Presumably we should say that the *object* of any such *de re* belief is the thing designated by the expression in the place of '*x*'.) Thus, in the case of (3), the *property attributed* is the property of being wise (and the *object* to which it is attributed is the tallest man). And let us say that the predicative expression in the place of 'F' expresses the *content of the property attributed*. Thus, in (3), the word 'wise' expresses the content of the property attributed.

We will now distinguish two fallacies and illustrate them by supposing that the following is true:

> (4)   The property most frequently attributed to Solomon is the property of being wise.

Given our use of 'attributes' and D.C.2 above, we may note that (1) and (4) together imply

> (5)   The property most frequently attributed to Solomon is attributed by Jones to the tallest man.

I shall call the first fallacy 'the fallacy of inferring the content of the property attributed from an accidental description of the property attributed'. One commits this fallacy if one supposes that (4) and (5) together imply

> (6)   The tallest man is such that Jones believes that he has the property most frequently attributed to Solomon.

Suppose that (1) and (4) and therefore also (5) are true, but that Jones does not have the concepts requisite for understanding what is meant by 'the property most frequently attributed to Solomon'; perhaps he doesn't know what attribution is or he doesn't know what a property is. Then (6) will be false.

In thus committing 'the fallacy of inferring the content of the property attributed from an accidental description of the property attributed', one argues in the following way. The premises of the argument tell us that there is a certain property x which a man attributes to something, but they characterise x by means of an accidental definite description and not by means of an essential definite description. And the conclusion of the argument contains an essential description of the property x and thus tell us *what* the property is that the man has attributed. (The point of 'accidental description' will be clear if we look back to (4). 'The property most frequently attributed to Solomon' is an accidental description of a certain property; it doesn't tell us *what* the property is. But 'the property of being wise' is non-accidental; it *does* tell us *what* the property in question is.)

I shall call the second fallacy 'the fallacy of inferring the property attributed from a partial description of its content'. One commits this fallacy if one takes (6) and (4) to imply (1). Let us imagine that (6) and (4) are true. Jones mistakenly thinks that the property most frequently attributed to Solomon is that of being honest; the tallest man is thought by Jones to be honest; and, reflecting on these two facts, Jones concludes, with respect to the tallest man, that he has the property most frequently attributed to Solomon. But these assumptions are quite consistent with our supposing also that the tallest man is thought by Jones to be stupid and not to be wise at all.

In thus committing 'the fallacy of inferring the property attributed from a partial description of its content', one argues in the following way. The premise tells us *what* property a man has attributed and thus gives us the content of that property. In describing this property, the premise makes use of an accidental description of a certain *other* property x. And the conclusion tells us that x is the property that the man has attributed.

Analogous points could now be made about endeavour. To make them, we have only to replace the two expressions 'x is believed by s to be F' and 's attributes the property of being F to x', respectively, by 'x is such that s acts with the intention of bringing it about that it is F' and 'The property of being F is such that s undertakes to cause s to have it'. Then we could have this definition:

> D.C.4 x is such that s acts with the intention of bringing it about that it is F $=$Df The property of being F is one such that s undertakes to cause x to have it.

By considering the analogues of our statements (1) through (6) above, we could then distinguish 'the fallacy of inferring the content of the property endeavoured from an accidental description of the property endeavoured' and 'the fallacy of inferring the property endeavoured from an accidental description of its content'.

4 *Belief* De Re *as a Species of Belief* De Dicto

Can we exhibit belief *de re* as an instance of belief *de dicto*? In other words, can we define 's attributes the property of being F to x' by reference to such *de dicto* concepts as 's accepts the proposition that p'?

When the locution 's believes x to be F' ('s attributes the property of being F to x') is warranted, then one may say of the thing in question: 'One of its properties is that of being believed by s to be F.' If a thing x *is* thus an object of a person's belief, then the person has, so to speak, gone 'outside the circle of his own ideas'. His thoughts are directed, at least in part, upon the thing x. In order for this to happen, should the person bear some intimate epistemic relation to x, or is it enough that he accept a proposition implying x to have a certain property?

There is some disagreement about the answers to such questions and there would seem to be no obvious procedure for arriving at agreement.[3] We may ask: 'When would we *say*, of a thing x, that it's believed by someone to be something or other?' But an investigation of our language habits suggests two things: first that, on some occasions, we require very little of a person s in order to be able to say of a thing x that it is believed by s to be something or other; and secondly that, on other occasions, we require a considerable degree of epistemic intimacy between s and x before we will allow ourselves to say that x is the object of s's beliefs.

If, instead of considering the language we might use in talking about s and x, we restrict ourselves to descriptive psychology, or 'phenomenology', and just consider our own doxastic states, then, it would seem, there is no obvious difference between *de re* and *de dicto* belief. The distinction between the types of belief is not like that, say, between belief and desire. One may say with perfect certainty: 'This is a matter of belief and not of desire, and that is a matter of desire and not of belief.' But one may not say with any certainty at all: 'This is a matter of *de re* and not of *de dicto* belief, and that is a matter of *de dicto* and not of *de re* belief.'

It is fairly easy to set forth criteria enabling us to reduce the *de re* locution to the *de dicto* locution. In what follows, I will discuss two different criteria. The first is latitudinarian, or permissive, in that it requires very little of the subject s. The second is more rigoristic in that it does require of s a certain amount of epistemic achievement before we can thus say he has gone 'beyond the circle of his own ideas'. Other possible criteria are even more rigoristic, but I will here defend the second.

Let us recall the following concepts that were introduced in Chapter I:

D.I.3 p entails the property of being F $=$Df p is necessarily such that (i) if it obtains then something has the property of being F and (ii) whoever accepts p believes that something is F.

D.I.4   c is an individual concept $=$Df c is a property such that (i) it is possible that something has c and (ii) it is not possible that more than one thing has c at a time.

D.I.6 p implies x to have the property of being F $=$Df There is a property G such that (i) G is an individual concept, (ii) p entails the conjunction of G and the property of being F, and (iii) x has G.

The latitudinarian conception of *de re* belief would now be this:

s attributes the property of being F to x $=$Df s accepts a proposition which implies x to have the property of being F.

The proposed definition requires, as it should, that if x is to be believed by s to be F, then there must *be* such a thing as x. But otherwise the definition would seem to be overly latitudinarian or permissive.[4] One could object: 'If s's belief is actually to pertain to the particular individual x, then s must bear *some* kind of intimate epistemic relationship to x. s must be able to get outside the circle of his own ideas and direct his belief precisely upon *that* particular individual.'

I think that the objection is sound and therefore that any adequate definition of *de re* belief should contain an epistemic component. The following definition, unlike the one just considered, does contain such a component:

D.C.5   s attributes the property of being F to x $=$Df There is an individual concept c such that (i) s knows a proposition implying x to have c and (ii) s accepts a proposition which implies x to have the property c and the property of being F.

The concept of knowledge, referred to in the definiens, will be discussed in Appendix D.[5] We suggested in D.C.3 above that 's believes x to be F', or 's believes with respect to x that it is F', may be taken to abbreviate 's attributes the property of being F to x'. And so definition D.C.5 completes our account of *de re* belief. Let us now illustrate the account by altering Russell's example.

If Scott is the author of *Waverley*, and if the proposition that the author of *Waverley* is Scottish is one that is known by George, then, whether or not George has any idea that Scott might have written *Waverley*, Scott may be said to be such that George believes him to be Scottish. And this will be so even if George accepts the proposition that Scott is not Scottish.

What if Scott is also the author of *Marmion* and George accepts the proposition that the author of *Marmion* is not Scottish? It will still be the case, given our definition, that Scott – i.e. the author of *Marmion* – is believed by George to be Scottish.

Suppose that, in addition, the proposition that the author of *Marmion* wrote many works is one that George also knows to be true. Since, we are assuming, George accepts the proposition that the author of *Marmion* is not Scottish, must we now say that Scott is believed by George to be both Scottish and not Scottish? We are not entitled to say this. We can say that George believes with respect to Scott that he is Scottish and *also* that George believes with respect to Scott that he is not Scottish. But we cannot say that George believes with respect to Scott that he is both Scottish and not Scottish. It would be unjust, therefore, to say that George has a contradictory belief or even that he has beliefs that contradict each other.[6]

Let us consider now three possible objections to this definition of *de re* belief.

The first objection is this. 'Your definition is overpermissive. If Robinson knows that the tallest spy is a spy and believes that all spies are secretive, then, if he puts two and two together, he will believe that the tallest spy is secretive. Your account, therefore, would require you to say that the tallest spy is believed by Robinson to be secretive. But, surely, his knowledge that the tallest spy is a spy is much too easily acquired. It hardly brings him into the requisite relationship with the tallest spy.'

The reply is that the objection does not take the concept of *knowledge* sufficiently seriously. The knowledge in question is *not* easily acquired. To say of a proposition that it is *known* by a given person is not merely to say that the proposition is one that he is justified in accepting. Nor is it to say merely that the proposition is one that for him is beyond reasonable doubt. It is to say that the proposition is one on which he has a right to rely – one that he may, so to speak, include in his evidence-base and appeal to when he is considering the epistemic status of other propositions.[7]

To *know* that the tallest spy is a spy, one must know, not only that there are spies, but also that there are not two or more spies such that they are of the same height and taller than all other spies. And to know that the latter one must have information that probably *no one* has.

The second objection to the proposed definition of *de re* belief is this. 'Suppose c is the property of being identical with the President; q is the proposition that the President is a Republican; and p is the proposition that the President is a resident of California. Imagine now a well-informed Washington correspondent who had been asleep for a week and woke up on 10 August, 1974, still believing that Mr Nixon was President and still believing that the President was a resident of California. Since the proposition q, that the President is a Republican, is a proposition that the correspondent knew to be true, your definition would have the absurd consequence that this well-informed correspondent believes, with respect to Mr Ford, that *he* is a resident of California.'

This objection, like the preceding one, does not take the concept of knowledge sufficiently seriously. It is now clear that, if a person *knows* a proposition to be true, then, not only must the proposition be evident or justified, but also it should be such that the ground or basis that it has does not justify or make evident any false proposition. (This point will be discussed and made more precise in Appendix D.) But the ostensible knowledge referred to in the proposed counter-example does not fulfil this condition. The well-informed correspondent did not know that the President is a Republican; for the basis *he* had for this proposition made evident the false proposition that Mr Nixon is President.[8] And so, too, for any of the other things he might be thought to know about the President.

The third and final objection to our account of *de re* belief is this: 'If there is a person such that Jones believes, with respect to him, that he is the next President, then Jones knows who that person is. And more generally, if there is an entity x which a person s has a belief about, then s knows who or what that entity is. But the conditions of your definition could be satisfied even if Jones didn't know who the next President is. Therefore your account is overpermissive.'

But is it correct to say that a person s cannot have a belief with respect to a thing *x* unless s *knows who,* or *knows what x* is? Surely not. I can believe, with respect to a man I see standing on the corner, that he is wearing a hat – without knowing who the man is. A visitor from another country could visit one of our political conventions and be led to believe, with respect to the speaker on the rostrum, that *he* is our next President – without having any idea as to who the speaker might in fact be. It is a mistake, then, to equate an explication of *de re* with an explication of the extraordinarily elusive concepts of *knowing who* and *knowing what.* (But we will consider these further in the following section.)

It is possible, of course, to formulate more restrictive characterisations of *de re* belief. Thus one might define 's attributes the property of being F to *x*' by saying: 'There is a *q* such that s knows *q* to be true and *q* implies *x* to be F.' Or one could restrict the objects of *de re* belief to the objects of direct aquaintance, or to the objects of direct acquaintance and perception. But I think that the present account has the advantage of being neither excessively rigoristic nor excessively latitudinarian.[9]

Once again we may note the analogy between belief and endeavour. Thus if we were to follow the latitudinarian conception of *de re* belief we would characterise *de re* endeavour this way:

> The property of being F is one such that s undertakes to cause *x* to have it =Df There is a state of affairs which s endeavours to bring about and which implies *x* to be F.

But our account of such endeavour will be more rigoristic. We will say:

> D.C.6 The property of being F is one such that s undertakes to cause *x* to have it =Df There is an individual concept c that: (i) s knows a proposition implying *x* to have c; and (ii) s endeavours to bring about a certain state of affairs which implies *x* to have c and s to have the property of causing what has c to be F.

Here, too, more rigoristic accounts are possible. But I believe that the present account of *de re* endeavour, like our account of *de re* belief, falls between the extremes of excessive rigorism and excessive latitudinarianism.

5 A Note on 'Knowing Who'

In reply to the question 'Who robbed the bank?' one may be able to say, truly, 'The man who drove the Buick is the man who robbed the bank' or 'Utterson is the man who robbed the bank'. Under some conditions these true sentences might constitute an answer to the question 'Who robbed the bank?' But under other conditions these same true sentences might not constitute an answer, even if the questioner had not previously known that they were true; in such cases, the questioner might well go on to ask, 'Yes, but *who* is the man who drove the Buick?' or 'But who *is* Utterson?' More generally, of various true and informative sentences, '*a* is the one who is F', '*a* is the one who is G', '*a* is the one who is H', some but not others will constitute an adequate answer to the question 'Who is *a*?' The philosophical problem is: what is it in virtue of which some of these true sentences constitute an adequate answer and some do not? I am inclined to think that this philosophical problem has a pragmatic solution, but others have suggested that its solution can only be metaphysical.

The pragmatic solution would be something like this: the question 'Who is *a*?' presupposes a certain context of inquiry, and this context determines which, of the various true (and informative) sentences of the form '*a* is the one who . . .', actually constitutes an answer. For example, if I ask you 'Who is that man?' my question might be one that could be made more explicit by asking: 'Of the people who are coming to the party – the banker, the professor, the artist – which one is that man?' If you make a true statement about the man (e.g. 'He is the brother of the man beside him'), but one which does not enable me to infer that he is the banker, or that he is the professor, or that he is the artist, then although you may have made a true and informative statement of the form 'That man is the person who is F' you will not have told me *who* he is. We could also say, similarly, that the question 'What is *a*?', as well as such statements as 'I know *who* he is' and 'I wonder *what* that is', presupposes a certain context of discussion or inquiry, and that 'who' and 'what' refer to a position within that context.

The metaphysical solution is suggested by the traditional treatment of the following sophism: 'Do you know Coriscus?' 'Yes.' 'Do you know the man who is approaching?' 'No.' 'But he is Coriscus. Therefore you know who he is and you do not know who he is.'[10] The traditional solution is to distinguish between knowing Coriscus *per se* and knowing Coriscus *per accidens*: to know *who* Coriscus is is to know, with respect to certain properties that are *essential* to Coriscus and to no one else, that Coriscus is the man who has these properties; but the property of being the man who is approaching is not essential to Coriscus; hence from the fact that you do not know who the man approaching is, it does not follow that you do not know who Coriscus is – despite the fact that Coriscus *is* the man approaching.[11]

This view suggests that, no matter how much you may know about a person, if you do not know a proposition implying his individual essence or haecceity, then you do not know who he is.[12] This metaphysical account of 'knowing who' could readily be explicated in the terms that we have been using here. Thus we could say:

> D.C.7 s knows who *x* is = Df There is an individual essence (or haecceity) H such that s knows a proposition implying *x* to have H.

This definition might be said to give us an explication of the strict and philosophical sense of 'knowing who'. If what we have said in Chapter I is correct, then, in this strict and philosophical sense, each person is such that he himself can be said to be the only person who knows who he is.

But, as we have said, an explication of the strict and philosophical sense of *de re* belief need not involve an explication of *knowing who*.

6 Some Interrelations Between De Dicto and De Re

The following summary may now throw light upon what has been said about the objects of belief and endeavour. The letters 'F' and 'G' occupy the places of predicative expressions and 'the F' is short for 'the thing which is 'F''.

(a) s believes that the F is G.

(b) The F is believed by s to be G.

(c) s believes that the proposition that the F is G is true.

(d) The proposition that the F is G is believed by s to be true.

(e) The proposition that the F is G is accepted by s.

(f) s believes that the F has the property of being G.

(g) The F is believed by s to be such that it has the property of being G.

(h) s attributes the property of being G to the F.

These eight locutions are easily confused with each other and such confusion sometimes infects what has been written about the philosophy of belief. But the foregoing considerations should help us to distinguish them.

It is sometimes thought that belief *de dicto* is only a special instance of belief *de re*. According to this view, to believe (*de dicto*) that Socrates is mortal is simply to believe (*de re*), with respect to the proposition that Socrates is mortal, that that proposition is true. This view presupposes, mistakenly, that (a) is equivalent to (d).[18] But (a) does not imply (d), and (d) does not imply (a).

Let us ask, with respect to each of these locutions, which ones of the others it entails. (I here use 'entail' in the way defined in D.IV.2. A proposition *p* may be said to entail a proposition *q*, provided only: *p* is necessarily such that (a) if it obtains then *q* obtains and (b) whoever accepts it accepts *q*.)

If 'accepts' and 'attributes' are restricted in the ways in which I have proposed, and if definitions D.C.1 and D.C.3 are accepted, then we may assert that the following entailment relations hold:

  a entails *e*
  b entails *h*
  c entails *a*, *d* and *e*
  e entails *a*
  f entails *a* and *e*
  g entails *b* and *h*
  h entails *b*.

But no additional entailment relations hold between any two of these eight locutions.

Once again we could make precisely analogous points about endeavour. Thus (a) would be replaced by 's acts with the intention of bringing it about that the F is G'; (b) would be replaced by 'The F is such that s acts with the intention of bringing it about that it is G'; and analogously for (c) through (g).

APPENDIX D

KNOWLEDGE, EVIDENCE AND REASONABLE BELIEF

1 Epistemic Preferability

We may think of the theory of evidence as a branch of the theory of preference, or, more accurately, of the theory of *right* preference, or preferability. Let us take *epistemic preferability* as our undefined epistemic concept. Thus we begin with the locution, '*p* is epistemically preferable to *q* for s at t', where the expressions occupying the place of '*p*' *and* '*q*' are terms referring to states of affairs (or propositions) and where 's' and 't', respectively, refer to a particular person and to a particular time.

There are two ways of throwing light upon what is intended by an undefined expression. The first is to paraphrase it into a different terminology. And the second is to make explicit the basic assumptions it is used to formulate.

So far as the first is concerned, we might paraphrase the locution '*p* is epistemically preferable to *q* for s at *t*' by reference to the concept of an *intellectual requirement*. I assume that every person is subject to a certain purely intellectual requirement – that of trying his best to bring it about that, for every proposition *h* that he considers, he accept *h* if and only if *h* is true. We could say that this is the person's duty or responsibility *qua* intellectual being. But as a requirement, it is only a *prima facie* duty; it may be, and usually is, overridden by other, nonintellectual requirements and it may be fulfilled more or less adequately. One way, then, of re-expressing '*p* is epistemically preferable to *q* for s at *t*' is to say this: 's is so situated at *t* that he can better fulfil his intellectual requirement, his responsibility as an intellectual being, by bringing about *p* than by bringing about *q*.'[1]

So far as the second method of explicating an undefined concept is concerned, we may set forth the following six principles as axioms of epistemic preferability.

(1) Epistemic preferability, like other types of preferability, is such that, for any states of affairs *p* and *q*, if *p* is preferable to *q* for s at *t*, then it is not the case that *q* is preferable to *p* for s at *t*. (2) Again like other types of preferability, epistemic preferability is such that, for any states of affairs, *p*, *q* and *r*, if it is

not the case that p is preferable to q, and if it is not the case that q is preferable to r, then it is not the case that p is preferable to r. (3) For any propositions h and i, accepting h is epistemically preferable to accepting i for s at t, if and only if, accepting not-i is epistemically preferable to accepting not-h for s at t. (4) For any proposition h, if withholding h (that is, neither accepting h nor accepting not-h) is *not* epistemically preferable to accepting h, then accepting h is epistemically preferable to accepting not-h. 'If agnosticism is not epistemically preferable to theism, then theism is epistemically preferable to atheism.' (5) For any propositions h and i, withholding h is the same in epistemic value as withholding i for s at t, if and only if, either accepting h is the same in epistemic value as accepting i for s at t or accepting not-h is the same in epistemic value as accepting i for s at t. (To say that one state of affairs is 'the same in epistemic value' as another is to say that neither one is epistemically preferable to the other.) (6) For any proposition h and i, if accepting i is epistemically preferable to accepting h for s at t and also epistemically preferable to accepting not-h for s at t, then withholding h is epistemically preferable to withholding i for s at t.

In addition to these six epistemic principles, we presuppose general principles about states of affairs such as those set forth in Chapter IV. One such principle is that according to which every state of affairs is identical with the negation of its own negation.[2]

In order to explicate the basic concepts of the theory of epistemic preferability, we should consider what is involved in asking, for any given proposition and any given subject and any given time, which is epistemically preferable: accepting the proposition, disbelieving the proposition (that is, accepting the negation of the proposition), or withholding the proposition (neither accepting nor disbelieving the proposition). In this way, we may now explicate some of the epistemic terms that have been used in the present work. (We assume in the following definitions that a temporal reference is constant throughout, but for simplicity we keep it implicit.)

D.D.1 h is beyond reasonable doubt for s $=$Df Accepting h is more reasonable for s than is withholding h.

D.D.2 h has some presumption in its favour for s $=$Df Accepting h is more reasonable for s than accepting not-h.

D.D.3   *h* is acceptable for s =D*f* Withholding *h* is no more reasonable for s than accepting *h*.

These definitions may be said to define three *de dicto* epistemic concepts.[3] The corresponding *de re* concepts may be analysed in accordance with the general method set forth in Appendix C. Thus:

D.D.4   *x* is such that it is beyond reasonable doubt for s that it is F =D*f* There is an individual concept C such that: (i) s knows a proposition implying *x* to have C; and (ii) there is a proposition which is beyond reasonable doubt for s and which implies *x* to have the property C and the property of being F.

The definitions of the other *de re* epistemic concepts would be analogous.[4]

2 The Certain and the Evident

The concept of epistemic certainty was defined in Chapter I as follows:

D.I.2   *h* is certain for s at *t* =D*f* (i) Accepting *h* is more reasonable for s at *t* than withholding *h* and (ii) there is no *i* such that accepting *i* is more reasonable for s at *t* than accepting *h*.

Given D.D.1 above, we may replace the first clause in the definiens by: '*h* is beyond reasonable doubt for s at *t*'.

The ordinary things we know are more than merely beyond reasonable doubt but they are less than certain. How, then, do we find a place between these two categories?

An evident proposition, like a proposition that is certain, is one such that accepting it is epistemically preferable to withholding it, but it may fall just short of certainty. We will say:

D.D.5   *h* is evident for s =D*f* (i) Accepting *h* is epistemically preferable for s to withholding *h* and (ii) for every *i*, if accepting *i* is epistemically preferable for s to accepting *h*, then *i* is certain for s.

This definition presupposes that being evident, like being certain, is not capable of degrees. And so we could say, in short, that an evident proposition is one that s may use in deciding upon the reasonableness or acceptability of *other* propositions.

We may assume that whatever is certain is also evident, but the converse is not true. And our definitions and axioms imply that: whatever is evident is beyond reasonable doubt; whatever is beyond reasonable doubt is acceptable; and whatever is acceptable is such as to have some presumption in its favour. But our definitions and axioms do not imply the converses of these propositions. Hence we have a hierarchy of epistemic concepts.

3 The Directly Evident

We next consider briefly a somewhat different type of epistemic concept.

Certain propositions may be said to be *directly evident* for a man at any given time. Of the propositions that are thus directly evident, some may be said to be empirical or *a posteriori*, and others may be said to be *a priori*. Leibniz referred to these two types of directly evident proposition as 'the first truths of fact' and 'the first truths of reason' respectively.[5]

We may characterise 'the first truths of fact' by reference to the concept of self-presentation that was introduced in Chapter I. We there proposed the following:

D.I.1 h is such that it is self-presenting for s at t =Df h occurs at t and is necessarily such that, whenever it occurs, then it is certain for s.

We make the temporal reference explicit in this definition in order to bring out the facts that what is self-presenting is evident at the time at which it occurs. We could obtain a somewhat more restrictive, and possibly more useful, definition of self-presentation by further restricting the definiens. Thus we might say: 'h occurs, s considers h, and necessarily whenever h occurs and s considers h, then h is evident for s'. The references to s's *considering* or *entertaining* the state of affairs h might have these advantages: it would restrict self-presentation to those states of affairs that s is able to grasp or understand (for one cannot consider or entertain a state of affairs one is able to grasp); and it would restrict self-presentation to those states of affairs that s actually notices.

The proposition I would express by 'I exist' is directly evident *a posteriori* but it is not self-presenting. (If I'm asleep the proposition is true but it may not be evident to me.) We may characterise the directly evident *a posteriori* by reference to what is self-presenting:

D.D.6 h is directly evident *a posteriori* for s =Df h is logically contingent; and there is an e such that (a) e is self-presenting for s and (b) necessarily, whoever accepts e accepts h.

What now of that which is directly evident *a priori*? It is traditional to say that an *a priori* proposition is a proposition that is 'independent of experience' and is such that 'if you understand it then you can see that it is true'. To get at what is intended by these descriptions, we will first say what it is for a proposition to be an axiom:

> D.D.7   *h* is an axiom =Df *h* is necessary such that (a) it is true and (b) for every s, if s considers *h*, then s accepts *h* and *h* is evident for s.

(It may be noted that we here make use once again of the concept of considering or 'entertaining' a state of affairs.) Next we say what it is for a proposition to be *axiomatic* for a given person:

> D.D.8   *h* is axiomatic for s = Df (i) *h* is an axiom and (ii) s considers *h*.

We may now characterise the *a priori* as that which can be derived from what is axiomatic. Or, more exactly:

> D.D.9   *h* is directly evident *a priori* for s = Df There is an *e* such that (a) *e* is axiomatic for s, (b) the proposition, if *e* occurs then *h* occurs, is axiomatic for s and (c) s considers *h*.

The directly evident, then, is whatever is either directly evident *a posteriori* or directly evident *a priori*. It will be useful to be able to contrast this concept of the directly evident with the following concept of a *basic proposition*:

> D.D.10   *e* is a *basic proposition* for s = Df *e* is strictly equivalent to a conjunction of propositions, each of which is either self-presenting or axiomatic for s.[6]

4 Making Evident

What is it for one proposition to make another proposition evident for a subject s?

In order to characterise the concept of making evident, let us first say what it is for one proposition to be such that it is a *basis* for another proposition:

> D.D.11   *e* is a basis of *h* for s = Df *e* is self-presenting for s; and necessarily, if *e* is certain for s, then *h* is evident for s.

I assume that, for anything *h* that is evident for s, there is something *e* which is a basis of *h* for s.[7] (This assumption might be said to characterise 'foundationalism'.) And now we may formulate our definition of making evident:

D.D.12   *e* makes *h* evident for s =Df *e* is evident for s; and for every *b*, if *b* is a basis of *e* for s, then *b* is a basis of *h* for s.

It should be noted that, if *e* is a basis of *h* for s, then *e* makes *h* evident for s. But *e* may make *h* evident for s without *e* being thereby a basis of *h* for s. It may be, for example, that there are propositions about Neptune and astronomy that make evident, for some astronomer, a number of propositions about the motions of Uranus. But the former propositions do not provide a *basis* (in the sense of D.D.11) for the latter propositions, since the former cannot be said to be certain in the strict sense defined in D.I.2 above.

We may also note that, if *e* is a *basis* of *h* for s, then *e* is necessarily such that, if it is certain for s, then *h* is evident for s. But if *e makes h evident* for s, then it is possible for it to be the case that *e* is evident for s and *h* is *not* evident for s. The latter possibility would be realised if *e*'s contribution toward *h* being evident is *defeated* or *overridden* – if there is some proposition *i* such that *i* is evident for s and the conjunction, *e* and *i*, does not make *h* evident. But if *e* is a *basis* for *h*, *e*'s contribution cannot thus be defeated or overridden; as long as *e* is certain for s, *h* will be evident for s.[8]

By modifying these definitions in obvious ways, we may also define such concepts as those suggested by '*e* makes *h* such as to be beyond reasonable doubt for s' and '*e* makes *h* such as to have some presumption in its favour for s'. The latter concept is the one that is sometimes expressed by '*e* confirms *h* for s'.[9]

5 Knowledge

According to the traditional conception of knowledge, a man can be said to know a proposition *h* provided the following three conditions are fulfilled: (1) he accepts *h*; (2) *h* is true; and (3) *h* is evident for him.[10]

But the traditional conception of knowledge has been shown to be inadequate by Edmund L. Gettier, Jr, in his classic paper entitled 'Is Justified True Belief Knowledge?'[11] The inadequacy of the traditional conception derives from the fact, referred to above, that some of the things we know are such that they are not logically implied by the evidence we have for them – the fact, in other words, that our evidence for some of the things we know is non-demonstrative or inductive. This fact implies that one proposition may make another proposition evident for a subject s even though the second proposition is *false*, and hence that a proposition may be both evident and false. And this fact proves disastrous for the traditional conception of knowledge.

According to the traditional conception a proposition isn't known unless it is both evident and *true*. Why, then, should the possibility of evident falsehoods make a difficulty? Suppose an evident falsehood makes evident still another proposition – and that the other proposition, as luck would have it, happens to be *true*. Then the traditional conception would require us to say that the latter proposition is known to be true, but it may be in fact that the latter proposition is *not* known to be true.

The following example, somewhat oversimplified, will illustrate this situation. Suppose s mistakes a dog for a sheep, but under such conditions that the false proposition he would express by 'I see a sheep in the field' is evident to him. Then the proposition he would express by 'A sheep is in the field' will also be evident to him. Suppose further that, as luck would have it, there *is* a sheep in the field – but elsewhere in the field and not seen or even thought of by s. This situation, obviously, would not warrant our saying that s *knows* that there is a sheep in the field. But it satisfies the terms of the traditional definition of knowledge, for the proposition that there is a sheep in the field is a proposition h which is such that: (1) s accepts h; (2) h is true; and (3) h is evident for s.

What went wrong in the situation described? Although the proposition h, 'There is a sheep in the field', was both true and evident, the only *basis* the man had for h was also a basis he had for the false proposition 'I see a sheep in the field'. Since we do not want to count h as a case of knowledge, we should say that, if a man knows a proposition to be true, then his basis for that proposition should not be such as to make a false proposition evident. To put this point more precisely, let us first introduce the concept of a proposition being 'nondefectively' evident:

    D.D.13   h is nondefectively evident for s =Df h is evident for s and is entailed by a conjunction of propositions each having for s a basis which is not a basis of any false proposition for s.

We may now define *de dicto* knowledge as follows:

D.D.14   *h* is known by s = Df *h* is accepted by s; *h* is true;
and *h* is nondefectively evident for s.

And so we need not say, of the man discussed above, that he
knows that there is a sheep in the field. The directly evident
propositions which make evident to him the proposition that
there is a sheep in the field also make evident to him the false
proposition he would express by saying 'What I take to be a
sheep is a sheep'. Hence the proposition that there is a sheep in
the field is not nondefectively evident for the man and it would
seem to be impossible to find a conjunction of nondefectively
evident propositions which entail it.[12]

In Appendix C, we introduced a schematic definition enabling
us to define the ordinary 'believes that' locution by reference
to the acceptance of propositions. This was:

D.C.1   s believes that *p* = Df s accepts the proposition that *p*.

The occurrence of '*p*' is here schematic and may be replaced by
any English sentence. The ordinary 'knows that' locution may
now be introduced in a similar way:

D.D.15   s knows that *p* = Df The proposition that *p* is known
by s.

The definition of the concept of *de re* knowledge is compara-
tively simple:

D.D.16   *x* is known by s to be F = Df There is a proposition
which is known by s and which implies *x* to be F.

APPENDIX E

SUMMARY OF DEFINITIONS

There follows a list of the definitions that have been presented in this book. They are listed in the order in which they have been introduced.

D.I.1   *h* is such that it is self-presenting to S at *t* =Df *h* occurs at *t* and is necessarily such that, whenever it occurs, then it is certain for S.

D.I.2   *h* is certain for S at *t* =Df (i) Accepting *h* is more reasonable for S at *t* than withholding *h* (i.e. not accepting *h* and not accepting not-*h*) and (ii) there is no *i* such that accepting *i* is more reasonable for S at *t* than accepting *h*.

D.I.3   *p* entails the property of being F =Df *p* is necessarily such that (i) if it obtains then something has the property of being F and (ii) whoever accepts *p* believes that something is F.

The letter 'F' in this definition and in D.I.6 is schematic; it may be replaced by any English predicate expression. The closely related concept expressed by '*p* entails [the proposition or state of affairs] *q*' is defined in D.IV.2 below.

D.I.4   C is an individual concept =Df C is a property such that (i) it is possible that something has C and (ii) it is not possible that more than one thing has C at a time.

D.I.5   G is an *individual essence* (or *haecceity*) =Df G is a property which is such that, for every *x*, *x* has G if and only if *x* is necessarily such that it has G, and it is impossible that there is a *y* other than *x* such that *y* has G.

D.I.6   *p* implies *x* to have the property of being F =Df There is a property G such that (i) G is an individual concept, (ii) *p* entails the conjunction of G and the property of being F, and (iii) *x* has G.

D.I.7   S is acquainted with *x* at *t* =Df There is a *p* such that (i) *p* is self-presenting for S at *t* and (ii) there is a property that *p* implies *x* to have.

This concept of *acquaintance* should be contrasted with the concept of *knowing how*, defined in D.C.7.

The following three definitions make use of the concept of '*p* is known by s' that is defined in D.D.16.

D.I.8   s has an individual concept of *x* =Df There is a proposition *p* and an individual concept c such that (i) *p* implies *x* to have c and (ii) *p* is known by s.

D.I.9   s individuates *x* =Df There is a *p* such that (i) *p* is known by s and (ii) there is a property *p* implies *x* to have.

D.I.10   s individuates *x per se* =Df There is a p such that (i) *p* is known by s, (ii) there is a property *p* implies *x* to have, and (iii) there is no individual thing *y* such that *y* is other than *x* and there is a property *p* implies *y* to have.

The concept of *individual thing* which appears in this definition is defined in D.IV.14.

D.I.11   s believes himself to be F =Df There is an individual essence c such that (a) a proposition implying s to have c is self-presenting for s and (b) s accepts a proposition which entails the conjunction of c and the property of being F.

It is suggested in Chapter I that clause (a) above is unnecessary.

The twenty definitions from Chapter II that follow make use of the undefined concepts of *physical necessity, causal contribution* and *endeavour*. The concept of *event* is defined in D.IV.7.

D.II.1   *p* is *physically possible* =Df It is not physically necessary that *p* does not occur.

D.II.2   *p* is *causally possible* =Df There does not occur an event *q* such that it is physically necessary that, if *q* occurs, then *p* does not occur.

D.II.3   *p* is a *sufficient causal condition* of *q* =Df *p* and *q* are events which are such that it is physically necessary but not logically necessary that, if *p* occurs at any time *t*, then *q* occurs at *t* or after *t*.

D.II.4   Determinism =Df The proposition that, for every event that occurs, there occurs a sufficient causal condition of that event.

D.II.5   s is *free at t to undertake p* $=$ Df There is a period of time which includes, but begins before, t and during which there occurs no sufficient causal condition either for s undertaking p or for s not undertaking p.

D.II.6 p is directly within s's power at t $=$ Df There is a q such that: s is free at t to undertake q; and either (a) p is s undertaking q or (b) there occurs an r at t such that it is physically necessary that, if r and s-undertaking-q occurs, then s-undertaking-q contributes causally to p.

D.II.7 p is within s's power at t $=$ Df p is a member of a series such that (i) the first is directly within s's power at t and (ii) each of the others is such that its predecessor in the series is a sufficient causal condition of its being directly within his power.

D.II.8 p is a *necessary causal condition* of q $=$ Df p and q are events such that it is physically necessary but not logically necessary that, if q occurs at any time t, then p occurs at t or prior to t.

D.II.9   s does something at t which contributes causally to p $=$ Df There is a q such that s's undertaking q at t contributes causally to p.

An alternative definition, to accommodate the concept of the *commission of an omission*, is set forth in D.II.9.1 (immediately following D.II.12 below).

D.II.10   s contributes causally at t to p $=$ Df Either (a) s does something at t that contributes causally to p, or (b) there is a q such that s undertakes q at t and s-undertaking-q is p, or (c) there is an r such that s does something at t that contributes causally to r, and p is that state of affairs which is s doing something that contributes causally to r.

D.II.11   By contributing causally at t to p, s contributes causally at t to q $=$ Df s contributes causally at t to p, and that event which is s contributing causally at t to p also contributes causally to q.

D.II.12   s deliberately omits undertaking p at t $=$ Df s considers at t undertaking p and s does not undertake p at t.

(It should be noted that this definition makes use of the undefined concept of *considering* ('entertaining') a proposition or state of affairs). The definition that follows is an alternative to D.II.9, providing for the concept of the *commission of an omission*.

D.II.9.1   s does something at *t* which contributes causally to *p* =Df There is a *q* which is such that either (a) s undertaking *q* at *t* contributes causally to *p*, or (b) s deliberately omits *q* at *t* and *p* is that state of affairs which is s deliberately omitting *q*.

D.II.13   s undertakes *p* and does so for the purpose of bringing about *q* =Df s undertakes to bring about (i) *p* and (ii) his-undertaking-*p* contributing causally to *q*.

D.II.14   *p* is for s a *mere means* to something else =Df (i) There is a *q* such that *p* is for s a means to *q* and (ii) for every *r*, if *p* is for s a means to *r*, then it is false that s undertakes *r* for the purpose of bringing about *p*.

The expression '*p* is for s a means to *q*', as used here, is an abbreviation for 's undertakes *p* and does so for the purpose of bringing about *q*' (defined in D.II.13 above).

D.II.15   *p* is an *ultimate end* or *end in itself* for s =Df (i) s undertakes *p* and (ii) it is false that *p* is for s a mere means to something else.

D.II.16   s intends *p* as a *preliminary step* towards bringing about *q* =Df s undertakes *p* and does so for the purpose of bringing it about that someone bring about *q*.

D.II.17   s *makes an attempt* to bring about *p* =Df s undertakes *p* and does not undertake anything as a preliminary step toward *p*.

D.II.18   s is *completely successful* in his endeavour at *t* to bring about *p* =Df (i) s makes an attempt at *t* to bring about *p* and (ii) everything he then undertakes for the purpose of bringing about *p* contributes causally to *p*.

D.II.19   s brings about *p* as a *basic act* at *t* =Df (i) s undertaking *p* contributes causally at *t* to *p* and (ii) there is no *q* such that s undertakes *q* at *t* for the purpose of bringing about *p*.

D.II.20   s brings about p *directly* at t =Df (i) s contributes causally at t to p and (ii) there is no q such that (a) s contributes causally at t to q and (b) q contributes causally to p.

The ten definitions from Chapter III that follow are intended to explicate the concept of an *ens successivum*. They are restricted to the concept of a table, or a 'successive table', but the term 'table' in these definitions may be replaced by counter-terms for other types of physical things. The definitions make use of the concept of *part* that is explicated in Appendix B ('Mereological Essentialism').

D.III.1   x is at t a direct table successor of y at t' =Df (i) t does not begin before t'; (ii) x is a table at t and y is a table at t'; and (iii) there is a z, such that z is a part of x at t and a part of y at t', and at every moment between t' and t, inclusive, z is itself a table.

D.III.2   x is at t a table successor of y at t' =Df (i) t does not begin before t'; (ii) x is a table at t and y is a table at t'; and (iii) x has at t every property P such that (a) y has P at t' and (b) all direct table successors of anything having P have P.

D.III.3   x constitutes at t the same successive table that y constitutes at t' =Df Either (a) x and only x is at t a table successor of y at t', or (b) y and only y is at t' a table successor of x at t.

D.III.4   x constitutes at t a successive table =Df There are a y and a t' such that y is other than x and x constitutes at t the same table that y constitutes at t'.

D.III.5   There is exactly one successive table at place P at time t =Df There is exactly one thing at place P at time t that constitutes a successive table at t.

D.III.6   G is rooted outside the times at which it is had =Df Necessarily, for any x and for any period of time t, x has the property G throughout t only if x exists at some time before or after t.

D.III.7   G may be rooted outside times at which it is had =Df G is equivalent to a disjunction of two properties one of which is, and the other of which is not, rooted outside times at which it is had.

D.III.8 The successive table that is a place P at time t is F at t =Df There is exactly one thing at place P at t that constitutes a successive table at t and that thing is F at t.

The letter 'F' as used in D.III.8 and in other definitions on this list is schematic.

D.III.9 The successive table that is at place P at time t has existed for at least 3 days =Df There is exactly one x such that x is at place P at time t and x constitutes a successive table at t; there are a y and a time t' such that x is at t a table-successor of y at t'; and t and t' are separated by a period of three days.

D.III.10 The successive table that is a place P at time t is constituted by x at t' =Df There is a y such that y is at place P at time t; y constitutes a successive table at t; and either x is identical with y and t is identical with t', or y constitutes at t the same successive table that x consitutes at t'.

D.III.11 There are, in the loose and popular sense, n so-and-so's at t =Df There are n things each of which constitutes a so-and-so at t and no two of which constitute the same so-and-so at t.

The following fourteen definitions from Chapter IV pertain to the theory of states of affairs. They presuppose the following undefined concepts: *acceptance* (an intentional concept relating a person and a state of affairs), *obtaining* (also expressible by 'occurring' and 'taking place'), and *times* and *places*.

D.IV.1 p is a state of affairs =Df It is possible that there is someone who accepts p.

D.IV.2 p entails q =Df p is necessarily such that (a) if it obtains then q obtains and (b) whoever accepts it accepts q.

D.IV.3 p is a proposition =Df p is a state of affairs, and it is impossible that there is a time t and a time t' such that p occurs at t and does not occur at t'.

It should be noted that the concept of *occurring at a certain time*, which is employed in this definition, is defined in D.IV.5 below.

D.IV.4   *e* is concretised by A at *t* = Df *e* occurs; for every property P, if *e* entails P, and if P is had only by contingent things, then some member of A has P at *t*; and there is no proper subset S of A which is such that, for every such P, some member of S has P.

A contingent thing is a thing which is not such that necessarily there is something that is identical with it.

D.IV.5   *e* occurs at time *t* = Df There is a set A such that *e* is concretised by A at time *t*.

D.IV.6   *e* occurs at place P = Df There is a set A and a time *t* such that *e* is concretised by A at *t*, and all the members of A are at place P at *t*.

D.IV.7   *p* is an event = Df *p* is a state of affairs which is such that: (i) it occurs; (ii) it is not a proposition; and (iii) it entails a property G which is such that (a) only individual things can exemplify G, (b) it is possible that no individual things exemplify G, and (c) G is not such that it may be rooted outside the times at which it is had.

The expression 'may be rooted outside the times at which it is had' was defined in D.III.7 above.

D.IV.8   A is such that at *t* it has concretised *p* exactly *n* times = Df There are *n* periods of time such that: no two of them are continuous with each other; none is later than *t*; A concretises *p* during each; and A does not concretise *p* at any other time within or prior to *t*.

D.IV.9   *p* is such that at *t* it has been concretised exactly *n* times = Df Consider each set that concretises *p* at *t* or prior to *t*; for each such set take that number which is the number of times such that the set at *t* has concretised *p* exactly that number of times; the sum of all such numbers is *n*.

The four definitions that follow are intended to show how certain *de re* concepts may be reduced to the corresponding *de dicto* concepts. They presuppose the *de dicto* concepts expressed by '*p* explains *q*', '*p* contributes causally to *q*', and 's perceives *p*'.

D.IV.10 p explains, with respect to x, why it has the property of being F $=$ Df There is a q which implies x to have the property of being F, and p explains q.

D.IV.11 x being F contributes causally at t to y being G $=$ Df Consider all those states of affairs which are such that they occur, they imply x to be F at t, and they do not imply y to be G; each such state of affairs contributes causally to a state of affairs which implies y to be G.

D.IV.12   s perceives x to have the property of being F $=$ Df There is a state of affairs p which is such that: s perceives p; and p implies x to have the property of being F.

D.IV.13   s perceives x $=$ Df There is a property such that s perceives x to have that property.

D.IV.14 x is an individual thing $=$ Df There exists at y such that y is identical with x and it is possible that there does not exist a y such that y is identical with x.

D.IV.15 x is a person $=$ Df x is an individual thing which is necessarily such that it is physically possible that there is something which it undertakes to bring about.

The six following definitions from Appendix B ('Mereological Essentialism') make use of the undefined expression 'x is an s-part of y'. The expression 's-part' is intended to indicate that 'part' (i.e. 'proper part') is here taken in a strict and philosophical sense. (The word 'part', as it is used in D.III.1 should be taken as synonymous with 's-part' as used here.) The first two definitions are adapted from Whitehead.

D.B.1 x is discrete from y $=$ Df (i) x is other than y, (ii) there is no z such that z is an s-part of x and z is an s-part of y, and (iii) x is not an s-part of y and y is not an s-part of x.

D.B.2 w is strictly made up of x and y $=$ Df (i) x is an s-part of w, (ii) y is an s-part of w, (iii) x is discrete from y, and (iv) no s-part of w is discrete both from x and from y.

D.B.3 x is strictly joined with y $=$ Df There is a w such that w is strictly made up of x and y.

D.B.4 x has y as an L-part at t =Df x is an *ens successivum*; and either y or something that constitutes y at t is an s-part of something that constitutes x at t.

The concept of an *ens successivum* may be obtained by generalising upon the concepts defined in D.III.4, D.III.8, D.III.9 and D.III.10.

D.B.5 x could have y as an L-part at t =Df There are a w and a v such that (i) w is an s-part of something that constitutes x at t, (ii) either x is identical with y or there is a time at which v constitutes y, and (iii) there is a possible world in which w is strictly joined with v.

The following definition, pertaining to 'the problem of increase', presupposes the concept expressed by 'x is larger than y'.

D.B.6 x is larger at t^2 than it is at t^1 =Df There exists a y and there exists a z such that (i) y constitutes x at t^1, (ii) z constitutes x at t^2 and (iii) z is larger than y.

The six definitions that follow are from Appendix C ('The Objects of Belief and Endeavour'). They presuppose the concepts of *acceptance* and *endeavour*.

D.C.1   s believes that p =Df s accepts the proposition that p.

In both D.C.1 and D.C.2, 'p' is used schematically; it may be replaced by any well-formed English sentence.

D.C.2   s acts with the intention of bringing it about that p =Df s undertakes to bring about the state of affairs that p.

It should be noted that D.C.3 and D.C.4, respectively, presuppose D.C.5 and D.C.6.

D.C.3 x is believed by s to be F =Df s attributes the property of being F to x.

D.C.4 x is such that s acts with the intention of bringing it about that it is F =Df The property of being F is one such that s undertakes to cause x to have it.

D.C.5   s attributes the property of being F to x =Df There is an individual concept C such that (i) s knows a proposition implying x to have C and (ii) s accepts a proposition which implies x to have the property C and the property of being F.

This definition and the one that follows presuppose the concepts defined in D.I.6 ('*p* implies *x* to have the property of F') and D.D.16 ('*h* is known by s to be true').

D.C.6   The property of being F is one such that s undertakes to cause *x* to have it =D*f* There is an individual concept C such that: (i) s knows a proposition implying *x* to have C; and (ii) s endeavours to bring about a certain state of affairs which implies *x* to have C and s to have the property of causing what has C to be F.

D.C.7   s knows who *x* is =D*f* There is an individual essence (or haecceity) H such that s knows a proposition implying *x* to have H.

This definition presupposes the concepts defined in D.I.5 ('G is an individual essence, or haecceity'), D.I.6 ('*p* implies *x* to have the property of being F') and D.D.16 ('*h* is known by s to be true').

The final eighteen definitions are from Appendix D ('Knowledge, Evidence and Reasonable Belief'). The first two definitions of Chapter I – i.e. D.I.1 ('*h* is such that it is self-presenting for s at *t*') and D.I.2 ('*h* is certain for s at *t*') – belong with this group. The following undefined concepts are presupposed: *acceptance* ('s accepts *p*'), *consideration* ('s considers, or entertains, *p*'), and *epistemic preferability* ('*p* is epistemically preferable to *q* for s at *t*'). The expression 'withholding *h*' is an abbreviation for 'neither accepting *h* nor accepting not-*h*'.

D.D.1   *h* is beyond reasonable doubt for s =D*f* Accepting *h* is more reasonable for s than is withholding *h*.

D.D.2   *h* has some presumption in its favour for s =D*f* Accepting *h* is more reasonable for s than accepting not-*h*.

D.D.3   *h* is acceptable for s =D*f* Withholding *h* is no more reasonable for s than accepting *h*.

These first three definitions are of *de dicto* epistemic concepts. The three definitions that follow are of the corresponding *de re* concepts; they presuppose the concept of *de dicto* knowledge that is defined in D.D.16.

D.D.4   *x* is such that it is beyond reasonable doubt for s that it is F =D*f* There is an individual concept C such that: (i) s knows a proposition implying *x* to have C; and (ii) there is a proposition which is beyond reasonable doubt for s and which implies *x* to have the property C and the property of being F.

D.D.5   *h* is evident for s =Df (i) Accepting *h* is epistemically preferable for s to withholding *h* and (ii) for every *i*, if accepting *i* is epistemically preferable for s to accepting *h*, then *i* is certain for s.

's decides *h* on *i*' abbreviates: '*h* is other than *i*; s undertakes to consider *h* and does so for the purpose of bringing about that he accept *i* if and only if *i* is true and that he accept not-*i* if and only if *i* is false'. The definition of *evident* thus presupposes the purposive concept defined in D.II.13.

D.D.6   *h* is directly evident *a posteriori* for s =Df *h* is logically contingent; and there is an *e* such that (a) *e* is self-presenting for s and (b) necessarily, whoever accepts *e* accepts *h*.

D.D.7   *h* is an axiom =Df *h* is necessarily such that (a) it is true and (b) for every s, if s considers *h*, then s accepts *h* and *h* is evident for s.

D.D.8   *h* is axiomatic for s =Df (i) *h* is an axiom and (ii) s considers *h*.

D.D.9   *h* is directly evident *a priori* for s =Df There is an *e* such that (a) *e* is axiomatic for s, (b) the proposition, if *e* occurs then *h* occurs, is axiomatic for s and (c) s considers *h*.

D.D.10   *e* is a *basic proposition* for s =Df *e* is strictly equivalent to a conjunction of propositions, each of which is either self-presenting or axiomatic for s.

The locution '*p* is strictly equivalent to *q*' may be taken to abbreviate '*p* entails *q* and *q* entails *p*', where *entailment* is taken in the way defined in D.IV.2.

D.D.11   *e* is a basis of *h* for s =Df *e* is self-presenting for s; and necessarily, if *e* is certain for s, then *h* is evident for s.

D.D.12   *e* makes *h* evident for s =Df *e* is evident for s; and for every *b*, if *b* is a basis of *e* for s, then *b* is a basis of *h* for s.

D.D.13   *h* is nondefectively evident for s =Df *h* is evident for s and is entailed by a conjunction of propositions each having for s a basis which is not a basis of any false proposition for s.

D.D.14   *h* is known by s = Df *h* is accepted by s; *h* is true; and *h* is nondefectively evident for s.

In D.D.14, the letter '*h*' serves as a variable; but in the following definition, D.D.15, the letter '*p*' is schematic and may be replaced by any well-formed English sentence.

D.D.15   s knows that *p* = Df The proposition that *p* is known by s.

D.D.16   *x* is known by s to be F = Df There is a proposition which s knows to be true and which implies *x* to be F.

The expression '*p* implies *x* to have the property F' is defined in D.I.6.

NOTES

NOTES TO INTRODUCTION

1 G. E. Moore, 'A Defence of Common Sense', in *Philosophical Papers* (London: George Allen & Unwin, 1959), pp. 32–59.
2 Compare Stuart Hampshire, *Thought and Action* (London: Chatto & Windus, 1959), pp. 80–2.
3 These terms and their interrelations are discussed in more detail in Appendix D.
4 P. T. Geach, *Mental Acts* (London: Routledge & Kegan Paul, 1958), p. 119.
5 Many philosophers speak as though the contrary were true. Thus Russell wrote: 'The subject, however, appears to be a logical fiction, like mathematical points and instants. It is introduced, not because observation requires it, but because it is linguistically convenient and apparently demanded by grammar. Nominal entities of this sort may or may not exist, but there is no good ground for assuming that they do. The functions that they appear to perform can always be performed by classes or series or other logical constructions, consisting of less dubious entities. If we are to avoid a perfectly gratuitous assumption, we must dispense with the subject as one of the actual ingredients of the world.' *My Philosophical Development* (London: George Allen & Unwin, 1959), pp. 135–6. Unfortunately Russell did not devote to the defence of this thesis about the subject the honest toil that he had devoted to the corresponding thesis about such entities as numbers. The question whether the subject is 'required by observation' will be discussed in the following chapter.
6 For the reader's convenience, they will be numbered in the order of their appearance. Thus the first definition of Chapter II will be numbered 'D.II.1' and the first definition of Appendix B will be numbered 'D.B.1'. All the definitions are listed in the final Appendix.
7 The logic of these concepts will be discussed in Appendix C ('The Objects of Belief and Endeavour').
8 The logic of this locution is discussed in detail in Appendix D ('Knowledge, Evidence and Reasonable Belief').
9 In Appendix B ('Mereological Essentialism'), I will set forth axioms which, I believe, will serve to distinguish this concept from other related concepts.

NOTES TO CHAPTER I

1 G. W. Leibniz, *Discourse on Metaphysics: Correspondence with Arnauld and Monadology* (La Salle, Ill.: The Open Court Publishing Co., 1937), p. 116.
2 Jean-Paul Sartre, *L'Être et le néant* (Paris: Librairie Gallimard, 1943), pp. 134, 145, 652–3.

3 Bertrand Russell, *Logic and Knowledge* (London: George Allen & Unwin, 1956), p. 305. In his early epistemological writings, Russell was inclined to say that we are directly acquainted with ourselves; see the chapter 'Knowledge by Acquaintance and Knowledge by Description' in *The Problems of Philosophy* (London: Oxford University Press, 1950), first published in 1912.

4 R. Carnap, *Der logische Aufbau der Welt* (Berlin: Weltkreis-Varlag, 1928), pp. 87–90.

5 A. Meinong, *On Emotional Presentation* (Evanston: Northwestern University Press, 1972), edited and translated by Marie-Luise Schubert Kalsi, Chapter I. The German edition, first published in 1917, may be found in A. Meinong, *Gesamtausgabe*, Band III, *Abhandlungen zur Werttheorie* (Graz: Akademische Druck- u. Verlagsanstalt, 1968), edited by Rudolf Haller and Rudolf Kindinger.

6 See Franz Brentano, *The True and the Evident* (London: Routledge & Kegan Paul, 1966), p. 132; *Psychologie vom empirischen Standpunkt*, Vol. III (Hamburg: Felix Meiner, 1968), pp. 5–6.

7 One may wonder whether 'occurs' in this definition should be replaced by 'is true'. This point is discussed in Chapter IV. For the present we will use 'proposition' and 'state of affairs' more or less interchangeably, but in Chapter IV we will suggest that propositions constitute a sub-species of states of affairs.

8 Compare Alvin Plantinga, *The Nature of Necessity* (Oxford: The Clarendon Press, 1974). In Appendix B ('Mereological Essentialism'), I defend the view that every compound object is necessarily such that it has the parts that it has.

9 Note we should distinguish between saying a property P *includes* a property Q ('Necessarily whatever has P has Q') and saying a property P *involves* a property Q ('Necessarily if something has P then something has Q'). The property of being a wife includes the property of being female and involves but does not include the property of being a husband.

10 An alternative to 'more reasonable than' is 'epistemically preferable to'.

11 The relation between 'accepts' and 'believes that' will be discussed in detail in Appendix C ('The Objects of Belief and Endeavour').

12 Leibniz and Arnauld took 'individual concept' in this more narrow sense, to mean the same as 'individual essence' or 'haecceity'; see their correspondence in G. W. Leibniz, *Discourse on Metaphysics: Correspondence with Arnauld and Monadology:* (La Salle, Ill.: The Open Court Publishing Co., 1937), esp. pp. 93–9, 126–7. Compare the remarks below about Scotus's use of 'Haecceitas' and St Thomas's use of 'individual intention'. In more recent times, Carnap has used 'individual concept' in approximately the way I have defined it here; see R. Carnap, *Meaning and Necessity* (Chicago: The University of Chicago Press, 1947), pp. 40–1.

13 If we say that non-individuals, e.g. numbers, have individual essences, we may wish to leave open the possibility that they have more than one individual essence.

14 In other words, 'being identical with me', when I use it, has as its intention my haecceity; when another English-speaking person uses it, it has as its intention that person's haecceity. There is no contradiction or absurdity in affirming this and also affirming that 'being identical with *him*' does not intend anyone's haecceity. This latter view will, in fact, be suggested below.

15 Philosophers have sometimes spoken of 'constituents' of propositions and states of affairs. Our definition D.I.6 could be said to define one sense of 'constituent': a constituent of a state of affairs is a thing such that the state of affairs implies it to have some property. Note that all men being mortal does not have any men as its constituents (for it doesn't imply with respect to any particular man, in the way spelled out in D.I.6, that that man is mortal; but it could be said to have as constituents the properties of *being a man* and *being a mortal*, for it does imply, with respect to them, that they have certain properties. Compare Russell's observation about the proposition that Socrates was before Aristotle: 'Here it seems obvious . . . that the constituents of the proposition (as well as the corresponding fact) are simply the two terms and the relation, *i.e.* Socrates, Aristotle, and *before*.' *Introduction to Mathematical Philosophy* (London: George Allen & Unwin, 1920), p. 198. Compare also what Bolzano says about the *objects* of propositions, in Section 126 of *Theory of Science*, edited and translated by Rolf George (Oxford: Basil Blackwell, 1972).

16 The relation between knowledge and certainty is discussed in detail in Appendix D.

17 Moreover, if a man feels depressed, then not only does he have the *de dicto* knowledge that he might put by saying 'I feel depressed'; he also has the *de re* knowledge that we might put by saying 'He is known by himself to feel depressed'. See Appendix C and Appendix D.

18 My thought on this question has been influenced by correspondence with Arnold Levison and by David Wiggins. 'The Individuation of Things and Places', in M. J. Loux, ed., *Universals and Particulars: Readings in Ontology* (Garden City, N.Y.: Doubleday, 1970), pp. 307–35.

19 Putting the matter in terms of language, we could say, with Sydney Shoemaker: 'In no sense do I use the word "I" as an abbreviation for any physical description of myself. If it should turn out that I am having an hallucination, and that the description "the tall man sitting at the typewriter" does not apply to me, I would have to withdraw or amend the statement "The tall man sitting at the typewriter has a toothache," but would not have to withdraw or amend my statement "I have a toothache." ' Sydney Shoemaker, *Self-Knowledge and Self-Identity* (Ithaca, N.Y.: Cornell University Press, 1963), p. 16. It may be noted that, since there is more than one typewriter, the descriptive phrase 'the typewriter' in the above passage must be taken as short for a longer expression. It is instructive to ask: What might the longer expression be?

20 Compare Frege: 'Now everyone is presented to himself in a particular and primitive way, in which he is present to no-one else. So, when Dr Lauben thinks that he has been wounded . . . and says "I have been wounded," he must use the "I" in a sense which can be grasped by others, perhaps in the sense of "he who is speaking to you at this moment" . . .' Gottlob Frege, 'The Thought: A Logical Inquiry', *Mind*, LXV (1956), 289–311; the quotation is on page 398. Compare also Husserl: 'The word "I" names a different person from case to case, and does so by way of an ever altering meaning. What its meaning is at the moment, can be gleaned only from the living utterance and from the intuitive circumstances which surround it. If we read the word without knowing who wrote it, it is perhaps not meaningless, but is at least estranged from its normal sense . . . In solitary speech the meaning of "I" is essentially realized in the immediate idea of one's own personality . . . Each man has his own I-presentation [*Ichvorstellung*] (and with it his

individual notion of I [*seinen Individualbegriff von ich*], and that is why the word's meaning differs from person to person.' E. Husserl, *Logical Investigations* (London: Routledge & Kegan Paul, 1970), pp. 315–16 (Investigation I, Section 26).

21 Compare H. D. Lewis: 'When I lose my memory I am no longer aware of who I am – in one sense, namely that I do not remember my name, where I live, what I have been doing in the past and so on. I cannot place myself in the sense in which the outside observer would place me on the basis of what is known about me. But I do all the same recognize myself as the unique person I am. It is particulars of my past history and situation that I cannot recover. In a more basic sense I have no doubt who I am – I am myself, the being I expressly recognize myself to be in a way which is not possible for knowledge of any other.' *The Elusive Mind* (London: Allen & Unwin, 1969), p. 235.

22 St Augustine, *Contra Academicos*, Book III, Section 26; English edition published as *St Augustine Against the Academicians*, ed. Sister Mary P. Garvey (Milwaukee: Marquette University Press, 1942), p. 69. The italics are mine.

23 'For it is plain that the singular is sensed *properly* and *per se*, but nevertheless sense is in a certain way even of the universal. For he knows Callias not only as he is Callias, but also as he is this man, and Socrates as he is this man.' St Thomas Aquinas, *Exposition of the Posterior Analytics of Aristotle*, translated by Pierre Conway, O. P. (Quebec: M. Doyon, 1956), Part II, Lecture 20, Paragraph 14, p. 431. Compare *Summa Theologica*, Part I, Q. 84, Article 7, Duns Scotus writes: 'The singular adds an entity over and above the entity of the universal. Consequently the apprehension of the universal is not the complete ground of an apprehension of the singular.' Quoted in D. J. B. Hawkins, *A Sketch of Medieval Philosophy* (New York: Sheed & Ward, 1947), p. 124. He also observes: 'The thisness of this is by its very notion different from the thisness of that.' *Op. cit.*, p. 125. St Thomas speaks of 'individual intentions' in *Summa Contra Gentiles*, Book II, Chapter 60, Paragraph 1. For a contemporary defence of the doctrine, see Plantinga's *The Nature of Necessity*, Chapter V.

24 The first of these observations is due to Gary Rosenkrantz. The second will be defended in Chapter III.

25 In this case, the sentence 'The thing I'm now looking at has to be the thing I'm now looking at and couldn't be anything else', might be re-expressed as 'There is just one *x* such that I am now looking at *x*, *x* is necessarily identical with *x*, and for every *y*, if *y* is other than *x*, then *y* is necessarily other than *x*', *provided* that the new sentence is *not* taken to imply 'The thing that I am now looking at is necessarily such that I am now looking at it'. Compare A. F. Smullyan, 'Modality and Description', *Journal of Symbolic Logic*, III (1948), 31–7.

26 Vere Chappell, 'Ego and Person: Phenomenology of Analysis', *The Monist*, XLIX (1965), 18–27; the quotation is on page 26. Compare P. F. Strawson, *Individuals: An Essay in Descriptive Metaphysics* (London: Methuen, 1959), p. 104; the doctrine is qualified on page 99n.

27 C. J. Ducasse, *Nature, Mind, and Death*, The Paul Carus Lectures, Eighth Series (La Salle, Ill.: The Open Court Publishing Co., 1951), p. 425. Compare Sydney Shoemaker, *Self-Knowledge and Self-Identity*, p. 35.

28 *Summa Theologica*, Part I, Question 11, Article 2, ad 4. Compare the *Commentary on the Metaphysics of Aristotle*, 1996–1998.

29 Can I individuate me by saying something and adding 'I am the utterer of this sentence-token'? Only if I can know that I am the only one who is uttering the sentence-token. These considerations suggest that Russell was mistaken in saying that 'I' might be defined in terms of 'this'; compare *Human Knowledge: Its Scope and Limits* (New York: Simon and Schuster, 1948), p. 85. What Russell had written much earlier, contrasting our knowledge of Bismarck with Bismarck's own knowledge of himself, seems to me to be much more nearly correct; he suggests that our descriptions of Bismarck, unlike Bismarck's own, are 'accidental' and that we cannot grasp the propositions Bismarck would express in the first person. Compare *Mysticism and Logic* (New York: W. W. Norton, 1929), pp. 216–18. Compare the quotations from Frege and Husserl, in footnote 20 on p. 199 above, and the following from Stuart Hampshire: '. . . the pronoun "I", and the first person singular form in general, is more than just one more demonstrative device in language, parallel and on the same level with "this" and "that", and with the other personal pronouns. The first person singular is the nucleus on which all the other referential devices depend . . . The final point of reference, by which a statement is attached to reality, is the speaker's reference to himself, as one thing, and one person, among others.' *Thought and Action* (London: Chatto & Windus, 1959), p. 87.

30 Compare Hector-Neri Castañeda, ' "He": A Study in the Logic of Self-Consciousness', *Ratio*, VII (1966), 130–57, and 'On the Phenomeno-Logic of the I', *Atken des XIV Internationalen Kongresses fur Philosophie*, Vol. III (University of Vienna, 1969), 260–6.

31 Husserl wrote of Hume: 'Dessen genialer *Treatise* hat bereits die Gestalt einer auf strenge Konsequenz bedachten struckturellen Durchforschung der reinen Erlebnissphare, [ist] in gewisser Weise also der erste Anheib einer "Phänomenologie".' E. Husserl, *Phänomenologische Psychologie* (The Hague; Martinus Nijhoff, 1962), p. 264. The members of the Vienna Circle traced the 'scientific world-outlook' to the same source; see *Wissenschaftliche Weltauffassung* (Vienna: Artur Wolf Verlag, 1929), p. 12.

32 Thomas Reid makes this autobiographical remark about his own investigations of Hume's philosophy: 'For my own satisfaction, I entered into a serious examination of the principles upon which this sceptical system is built; and was not a little surprised to find that it leans with its whole weight upon a hypothesis, which is ancient indeed, and hath been very generally received by philosophers, but of which I could find no solid proof.' See the preface to *An Inquiry into the Human Mind on the Principles of Common Sense* (1764).

33 The passage may be found on page 194 of Charles W. Hendel's edition of Hume's *An Enquiry concerning Human Understanding* (New York: The Liberal Arts Press, 1955). Compare Bishop Berkeley: 'And as several of these [ideas] are observed to accompany each other, they came to be marked by one name, and so to be reputed as one thing. Thus, for example, a certain colour, taste, smell, figure and consistence having been observed to go together, are accounted one distinct thing, signified by the name *apple*; other collections of ideas constitute a stone, a tree, a book . . .' *The Principles of Human Knowledge*, Part I, Paragraph 1 (Open Court edition, pp. 29–30).

34 *New Essays Concerning Human Understanding*, Book II, Chapter xxiii, Section 1: ' . . . it is rather the *concretum*, as wise, warm, shining, which arises in our mind, than the *abstractions* or qualities (for these

and not the ideas are in the substantial object), as knowledge, heat, light, etc., which are much more difficult to comprehend.'

35 *A Treatise of Human Nature*, Book I, Part IV, Section vi ('Of Personal Identity').

36 H. H. Price, *Hume's Theory of the External World* (Oxford: The Clarendon Press, 1940), pp. 5–6. Compare P. F. Strawson, *Individuals* (London: Methuen, 1959), pp. 96–7, and Sydney Shoemaker, *Self-Knowledge and Self-Identity*, Chapters 2 and 3.

37 *Critique of Pure Reason*, ed. Norman Kemp Smith (London: Macmillan, 1933), p. 334.

38 *Op. cit.*, pp. 331, 337. It should be noted that Kant does not himself use a term corresponding to 'direct acquaintance'. The final phrase, beginning with 'without', is intended to translate: 'ohne die mindest Eigenschaft desselben zu bemerken, oder uberhaupt etwas von ihm zu kennen oder zu wissen'. The passage appears on page 350 of the first edition of the *Critique*.

39 That Kant may have had the third interpretation in mind is suggested by such passages as the following: 'People have long since observed, that in all substances the proper subject, that which remains after all the accidents (as predicates) are abstracted, remains unknown.' *Prolegomena to any Future Metaphysics*, Section 46 (Open Court edition, p. 99). A somewhat more charitable account of what Kant may have had in mind is to be found in Wilfrid Sellars, ' . . . this I or he or it (the thing) which thinks', *Proceedings and Addresses of the American Philosophical Association*, XLIV (1970–1), 5–31; the article is reprinted in Sellars's *Essays in Philosophy and Its History* (Dordrecht: D. Reidel, 1974). Whatever Kant may have held in fact, the views I have attributed to him call for criticism.

40 Compare A. E. Taylor: 'What we call one *thing* is said, in spite of its unity, to have many *qualities*. It is, *e.g.* at once round, white, shiny, and hard, or at once green, soft, and rough. Now, what do we understand by the *it* to which these numerous attributes are alike ascribed, and how does it possess them? To use the traditional technical names, what is the substance to which the several qualities belong or in which they inhere, and what is the manner of their *inherence*? . . . The notion that things have a *that* or substance prior to their *what* or quality . . . is thus unmeaning as well as superfluous.' *Elements of Metaphysics*, Fifth Edition (London: Methuen, 1920), pp. 128, 133.

41 'Ainsi le Pour-soi en tant qu'il n'est pas *soi* est une présence à soi qui manque d'une certaine présence à soi et c'est en tant que manque de cette présence qu'il est présence à soi.' *L'Être et le néant* (Paris: Librarie Gallimard, 1948), p. 145.

42 *An Inquiry into Meaning and Truth* (London: Allen & Unwin, 1948), p. 97.

43 Compare Edwin B. Allaire, 'Bare Particulars', in *Philosophical Studies*, XVI (1963); and Michael J. Loux, 'Kinds and the Dilemma of Individulation', *Review of Metaphysics*, XXVII (1974), pp. 773–84.

44 'A *substance* – that which is called a substance most strictly, primarily, and most of all – is that which is neither said of a subject nor in a subject; for example, the individual man or the individual horse.' Aristotle, *Categories,* Chapter 5; 2a 11. Compare St Thomas Aquinas, *Summa Theologica*, Part III, Question 77, Article 2.

45 We have considered just that side of Kant's scepticism which is derived from his theory of conception. But he also appeals to a somewhat

different consideration: ' . . . what use am I to make of this concept of substance? That I, as a thinking being, *persist* for myself, and do not in any natural manner either *arise* or *perish* can by no means be deduced from it. Yet there is no other use to which I can put the concept of the substantiality of the thinking subject, and apart from this I could very well dispense with it.' *Critique of Pure Reason* (p. 349 of the first German edition; Kemp-Smith edition, pp. 333–4). These points will be considered in Chapter III.

46 Compare the use of 'Inner perception' in the writings of Franz Brentano; e.g. in *Psychology from an Empirical Standpoint* (London: Routledge & Kegan Paul, 1973), *passim*.

47 When Russell wrote about what he called 'knowledge by acquaintance', he vacillated with respect to the question whether we are directly acquainted with ourselves. I suspect that what inclined him to say that we are not acquainted with ourselves was the fact that such acquaintance differs in the way just described from external perception.

48 Jean-Paul Sartre, *The Transcendence of the Ego*, trans. Forrest Williams and Robert Kirkpatrick (New York: Farrar, Strauss & Cudahy, 1957), p. 51.

49 I am indebted to Keith Lehrer for this point. I am also indebted to him and to Charles Caton for criticisms enabling me to correct an earlier version of this chapter.

50 See H. A. Prichard, *Knowledge and Perception* (Oxford: The Clarendon Press, 1950), p. 213. Compare his much earlier *Kant's Theory of Knowledge* (Oxford: The Clarendon Press, 1909) and his 'Appearances and Reality', first published in *Mind* in 1906 and republished in Roderick M. Chisholm, ed., *Realism and the Background of Phenomenology* (Glencoe, Ill.: The Free Press, 1960), pp. 143–50.

51 A. O. Lovejoy, *The Revolt against Dualism* (La Salle, Ill.: The Open Court Publishing Co., 1930), p. 305.

52 'The general rule which one may derive from these examples is that the propositions we ordinarily express by saying that a person A is perceiving a material thing M, which appears to him to have the quality x, may be expressed in the sense-datum terminology by saying that A is sensing a sense-datum s, which really has the quality x, and which belongs to M.' A. J. Ayer, *The Foundations of Empirical Knowledge* (New York: Macmillan, 1940), p. 58.

53 Compare Thomas Reid: 'When I am pained, I cannot say that the pain I feel is one thing, and that my feeling of it is another thing. They are one and the same thing and cannot be disjoined even in the imagination.' *Essays on the Intellectual Powers*, Essay I, Chapter 1.

54 Compare John L. Pollock, *Knowledge and Justification* (Princeton: Princeton University Press, 1974), pp. 71–5.

55 And so are 'thoughts'. Consider a man who is thinking about a unicorn. Though we say, quite naturally, that the unicorn is the object of the man's thought, it would be less misleading to say that the unicorn is the object of the man to the extent that he is thinking. For thinking, like feeling and like what we may call 'sensing', is an affection, modification, or state of the man. Compare Leibniz's assertion that ideas are 'affections or modifications of the mind', in his 'Thoughts on Knowledge, Truth, and Ideas' in Erdmann's edition of Leibniz's *Opera Philisophica*, p. 81. Sartre, too, has said that the appearance is 'the manner in which the subject is affected [la manière dont le sujet est affecté]', but he adds,

unfortunately, that 'consciousness has nothing of the substantial [la conscience n'a rien de substantiel]'; *L'Être et le néant*, pp. 13, 23.

56 *Treatise of Human Nature*, Book I, Part IV, Section 5; my italics.

57 I have tried to say what these conditions are in *Theory of Knowledge* (Englewood Cliffs, N.J.: Prentice-Hall, 1966), Chapter 3, and in *Perceiving: A Philosophical Study* (Ithaca: Cornell University Press, 1957). A general summary of this view of perception may be found in Keith Lehrer, 'Scottish Influences on Contemporary American Philosophy', *The Philosophical Journal*, v (1968), pp. 34–42. Compare also James W. Cornman, 'Chisholm on Sensing and Perceiving', in Keith Lehrer, ed., *Analysis and Metaphysics* (Dordrecht: D. Reidel, 1975), pp. 11–33.

58 Compare Brentano's remark about the concept of substance: 'Those who say that this concept is not included in any perception are very much mistaken. Rather it is given in every perception, as Aristotle had said . . .' Franz Brentano, *Versuch uber die Erkenntnis* (Leipzig: Felix Meiner, 1970), p. 28. Referring to the thesis according to which we know only 'phenomena' and not 'things in themselves', he wrote: 'But what does it mean to say that one apprehends something as a phenomenon? Simply that one apprehends it as a phenomenon to the one for whom it is a phenomenon. This means, in other words, that one apprehends that one is presented with or intuits the phenomenon in question and hence that one apprehends the one to whom it is presented, the one who intuits. But this a thing that one apprehends in itself.' *Die Vier Phasen der Philosophie* (Leipzig: Felix Meiner, 1926), p. 92.

NOTES TO CHAPTER II

1 *Summa Theologica*, Part I, Question 29, Article II; compare also *On the Power of God*, Question 9, Articles 1 and 2. St Thomas here defends the definition of person given by Boethius: 'A person is an individual substance of a rational nature.'

2 For a discussion of such general abilities, see Timothy Duggan and Bernard Gert, 'Voluntary Abilities', *American Philosophical Quarterly*, IV (1967), 127–35; reprinted in Myles Brand, ed., *The Nature of Human Action* (Glenview, Ill.: Scott, Foresman & Co., 1970), pp. 204–16.

3 Compare Kurt Baier, 'Could and Would', *Analysis*, XXIII (1961), supplement, 20–9.

4 Hobbes had said that we call propositions contingent 'because we do not yet know whether they be true of false'; See *De Corpore*, Chapter 10. Compare the criticism of this view, and some of the others noted here, in Richard Taylor, *Action and Purpose* (Englewood Cliffs, N.J.: Prentice-Hall, 1966), Chapter 4. My thinking in these questions was profoundly influenced by discussions some years ago with Taylor.

5 There are still other objections to the first of these two if-then formulae that do not apply to the second. Some of these were pointed out by J. L. Austin in 'Ifs and Cans'; see his *Philosophical Papers* (Oxford: The Clarendon Press, 1961), esp. p. 166. In 'J. L. Austin's Philosophical Papers', *Mind*, LXXIII, 289 (January 1964), 1–26, I noted that certain other objections are applicable to the first formula and are not applicable to the second; see esp. pp. 23–4. Further difficulties with this approach to our problem are indicated by Donald Davidson in 'Free-

dom to Act', in Ted Honderich, ed., *Essays on Freedom and Action* (London: Routledge & Kegan Paul, 1973), pp. 137–56. Compare also Keith Lehrer, 'Cans Without Ifs', *Analysis*, xxviii (1968), 29–32.

6 Presumably it was for reasons such as these that George Washington was said to be unable to tell a lie. The point was, not that he lacked the wit or skill or opportunity to do it, but that he was so good that he couldn't bring himself to deceive. Bayle quotes a seventeenth-century Walloon theologian, one de Wolzogue, who pointed out that, although God would have no difficulty in deceiving if he chose to deceive, nonetheless he *cannot* deceive since he *cannot choose* to deceive. De Wolzogue wrote: 'God can deceive if he will . . . but it is impossible for him to have such a will to deceive; it is also impossible for him to endeavor to employ his power for the execution of a deceit, whence I conclude that it is impossible for him to deceive.' See Pierre Bayle, *A General Dictionary, Historical and Critical*, article 'Rimini (Gregorio de)', note C. According to some Christians, an important point of difference between Mary and Jesus was that, while Mary could sin but never did, Jesus 'has not merely never actually sinned, but also could not sin', the point being, again, that he could not undertake (choose, will try, set out) to sin. Compare Ludwig Ott, *Fundamentals of Catholic Dogma* (Cork: Mercier Press, 1952), p. 169. Compare St Thomas's treatment of the question, 'Can God Do What Others Do?', in *On the Power of God*, Question I, Article 6.

7 G. H. von Wright, *Norm and Action: A Logical Inquiry* (London: Routledge & Kegan Paul, 1963), p. 50.

8 Compare Nicholas Rescher, *Hypothetical Reasoning* (Amsterdam: North-Holland Publishing Co., 1964); R. S. Walters, 'Contrary-to-Fact Conditional', in Paul Edwards, ed., *The Encyclopedia of Philosophy* (New York: Crowell Collier & Macmillan, 1967), Vol. II, pp. 212–16; William Kneale, 'Natural Laws and Contrary-to-Fact Conditionals', *Analysis*, x (1950), 121–5; Roderick M. Chisholm, 'Law Statements and Counterfactual Inference', *Analysis*, xv (1955), 97–105.

9 It might be supposed that causal contribution could readily be defined in terms of sufficient causal condition; e.g. that 'c contributes causally to e' might be defined as saying 'there occurs an event s such that s is a sufficient causal condition of e, and c is a part of s'. But this definition is not satisfactory, since sufficient causal conditions may have parts that are superfluous. For if s is a sufficient causal condition of e, and if c occurs before e, than $c\&s$, no matter what c may be, will also be a sufficient causal condition of e; and so c may be a part of a sufficient causal condition of e without c itself contributing causally to e. The problem thus becomes that of finding a suitable definition of 'a causally superfluous part of a sufficient causal condition of e'. The problem is discussed by J. L. Mackie, in 'Causes and Conditions', *American Philosophical Quarterly*, i (1965), 245–64. As a result of lengthy discussions and correspondence with Robert S. Keim and Ernest Sosa, I am convinced that no solution to this problem is at hand.

10 G. E. Moore, *Commonplace Book 1919–1953*, edited by C. Lewy (London: George Allen & Unwin, 1962), p. 410.

11 Presumably if determinism is true, then whatever is causally necessary at any time t is also causally necessary at any time prior to t. But what I have said presupposes that, if determinism is not true, then the occurrence of a certain event at a certain time t may be causally necessary at one time and causally non-necessary at some earlier time. One might

object to this presupposition in the following way: 'You cannot consistently say, both (i) that there occurred at 10 a.m. a sufficient causal condition c for an event e occurring at 2 p.m., and also (ii) that there did *not* occur any sufficient causal condition at 9 a.m. any sufficient causal condition for e occurring at 2 p.m. For if c was a sufficient causal condition of e that occurred at 10, then c *occurs at 10* and c *will occur in an hour* are sufficient causal conditions of e that occurred at 9 a.m.' The reply to this objection is (a) that a sufficient causal condition is an *event* or a conjunction of events, and (b) that the state of affairs c *occurs at 10* and c *will occur in an hour* are not events. This conception of events, as constituting a certain subspecies of states of affairs, will be defended in Chapter IV. It will there be shown that 'c occurs at 10' and c will occur in an hour' do not refer to *events*.

12 Aristotle, *Ethics*, Book III, Chapter 5, 1113b; St Thomas Aquinas, *Commentary on the Nichomachean Ethics*, Paragraph 497. Unfortunately St Thomas goes on to say that 'as a consequence we must conclude that wherever affirmation is within our power, negation is also' (Paragraph 498). The most he has a right to infer is, of course, that wherever affirmation is within our power, *not* affirming is also within our power. This observation is relevant to what will be said in the following section about desires that 'incline but do not necessitate'.

13 Why not put the second clause more simply and say: 'There occurs an r such that it is physically necessary, if r and s-undertaking-q occur, then p occurs'? The simpler formulation would guarantee that, if s-undertaking-q occurs, then there would occur a sufficient causal condition of p. But it would not guarantee that s-undertaking-q contributes causally to p. For the simpler formulation is consistent with supposing that s-undertaking-q is a superfluous part of the sufficient causal condition of p.

14 The conception of states of affairs that is here presupposed is discussed in detail in Chapter IV.

15 *Essay Concerning Human Understanding*, Book II, Chapter xxi.

16 See Edwards's *Freedom of the Will* (1754), *passim*.

17 The classic statement of this distinction is in the *Summa Theologica*, First Part of the Second Part, Question I, Article 1 ('Whether it Belongs to Man to Act for an End').

18 In the Preface to the *Metaphysical Elements of Ethics*, in T. K. Abbott, ed., *Kant's Critique of Practical Reason and Other Works on the Theory of Ethics* (London: Longman, Green, 1959), p. 303.

19 Must we say, then, that in addition to states of affairs, there are such things as the *occurrences* of states of affairs? This question is discussed in the final section of Chapter IV.

20 Compare Alvin I. Goldman, *A Theory of Human Action* (Englewood Cliffs, N.J.: Prentice-Hall, 1970): 'When s's act A causes event E, we say s exemplified the property of causing E. In other words, we say that the even E was caused, or brought about, by the *agent* s.' (p. 25).

21 I would assume, however, that what is intended by most such action expressions could be paraphrased (doubtless sometimes cumbersomely) into our 'undertaking' and 'making happen' vocabulary without using terms that themselves designate actions. But an adequate explication of *some* action expressions ('His signalling for a turn', 'His checkmating his opponent') would also involve reference to what is *required* by certain laws, customs, rules or conventions. This point is stressed by H. L. A. Hart in 'Ascription of Responsibility and Rights', *Proceedings*

of the Aristotelian Society, XLIX (1949), 171–94, and by A. I. Melden in Free Action (London: Routledge & Kegan Paul, 1961). I would disagree, however, with the suggestion that such reference to laws, rules, customs or conventions constitutes the *mark* of action.

22 F. Suarez, *Disputationes Metaphysicae*, Disputation XVIII, Section 10, Paragraph 6. Compare Robert Binkley, 'A Theory of Practical Reason', *Philosophical Review*, LXXIV (1965), 423–48. Binkley there takes as axiomatic the principle that, if a man brings about p, then he brings it about that he brings about p.

23 Thomas Hobbes, in *The Questions Concerning Liberty, Necessity, and Chance*; the quotation may be found on page 42 of the excerpt reprinted in Sidney Morgenbesser and James Walsh, *Free Will* (Englewood Cliffs, N.J.: Prentice-Hall, 1962).

24 All but the first of these examples are taken from Alvin I. Goldman, *A Theory of Human Action* (Englewood Cliffs, N.J.: Prentice-Hall, 1970), pp. 23–7. They all illustrate what he calls 'act generation', one act, so to speak, arising out of another. The first example is from G. E. M. Anscombe, *Intention* (Oxford: Basil Blackwell, 1968), pp. 40ff.

25 Compare Oskar Kraus, 'Das Dogma von der Ursachlichkeit der Unterlassung', *Juristiche Vierteljahrsschrift*, Bd. 30 (Bd. 14, N. F.) (1898), 1–82; and Stephan Körner, *Experience and Theory* (London: Routledge & Kegan Paul, 1966), p. 215.

26 And so, if we say that, when a person undertakes to bring about a certain state of affairs, he thereby *wants* to bring about that state of affairs, we should recognise that this use of 'want' involves no reference to discomfort, urges, or felt desires and we should not suppose that the statement 'He undertakes only what he wants' says anything of significance. G. E. M. Anscombe takes 'want' in this way and notes: 'The wanting that interests us, however, is neither wishing nor hoping nor the feeling of desire, and cannot be said to exist in a man who does nothing toward getting what he wants. The primitive sign of wanting is *trying to get . . .*' *Op. cit.*, pp. 67–8. Compare A. I. Melden: 'the connection between wanting and doing is logical'; *op. cit.*, p. 166.

27 It should be noted that this principle does not imply the following principle, which is more general: 'If a man acts with the intention of bringing about a certain state of affairs p and if he believes that another state of affairs q obtains, then he acts with the intention of bringing about that conjunctive state of affairs which is p and q.'

28 This situation may recall the scholastic distinction between the *finis operantis*, the aim of the operator or agent, and the *finis operationis*, the aim of his operation or activity. Compare the discussion of means-end reasoning in Robert W. Binkley, 'A Theory of Practical Reason', *Philosophical Review*, LXXIV (1965), 423–48: '. . . means-end reasoning requires not merely a judgment about the inter-connections of things, but also a kind of self-conscious judgment of one's own effectiveness as an agent causing things to happen'. (p. 443).

29 Annette Baier, 'Act and Intent', *Journal of Philosophy*, LXVII (1970), 648–58; the quotation is from pp. 648–9.

30 In the formulation of the definition criticised by Professor Baier, it was said that if a person undertakes p for the purpose of bringing about q, then he intends to bring it about that 'by bringing about p he will bring about q'. The point is that the agent need not intend that p contribute causally to q.

31 Compare the remarks above in connection with D.II.11 (the definition of 'By contributing causally to p at t, s contributes to q at t').

32 Thus we could define 's contributes causally to p for the purpose of bringing about q' by saying: 'There is an r such that: (1) s undertakes r for the purpose of bringing about that state of affairs which is (i) r and (ii) his-undertaking-r contributing causally to q; and (2) his under-taking-r contributes causally to p.' If the assassin of our earlier example succeeded in blowing up the palace, we may say that he did so for the purpose of bringing about the death of the king. Or if he didn't succeed in either of these ends, but blew himself up instead, we may say he contributed causally to his own death and did so for the purpose of blowing up the palace and also for the purpose of bringing about the death of the king. The state of affairs referred to by the 'p' in just the expression defined, unlike that referred to by the 'p' in D.II.13, need not be one that the agent undertakes.

33 An objection of this sort is suggested (but not formulated as above) by Terence Penelhum, in 'Doing, Desiring, and Making Happen', *Journal of Philosophy*, LXI (1964), 625–7; by Irving Thalberg in 'Do We Cause Our Own Actions?', *Analysis*, XXVII (1967), 196–201; and by Annette Baier, *op. cit.*

34 *Ethics*, Book X, Chapter 6, 1176b.

35 Compare St Thomas, *Commentary of Aristotle's Ethics*, Paragraph 109: 'We find also an object is indeed desirable on account of what it is, but besides, it is desired for something else, like sweet-tasting medicine.'

36 The expression 'p is for s a means to q', as it appears in this definition, may be thought of as abbreviating 's undertakes p for the purpose of bringing about q'.

37 But compare: 'I say unto you, That whosoever looketh on a woman to lust after her hath committed adultery with her already in his heart.' (Matthew 5: 28)

38 The term 'attempt', as it is restricted in law, would seem to differ from that defined here in that it implies failure along with a significant degree of success: the agent fails to achieve the end he attempts but he is sufficiently successful with respect to *means* to come dangerously close. See Jerome Michael and Herbert Wechsler, *Criminal Law and Its Administration* (Chicago: The Foundation Press, 1940), p. 587. Contrast these two men: one makes an attempt at killing the king by shooting him through the heart and is completely successful; another attempts precisely the same thing but mistakes a toy for a pistol and a post for the king. It is easy to understand why the state would not charge either with 'making an attempt': the first man is subject to a more serious charge, and the second man is not dangerous enough to trouble with. But so far as intentionality is concerned, their states of mind could have been the same.

39 Taking precautions involves the undertaking of conditionals.

40 The term 'basic act' and the expression 'repertoire of basic acts' are due to Arthur Danto; see his 'What We Can Do', *Journal of Philosophy*, LX (1963), 435–45, reprinted in Alan R. White, *The Philosophy of Action* (London: Oxford University Press, 1968). Compare St Augustine, *The City of God*, Book XIV, Chapter 24: 'We know, too, that some men are differently constituted from others and have some rare and remarkable faculty of doing with their body what other men can by no effort do, and, indeed, scarcely believe when they hear of others doing.

There are persons who can move their ears, either one at a time, or both together. There are some who, without moving the head, can bring the hair down upon the forehead, and move the whole scalp backwards and forwards at pleasure. Some, by lightly pressing their stomach, bring up an incredible quantity and variety of things they have swallowed, and produce whatever they please, quite whole, as if out of a bag. Some so accurately mimic the voices of birds and beasts and other men, that unless they are seen, the difference cannot be told. Some have such command of their bowels, that they can break wind continuously at pleasure, so as to produce the effect of singing. I myself have known a man who was accustomed to sweat whenever he wished. It is well known that some weep when they please, and shed a flood of tears . . .' (Translated by M. Dods)

41 Compare Arthur Danto, *op. cit.*

42 Compare Joseph Rickaby, *Free Will and Four English Philosophers* (London: Burns & Oates, 1906), p. 177. St Thomas is speaking of *immanent action* in the following passage: 'For action and production differ, because action is an operation that remains in the agent itself, as choosing, understanding and the like (and for this reason the practical sciences are called moral sciences), whereas production is an operation that passes over into some matter in order to change it, as cutting, burning and the like (and for this reason the productive sciences are called mechanical arts).' *Commentary on the Metaphysics of Aristotle* (Chicago: Henry Regnery, 1961), Paragraph 1152.

43 I suggest that such an identification would be correct only if we ourselves are identical with our brain or with some proper part of our brain. The following two chapters are concerned with questions bearing upon such identification.

44 There are more complex ways of dealing with this situation. See the discussion in Chapter IV of the 'event exemplification' theory and the 'under a description' terminology.

45 The quotation at the beginning is from Danto, 'Basic Actions'. *American Philosophical Quarterly*, 2 (1965), 141–2. Concerning this type of puzzle, compare G. N. A. Vesey, 'Do I Ever Directly Raise My Arm?' *Philosophy*, 42 (1967), 148–9.

NOTES TO CHAPTER III

1 *On the Intellectual Powers of Man*, Essay III, Chapter 14 in Sir William Hamilton, ed., *The Works of Thomas Reid, D.D.* (Edinburgh: Maclachlan & Stewart, 1854), p. 345.

2 Fragment 41–2, as translated in Milton C. Nahm, *Selections from Early Greek Philosophy* (New York: F. S. Crofts, 1934), p. 91.

3 See Plato, *Phaedo*, 58A and Xenophon, *Memorabilia*, 4, 8, 2. Leibniz speaks of the Ship of Theseus in the *New Essays Concerning Human Understanding*, Book II, Chapter 27, Section 4, noting that any ordinary physical body may be said to be 'like a river which always changes its water, or like the ship of Theseus which the Athenians were always repairing' (Open Court edition), p. 240.

4 Thomas Hobbes, *Concerning Body*, Chapter XI ('Of Identity and Difference'), Section 7.

5 Cf. W. V. Quine: 'Thus take the question of the biggest fresh lake. Is Michigan-Huron admissible, or is it a pair of lakes? . . . Then take the question of the longest river. Is the Mississippi-Missouri admissible, or is it a river and a half?' *Word and Object* (New York: John Wiley, 1960), p. 128.

6 Using terms not commonly applied to rivers, we may note for future reference that when our diagram is read from top to bottom it illustrates *fusion* and when it is read from bottom to top it illustrates *fission*.

7 See Note c of the article 'Carneades' in Pierre Bayle's *A General Dictionary: Historical and Critical*, trans. Rev. J. P. Bernard, Rev. Thomas Birch, John Lockeman *et al.* (10 vols; London: James Bettenham, 1734–41): 'He found uncertainty in the most evident notions. All logicians know that the foundation of the syllogism, and consequently the faculty of reasoning, is built on this maxim: Those things which are identical with a third are the same with each other (*Quae sunt idem uno tertio sunt idem inter se*). It is certain that Carneades opposed it strongly and displayed all his subtleties against it.'

8 Further aspects of this kind of problem are discussed in Appendix A ('The Doctrine of Temporal Parts').

9 Dissertation I, in *The Whole Works of Joseph Butler, LL.D.* (London: Thomas Tegg, 1839), pp. 263–70. But compare Locke's third letter to the Bishop of Worcester: 'For it being his body both before and after the resurrection, everyone ordinarily speaks of his body as the same, though, in a strict and philosophical sense, as your lordship speaks, it be not the very same.'

10 I have heard it suggested, however, that (a) whereas the evening star is strictly identical with the evening star, nevertheless (b) the evening star is identical but not strictly identical with the morning star. The facts of the matter would seem to be only these: the evening star (i.e. the morning star) is necessarily self-identical; it is not necessarily such that it is visible in the evening or in the morning; it would be contradictory to say that the evening star exists and is not identical with the evening star, or that the morning star exists and is not identical with the morning star; but it would not be contradictory to say that the morning star exists and the evening star exists and the morning star is not identical with the evening star; and whatever is identical with the evening star (i.e. with the morning star) has all the properties that it does

11 This example of the roads, like that of the rivers above ('the Mississippi-Missouri'), may suggest that the key to our puzzles about identity through time may be found in the doctrine of 'temporal parts'. According to this doctrine, every individual thing x is such that, for every period of time through which x exists, there is a set of parts which are such that x is made up of them at that time and they do not exist at any other time. (Compare: every individual thing x is such that, for every portion of space that x occupies at any time, there is at that time a set of parts of x which then occupy that place and no other place.) I consider this doctrine in detail in Appendix A. I there conclude that it will not help us with our problems about identity through time and that there is no sufficient reason for accepting it.

12 Contrast P. T. Geach, *Reference and Generality* (Ithaca: The Cornell University Press, 1962), p. 157: ' . . . different official personages may be one and the same man'. Possibly an illustration would be: 'The

fire-chief isn't the same personage as the Sunday-school superintendent (for one is charged with putting out fires and the other with religious instruction); yet Jones is both.' But here one seems to be playing loose with 'isn't', for what one has in mind, presumably, is something of this sort: 'Being the fire-chief commits one to different things than does being the Sunday-school superintendent, and Jones is both.'

13 There may be temptations in thus playing loose with 'is'. Suppose there were a monarchy wherein the subjects found it distasteful ever to affirm that the monarch vacated his throne. Instead of saying that there have been so many dozen kings and queens in the history of their country, they will say that the monarch has now existed for many hundreds of years and has had so many dozen different names. At certain times it has been appropriate that these names be masculine, like 'George' and 'Henry', and at other times it has been appropriate that they be feminine, like 'Victoria' and 'Elizabeth'. What, then, if we knew about these people and were to hear such talk as this: 'There has existed for many hundreds of years an x such that x is our monarch; x is now feminine, though fifty years ago x was masculine, and fifty years before that x was feminine'? We should not conclude that there was in that land a monarch who is vastly different from any of the people in ours. We should conclude rather that the speakers were either deluded or pretending.

14 Other examples are suggested by: 'He has a copy of *The Republic* on his desk and another on the table and he doesn't have any other books. How many books does he have?' 'He played the *Appassionata* once in the afternoon and once again in the evening, but nothing further. How many sonatas did he play?'

15 Compare P. T. Geach in *Logic Matters* (Berkeley and Los Angeles: The University of California Press, 1972), pp. 238–49; and *Reference and Generality* (Ithaca: Cornell University Press, 1962), pp. 149ff. The suggestion is criticised in detail by David Wiggins, in *Identity and Spatio-Temporal Continuity* (Oxford: Basil Blackwell, 1967), pp. 1–26. Compare W. V. Quine in a review of *Reference and Generality* in *Philosophical Review*, LXXIII (1964), 100–4, and Fred Feldman, 'Geach and Relativised Identity', *Review of Metaphysics*, XXII (1968), 547–55.

16 Compare P. T. Geach: 'Even if the man Peter Geach is the same person as the man Julius Caesar, they are certainly different men; they were for example born at different times to a different pair of parents.' P. T. Geach, *God and the Soul* (London: Routledge & Kegan Paul, 1969), p. 6. John Locke says very similar things; see the Fraser edition of the *Essay Concerning Human Understanding*, pp. 445, 450ff.

17 *A Treatise of Human Nature*, Book I, Part IV, Section VI; L. A. Selby-Bigge edition, p. 255.

18 Thomas Reid, *Essays on the Intellectual Powers of Man*, Essay III, Chapter IV. In *The Works of Thomas Reid, D.D.*, ed. Sir William Hamilton (Edinburgh: Maclachlan & Stewart, 1854), p. 346.

19 This thesis is discussed and defended in Appendix B ('Mereological Essentialism').

20 See *A Treatise of Human Nature*, Book I, Part iv, Section 6 (Selby-Bigge edition, p. 255): 'all objects, to which we ascribe identity, without observing their invariableness and uninterruptedness, are such as consist of a succession of related objects'. In this same section, Hume affirms a version of the principle of mereological essentialism.

21 We could define an *ens successivum* by saying, with St Augustine, that it is 'a single thing . . . composed of many, all of which exist not together'; see *Confessions*, Book IV, Chapter XI. St Thomas says in effect that a *successivum* is a thing such that some of its parts do not coexist with others of its parts ('una pars non est cum alia parte'); see the *Commentary on the Sentences*, Book I, Dist. VIII, Q. II, Art. I, ad 4. The term '*ens successivum*' has traditionally been applied to such things as periods of time (e.g. days, weeks, months) and events; compare Aristotle's *Physics*, Book III, Chapter VI, 206a.

22 Definition D.III.2 thus makes use of the general device by means of which Frege defined the ancestral relation; see G. Frege, *The Foundations of Arithmetic* (Oxford: Basil Blackwell, 1950), section 79. A more intuitive reading of clause (iii) might be: '(iii) x belongs at t to every class c which is such that (a) y belongs to c at t' and (b) all direct table successors of anything belonging to c belong to c'.

23 The distinction among these several types of property will be used in the following chapter to mark off those states of affairs that are *events*. (We had noted in the previous chapter that, although 'John is walking' refers to an event, 'John will walk' and 'John is such that either he is walking or he will walk' do not refer to events.)

24 Compare Hume: 'Tho' we commonly be able to distinguish pretty exactly betwixt numerical and specific identity, yet it sometimes happens that we confound them, and in our thinking and reasoning employ the one for the other.' *A Treatise of Human Nature*, Book I, Part IV, Section vi ('Of Personal Identity'), Selby-Bigge edition, pp. 257–8.

25 It may be noted that we have defined the loose and popular sense of the expression, 'There are n so-and-so's at t' and not the more general 'The number of so-and-so's that there ever will have been is n'. For the loose and popular sense of this latter expression is not sufficiently fixed to be explicated in any strict and philosophical sense. The following example may make this clear. In the infantry of the United States Army during World War II each private carried materials for half a tent – something like one piece of canvas, a pole and ropes. Two privates could then assemble their materials and create a tent which would be disassembled in the morning. On another night the two privates might find different tent companions. Occasionally when the company was in camp the various tent parts were collected, stored away, and then re-issued but with no attempt to assign particular parts to their former holders. Supposing, to simplify the matter considerably, that all the tents that there ever will have been were those that were created by the members of a certain infantry company, how, making use of our ordinary criteria, would we go about answering the question 'Just how many tents *have* there been?' Would an accounting of the history of the joinings of the various tent parts be sufficient to give us the answer?

26 And so if we say that men are mere *entia per alio* and that God is the only *ens per se*, it will follow that I am God and not a man. Compare Bayle's refutation of Spinoza's doctrine according to which men are modifications of God: '. . . when we say that a man denies, affirms, gets angry, caresses, praises, and the like, we ascribe all these attributes to the substance of his soul itself, and not to his thoughts as they are either accidents or modifications. If it were true then, as Spinoza claims, that men are modalities of God, one would speak falsely when one said, "Peter denies this, he wants that, he affirms such and such, a

thing"; for actually, according to this theory, it is God who denies, wants, affirm; and consequently all the denominations that result from the thoughts of all men are properly and physically to be ascribed to God. From which it follows that God hates and loves, denies and affirms the same things at the same time . . .'. From note N of the article 'Spinoza'; the passage may be found in R. H. Popkin, ed., Pierre Bayle, *Historical and Critical Dictionary: Selections* (Indianapolis: Bobbs-Merrill, 1965) 309–10.

27 *Critique of Pure Reason*, Kemp Smith edition, p. 342. The passage is from page 363 of the first edition of the *Kritik*.

28 Page 342 of the Kemp Smith edition; pp. 363–4 of the first edition.

29 *Essay Concerning Human Understanding*, Book II, Chapter xxiii ('Our Complex Ideas of Substance'); A. C. Fraser edition, p. 451.

30 *Op. cit.*, Fraser edition, p. 454.

31 *Op. cit.*, Fraser edition, p. 458.

32 The defence of this observation may be found in Section 4 of Chapter I.

33 Kant at least was clear about this point. When he states that the 'consciousness' of one substance may be transferred to another, as the motion of one ball may be transferred to another, and notes that the last of a series of such substances might be conscious of all the states of the previous substances, he adds that 'it would not have been one and the same person in all these states'; *Critique of Pure Reason*, Kemp Smith edition, p. 342 (first edition of *Kritik*, p. 364).

34 Compare Bernard Williams, *Problems of the Self* (Cambridge: The University Press, 1973), pp. 2ff.

35 ' "If the power to remember dies with the material body, has the question of any single person's future life after death any particular interest for him?" As you put the question, it is not whether the matter ought rationally to have an interest but whether as a fact it has; and perhaps this is the proper question, trusting as it seems to do, rather to instinct than to reason. Now if we had a drug which would abolish memory for a while, and you were going to be cut for the stone, suppose the surgeon were to say, "You will suffer damnably, but I will administer this drug so that you will during that suffering lose all memory of your previous life. Now you have, of course, no particular interest in your suffering as long as you will not remember your present and past life, you know, have you?" ' *Collected Papers*, Vol. V (Cambridge, Mass.: Harvard University Press, 1935), p. 355.

36 See Locke's *Essay*, Book II, Chapter xxvii, Section i: 'One thing cannot have two beginnings of existence.' Compare Thomas Reid, *Essays on the Intellectual Powers of Man*, Essay III, Chapter 4.

37 Some philosophers who have considered this type of situation have not presupposed, as I have, that persons are *entia per se*. Thus Derek Parfit has suggested it is a mistake to believe that in such cases the question 'Will I be he?' has a true answer. He writes: 'If we give up this belief, as I think we should, these problems disappear. We shall then regard the case as like many others in which, for quite unpuzzling reasons, there *is* no answer to a question about identity. (Consider "Was England the same nation after 1066?")' Derek Parfit, 'Personal Identity', *Philosophical Review*, LXXX (1971), 3–27; the quotation is on page 8. P. F. Strawson has expressed a similar scepticism: 'Perhaps I should say, not that I do not understand Professor Chisholm's notion of strict personal identity, but rather that I understand it well enough to think there can be no such thing.' P. F. Strawson, 'Chisholm on

Identity through Time', in H. E. Kiefer and M. K. Munitz, eds, *Language, Belief, and Metaphysics* (Albany: State University of New York Press, 1970), pp. 183–6; the quotation is on page 186. I think that the conception of persons set forth in Strawson's *Individuals* coheres more readily with the view that persons are *entia per se* than with the view that they are ontological parasites or *entia per alio*.

38 Compare Godfrey Vesey, *Personal Identity* (London: Macmillan, 1974), pp. 8*ff*., 80*ff*.; Bernard Williams, *Problems of the Self* (Cambridge: The University Press, 1973), pp. 8*ff*., 15*ff*; and Anthony Quinton, 'The Soul', *Journal of Philosophy*, LIX (1962), 393–409, and *The Nature of Things* (London and Boston: Routledge & Kegan Paul, 1973); and Richard Taylor, *With Heart and Mind* (New York: St Martin's Press, 1973), pp. 122–33.

39 I have attempted to throw light upon these distinctions in Chapter IV ('The Problem of the Criterion') of *Theory of Knowledge* (Englewood Cliffs, N.J.: Prentice-Hall, 1966). Compare the discussion of criteria of self-identity in Sydney Shoemaker, *Self-Knowledge and Self-Identity* (Ithaca: Cornell University Press, 1963), pp. 35–8, 211–12, 255–60.

40 G. W. Leibniz, *Discourse on Metaphysics*, Section XXXIV (Open Court edition, p. 58). Sydney Shoemaker cited this passage in criticising an earlier formulation of my views. This earlier formulation, Shoemaker's criticism, and my rejoinder may be found in Norman S. Care and Robert H. Grimm, eds, *Perception and Personal Identity* (Cleveland: Case Western Reserve Press, 1969), pp. 82–139.

41 Pierre Bayle, article 'Lucretius', Note Q, *A General Dictionary, Historical and Critical*, trans. Rev. J. P. Bernard, Rev. Thomas Birch, John Lockeman *et al.* (10 volumes: London, James Bettenham, 1734–41.)

NOTES TO CHAPTER IV

1 From the 'Dialogus de Connexione inter Res et Verba, et Veritatis Realitate', in G. W. Leibniz, *Opera Philosophica*, Vol. I, ed. J. E. Erdmann (Berolini: Sumtibus G. Eichleri, 1840), p. 76. I am indebted to Martha Browne for the translation of this passage.

2 These points will be put more precisely in the following section.

3 It has been suggested that the objects of propositional attitudes are sentence-tokens or inscriptions. 'Jones fears that there will be a war', according to this account, tells us that Jones bears the relation of *fearing-true* to some inscription or sentence-token of 'There will be a war'. It is difficult to know what to say about this view. We might compare it with an inscriptional view of causation. Suppose we were told, for example, that 'His walking regularly contributed causally to his feeling well' affirmed a relation between two sentence-tokens or inscriptions; an instance of 'his walking regularly' bears the relation of *causing-true* to an instance of 'his feeling well'. What could we say about *that* view? The first of these two views has been suggested by W. V. Quine and worked out in detail by Israel Scheffler. Compare W. V. Quine, *Word and Object* (New York: John Wiley, 1960), Chapter VI, and Israel Scheffler, *The Anatomy of Inquiry* (New York: Alfred A. Knopf, 1963). The second view, so far as I know, has not been advocated.

4   Gottlob Frege, *Philosophical Writings,* eds. Peter Geach and Max Black
    (Oxford: Basil Blackwell, 1952), p. 120. The quotation appears in
    Frege's article 'Negation'; compare his 'The Thought: A Logical
    Inquiry', in E. D. Klemke, ed., *Essays on Frege* (Urbana, Ill.: Univer-
    sity of Illinois Press, 1968), pp. 507–35. Compare W. E. Johnson's
    definition of a proposition as that which is capable of being asserted:
    Logic, Part I (Cambridge: The University Press, 1921), pp. 3–4. Com-
    pare also Marty's conception of states of affairs as constituting the
    possible content of judgement: Anton Marty, *Untersuchungen zur
    Grundlegung der allgemeinen Grammatik und Sprachphilosophie* (Halle:
    Max Niemeyer, 1908), pp. 288–362.
5   Bernard Bolzano, *Theory of Science,* ed. and trans. by Rolf George
    (Oxford: Basil Blackwell, 1972), p. 26. Bolzano adds that, although
    thinkability is a property of any proposition, 'it does not form part of
    the concept of a proposition. We can think the concept of a proposition
    in itself without reminding ourselves that it has the property of being
    thinkable. This makes it sufficiently clear that the indication of this
    property does not belong in the definition of this concept' (pp. 26–7).
    Bolzano's theory of definition is thus different from that presupposed
    in the present work. Bolzano also held that 'no proposition is real or
    exists' (p. 172; compare pp. 38–9). Evidently Bolzano accepted a
    version of what Meinong was to call the doctrine of *Aussersein*: that
    things may have a *Sosein* without having any *Sein* or, in other words,
    that things that do not exist or have any kind of being may yet have
    certain properties and stand in certain relations.
6   A. N. Whitehead, *Science and the Modern World* (New York: Mac-
    millan, 1937), p. 228; E. Husserl, *Logical Investigations,* Vol. I (London:
    Routledge & Kegan Paul, 1970), p. 285.
7   Hence we must be on guard against a certain ambiguity in the use of
    such terms as 'contingent' and 'noncontingent'. If we use 'contingent'
    to mean 'such that it is neither necessary nor impossible that it *exists*',
    then all states of affairs could be said to be noncontingent. But if we
    use 'contingent' to mean the same as 'such that it is neither necessary
    nor impossible that it *obtains*', then some states of affairs may be said
    to be contingent and others not.
8   For any state of affairs *q*, there are indefinitely many states of affairs *p*
    such that *p* contradicts *q*. Thus *Socrates being mortal* is contradicted,
    not only by *Socrates not being mortal*, but also by *Socrates not being
    mortal or two and two being five*. We could say that *a negation* of a
    state of affairs *p* is any state of affairs *q* of the following sort: *q* contra-
    dicts *p*, and for every *r*, if *r* contradicts *p*, then *r* is necessarily such
    that, if it is true, then *q* is true.
9   Perhaps the most thorough-going attempt to construct an adequate
    philosophy without commitment to such entities as events or states of
    affairs is that of Franz Brentano. See his *Psychology from an Empirical
    Standpoint* (London: Routledge & Kegan Paul, 1973); *The True and
    the Evident* (London: Routledge & Kegan Paul, 1966); *Kategorienlehre*
    (Hamburg: Felix Meiner, 1968); and R. M. Chisholm, 'Brentano's Non-
    propositional Theory of Judgment', *Midwest studies in Philosophy,* I
    (1976), 91–5. Compare also P. F. Strawson's 'Truth', *Proceedings
    of the Aristotelian Society,* XXIV (1950) and my criticism of this paper
    in 'J. L. Austin's Philosophical Papers', *Mind,* LXXIII (1964). And
    compare Tadeuz Kotarbinski, *Gnosiology: The Scientific Approach to the
    Theory of Knowledge* (Oxford: Pergamon Press, 1966), pp. 51*ff.*

10 See Jaegwon Kim, 'On the Psycho-Physical Identity Theory', *American Philosophical Quarterly*, III (1966), 227–34; 'Events and their Descriptions', in N. Rescher, ed., *Essays in Honor of C. G. Hempel* (Dordrecht: D. Reidel, 1971), pp. 198–215; 'Causation, Nomic Subsumption, and the Concept of an Event', *Journal of Philosophy*, LXX (1973), 217–36.

11 Kim suggests that the expression 'x is constituted by . . .' may be explicated in terms of set theory; e.g. 'x is an ordered triple having as its members . . .' It may be noted that, although this view restricts events to those that occur, it could easily be extended to allow for there being events that do not occur. Thus 'occur' could replace 'exist' in the above definition of the existence of an event. An event that *does not occur* would then be one such that its constitutive thing does not have the constitutive property at the constitutive time.

12 Compare in Donald Davidson: 'The Logical Form of Action Sentences', in N. Rescher, ed., *The Logic of Decision and Action* (Pittsburgh: The University of Pittsburgh Press, 1967), pp. 81–95; 'Agency', in R. Brinkley, R. Bronaugh and A. Marras, eds, *Agent, Action, and Reason* (Toronto: University of Toronto Press, 1971), pp. 3–25; 'Events as Particulars', *Nous*, IV (1970), 25–32; and 'The Individuation of Events', in N. Rescher, ed., *Essays in Honor of C. G. Hempel* (Dordrecht: D. Reidel, 1971), pp. 216–232.

13 C. I. Lewis, *An Analysis of Knowledge and Valuation* (La Salle, Ill.: The Open Court Publishing Co., 1946), Chapter III. Lewis there develops the view that states of affairs may be said to be *exemplified* in the actual world in the way in which properties are exemplified in the things that have them. I believe that the theory of concretisation to be set forth below is considerably simpler than Lewis's theory.

14 Compare G. H. von Wright, *Norm and Action* (London: Routledge & Kegan Paul, 1963), pp. 22–7.

15 Compare G. E. M. Anscombe, *Intention* (Oxford: Basil Blackwell, 1957): 'For moving his arm up and down with his fingers round the pump handle *is*, in these circumstances, operating the pump; and, in these circumstances, it *is* replenishing the house water-supply, and, in these circumstances it *is* poisoning the household. So there is one action with four descriptions . . .' (p. 46) 'We must always remember that an object is not what what is aimed at *is*; the description *under which* it is aimed at is that under which it is *called* the object." (p. 66) Compare also George Pitcher, ' "In Intending" and its Side Effects', *Journal of Philosophy*, LXVII (1970), 659–68: '. . . the (allegedly) two states of affairs – driving off in the car parked on the corner and driving off in the car that belongs to another man – are surely only one. There are two descriptions, but they are descriptions of the same state of affairs.' (p. 665)

16 See Richard Montague, 'On the Nature of Certain Philosophical Entities', *The Monist*, 53 (1969), 159–93.

17 A similar conception of events is suggested by the following passage in Carnap's 'Replies and Systematic Expositions': 'I believe that the informal thinking of the great majority of philosophers and scientists proceeds in terms of intensions, e.g., properties and propositions. It is true that the scientists usually do not use the term 'proposition' in this sense, but when they speak of possible cases, events, experimental results, distributions of the electric field or the like, they thereby mean what we call proposition.' See P. A. Schilpp, ed., *The Philosophy of*

Rudolf Carnap, Vol. 11 of the Library of Living Philosophers (La Salle, Ill.: The Open Court Publishing Co., 1963), p. 895. Compare Carnap's discussion of propositions in *Introduction to Semantics* (Cambridge: Harvard University Press, 1942, pp. 235–6, and *Meaning and Necessity* (Chicago: The University of Chicago Press, 1947), pp. 27–32. A variant of the view to be defended here is also suggested by Wilfred Sellars; see in particular Chapter X of *Essays in Philosophy and Its History* (Dordrecht: D. Reidel, 1974).

18 Compare the references to Carnap and Sellars above; also G. E. Moore, *Some Main Problems of Philosophy* (London: George Allen & Unwin, 1953), pp. 57–71, 258–60; and C. A. Baylis, 'Facts, Propositions, Exemplification, and Truth', *Mind*, LVII (1948), 459–79. C. I. Lewis, however, used the term 'proposition' to refer to linguistic expressions signifying states of affairs; compare *An Analysis of Knowledge and Valuation*, pp. 48–9. Compare Richard Cartwright, 'Propositions', in R. J. Butler, ed., *Analytical Philosophy*, First Series (Oxford: Basil Blackwell, 1962), pp. 81–103. It should be noted that although the word 'proposition' appears in the title of this important paper it does not appear in the paper itself.

19 Meinong saw this type of objection and felt it was not conclusive. He had noted that, where we may say 'The existence of the leaning tower in Pisa is actual' (or, at any rate, where a German-speaking person may say *'Die Existenz des schiefen Turmes in Pisa ist tatsächlich'*), we may not say 'The existence of the leaning tower in Pisa is true', this despite the fact that we may say both 'It is a fact that there is a leaning tower in Pisa' and 'It is true that there is a leaning tower in Pisa'. (In English 'There being a leaning tower in Pisa is true' would seem to be as natural, or as unnatural, as 'There being a leaning tower in Pisa is a fact'.) For Meinong's attempt to account for these differences in usage, see: *Über Annahmen*, second edition (Leipzig: Johann Ambrosius Barth, 1910), pp. 56, 95, 101; *Über Möglichkeit und Wahrscheinlichkeit* (Leipzig: Johann Ambrosius Barth, 1915), pp. 39–40; and *Über emotionale Präsentation* (Vienna: Alfred Holder, 1917), pp. 48–9. The latter two works have been published in *Alexius Meinong Gesamtausgabe*, Vol. III (Abhandlungen zur Werttheorie), ed. Rudolf Kindinger (Graz: Akademische Druck-u. Verlagsanstalt, 1968), and Vol. VI (1972). Compare also James Heanue, 'The Replacement of Dependent Clauses by Infinitive Expressions', in Rudolf Haller, ed., *Jenseits von Sein und Nichtsein* (Graz: Akademische Druck-u. Verlagsanstalt, 1972), pp. 179–86.

20 This puzzle is taken from Jaegwon Kim, 'Events and Their Descriptions' in N. Rescher *et al.*, eds, *Essays in Honour of Carl G. Hempel* (Dordrecht: D. Reidel, 1971), pp. 198–215; see page 210. Kim takes such puzzles to indicate that logically equivalent sentences may refer to different events.

21 It may be noted that the term 'set' or 'class' is not included in the minimum philosophical vocabulary that was set forth in the introduction to this book. As noted above, I assume that sets (or classes) may be reduced to properties (or attributes) in the way Russell has proposed. See A. N. Whitehead and Bertrand Russell, *Principia Mathematica*, Vol. I (Cambridge: The University Press, 1925), pp. 71*ff.* and 184*ff.* The definition of 'class' there used was first proposed by Russell in 'Mathematical Logic as Based on the Theory of Types', *American Journal of Mathematics*, XXX (1908), 222–62; see p. 249.

22 What we have said about properties may also be said about relations. Let c be the set consisting just of Brutus and Caesar; let s be the set of all those properties which are such that they are entailed by *Brutus killing Caesar* and only contingent things have them; and let R be the set of all those relations which are such that they are entailed by *Brutus killing Caesar* and only contingent things stand in them; if each of the members of s is had by members of c, then each of the members of R is such that it relates members of c to each other or to themselves. We may be confident of this since, for every relation (e.g. that expressed by '*x* kills *y*'), there are properties which are had if and only if things stand in that relation (e.g. being a killer and being killed).

23 Strictly speaking the second clause of the *definiens* ('there is no proper subset s . . .') is not needed to characterise concretisation; it is introduced here in order to simplify the account of *recurrence* to be given in Section 7 below. I am indebted to Ernest Sosa and to Fred Feldman who pointed out errors in earlier versions of this definition.

24 One may object: 'Suppose Jim Ryun runs a mile race by running four laps around a quarter-mile track and doesn't stop between any two laps. Your definition does not allow you to say that Ryun's running a lap recurs, for there is no gap in time between laps.' I suggest that, if Ryun's running a lap may be said to recur in this situation, then it is better described by the expression 'Ryun's completing his running a lap.' Describing the event this way, we see that it can be said to recur at four different points of time. The objection is taken from Major L. Johnson, Jr, 'Events as Recurrables', in Keith Lehrer, ed., *Analysis and Metaphysics* (Dordrecht: D. Reidel, 1975), pp. 209–26; this paper is an important contribution to the theory of recurrence.

25 This objection was first put to me by Fred Feldman. The present form of it is due to Edward Wierenga.

26 St Thomas Aquinas, *Commentary on Aristotle's Physics* (New Haven: Yale University Press, 1963), number 702 (p. 320). St Thomas is here commenting on Aristotle's query whether one and the same walking and one and the same cure can take place more than once. Concerning the cure, Aristotle said: 'But if Socrates once again passes through the same specific modification that he has passed through before, then, if we consider it possible for that which has perished to come into existence again and be individually and numerically one and the same, we may say that Socrates is making "one and the same" recovery, for instance; but if we do not admit the above-named possibility, we shall say that *h* is making "the same" recovery but not "one and the same".' *Physics*, Book V, Chapter IV, 228a.

27 St Augustine was troubled by one version of this puzzle (concerning the time of the coming into being of periods of time). See *Confessions*, Book XI, Chapter XV.

28 Compare Jaegwon Kim, 'Causation, Nomic Subsumption, and the Concept of Event', *Journal of Philosophy*, LXX (1973), 217–36.

29 What we have said about explanation and causation *de re* may throw light upon these remarks of G. E. M. Anscombe: '. . . I find it harmless to say that causal statements are intensional. But our considerations lead to raising the following question: What is at stake in maintaining or denying that an effect is properly described or presented in a *proposition*? I feel that something is at stake – but I don't know what it is. Whatever it is, in this issue one side is probably correctly represented by the insistence on the proposition; but I suspect – my

hunch is – that the other side is the right one, but is *not* correctly represented by objecting to the presentation in a proposition.' G. E. M. Anscombe, 'Causality and Extensionality', *Journal of Philosophy*, LXVI (1969), 152–9; the quotation is on pages 158–9. An excellent statement of the general problem of causation and extensionality may be found in Dagfinn Follesdal, 'Quantification into Causal Contexts', *Boston Studies in the Philosophy of Science*, Vol. II, ed. R. S. Cohen and M. W. Wartofsky (New York: Humanities Press, 1965), pp. 263–74.

30 See Appendix C ('The Objects of Belief and Endeavour').

31 It may be noted that 'perceptual acceptance' is a basic concept in H. H. Price's theory of perception. Compare H. H. Price, *Perception* (New York: Robert M. McBride, 1933), Chapter VI. Compare the discussion of perception in Stephan Körner, *Experience and Theory* (London: Routledge and Kegan Paul, 1966), pp. 199–202.

32 We may note, by ways of confirmation, that the present conception of events and states of affairs enables us to deal very simply with the so-called 'identity theory'. Is that 'mental event', which is Jones thinking about a unicorn, identical with that 'physical event', which is Jones's nerve cells vibrating in —— manner? (Let us pretend we know how to fill the blank.) The term 'event', in the formulation of the theory, could be taken either to refer to states of affairs (i.e. to those states of affairs which may be called 'events' in virtue of definition D.IV.7 above) or to some type of concrete event. If it is taken to refer to states of affairs, then, of course, the theory would be obviously false. And if the foregoing discussion is adequate, then it may be doubted whether there *are* such things as concrete events.

33 I have discussed some aspects of this question in 'Coming into Being and Passing Away: Can the Metaphysician Help?' in S. F. Spicker and H. T. Englehardt, eds, *Philosophical Medical Ethics: Its Nature and Significance* (Dordrecht: D. Reidel, 1976).

NOTES TO APPENDIX A

1 The quotations are from Edward's *Doctrine of Original Sin Defended* (1758), Part IV, Chapter II. This work is reprinted in C. H. Faust and T. H. Johnson, eds, *Jonathan Edwards* (New York: American Book Co., 1935).

2 Rudolf Carnap, *Introduction to Symbolic Logic* (New York: Dover Publications, 1958), pp. 213*ff*.

3 J. H. Woodger, *The Axiomatic Method in Biology* (Cambridge: Cambridge University Press, 1937); see especially pp. 55–63, and Appendix E by Alfred Tarski (pp. 161–72).

4 A thing *a* is said to be the *sum* of a class F, provided only every member of the class F is a part of *a*, and every part of *a* has a part in common with some member of the class. If, as these authors postulate, every non-empty class has a sum, there would be, for example, an *individual thing* which is the sum of the class of dogs. Every dog would be a part of this collective dog and every part of this collective dog would share a part with some individual dog. The same would hold for the class the only members of which are this man and that horse. An opposing view is that of Boethius: a man and a horse are not one thing. See D. P. Henry, *The Logic of Saint Anselm* (Oxford: The Clarendon Press,

1967), p. 56. In the following Appendix ('Mereological Essentialism'), a mereology or theory of part and whole is developed which does not presuppose that there are such sums.

5   Edwards is impressed by what he takes to be the analogy between space and time. To persuade his reader that God could reasonably regard Adam's posterity as being one with Adam, he asserts that there would be no problem at all if Adam's posterity *coexisted* with Adam. If Adam's posterity had 'somehow *grown out of him*, and yet remained *contiguous* and literally *united to him*, as the branches to a tree, or the members of the body to the head; and had all, before the fall, existed together at the *same time*, though in *different places*, as the head and members are in different places', surely then, Edwards says, God could treat the whole collection as 'one moral whole' with each of us as its parts. And if a collection of persons existing in different places can be thought of as a single moral whole, why not also a collection of persons existing at different times?

6   The doctrine implies, of course, that there are an infinite number of temporal parts of me – that there will have been an infinite number today and an infinite number tomorrow, if I can be said in any sense to persist into tomorrow. Hence it is misleading to speak, as we do above, of 'today's temporal part of me' and 'tomorrow's temporal part of me'. What we have to say could be put more precisely by speaking of 'any given one of my temporal parts of today' and 'any given one of my temporal parts of tomorrow'.

7   Jonathan Edwards's own argument for the doctrine might be put this way. '(i) At every moment of time God preserves or upholds all individual things that exist in time. But (ii) such preservation or upholding is equivalent to creation *ex nihilo*. And therefore (iii), for any moment at which an individual thing may exist, the thing is made up at that moment of things that exist only at that moment.'

8   C. S. Peirce, *Collected Papers*, Vol. I (Cambridge, Mass.: Harvard University Press, 1931), 1.494. But compare 1.493.

9   Quine's published discussions of these questions begin with his *o Sentido da Nova Logica* (Sao Paulo: Livraria Martins Editora, 1944), pp. 135–8, and continue in the works cited below, as well as in *Word and Object* (New York: John Wiley, 1960), pp. 114–18, 171–3.

10 This assumption, of course, is not essential to the doctrine of temporal parts. But given what we said in the Introduction about persons and processes, the assumption would bear directly on the question whether the temporal parts of persons are themselves persons and therefore capable of such things as hoping for rain.

11 *Methods of Logic* (New York: Holt Dryden, 1959), p. 210.

12 *From a Logical Point of View* (New York: Harper & Row, 1963), p. 65.

13 This view is suggested by St Thomas: 'The Seine river is not "this particular river" because of "this flowing water," but because of "this source" and "this bed," and hence is always called the same river, although there may be other water flowing down it; likewise a people is the same, not because of sameness of soul or of man, but because of the same dwelling place, or rather because of the same laws and the same manner of living, as Aristotle says in III *Politica*.' From *De Spiritualibus Creaturis*, Article IX, ad 16; *On Spiritual Creatures*, trans. M. C. Fitzpatrick and J. J. Wellmuth (Milwaukee: Marquette University Press, 1949), p. 109.

14 This is the procedure that Quine follows, but instead of 'cofluvial' he uses 'river kinship'. He writes: 'We begin, let us imagine, with momentary things and their interrelations. One of these momentary things, called *a*, is a momentary stage of the river Cayster, in Lydia, around 400 B.C. Another, called *b*, is a momentary stage of the Cayster two days later. A third, *c*, is a momentary stage, at this same latter date, of the same multiplicity of water molecules which were in the river at the time of *a*. Half of *c* is in the lower Cayster valley, and the other half is to be found at diffuse points in the Aegean Sea. Thus, *a*, *b*, and *c* are three objects, variously related. We may say that *a* and *b* stand in the relation of river kinship, and that *a* and *c* stand in the relation of water kinship. Now the introduction of rivers as single entities, namely, processes or time-consuming objects, consists substantially in reading identity in place of river kinship.' (*From a Logical Point of View*, p. 66).

15 A subtle defence of the doctrine of temporal parts may be found in Richard Cartwright's 'Scattered Objects', in Keith Lehrer, ed., *Analysis and Metaphysics* (Dordrecht: D. Reidel, 1975), pp. 153–71. Cartwright's defence presuppose (1) that for any two material things there is a material thing of which each is a part and (2) it is possible for a whole to survive the loss of some of its part. These two presuppositions are rejected in Appendix B ('Mereological Essentialism') that immediately follows.

NOTES TO APPENDIX B

1 See D. P. Henry, *Medieval Logic and Metaphysics* (London: Hutchinson University Library, 1972), p. 120.

2 *New Essays Concerning Human Understanding*, Book II, Chapter xxvii, Section 11 (Open Court edition, p. 247). Compare Hume, *Treatise of Human Nature*, Book I, Part IV, Section 6.

3 *Philosophical Studies* (London: Kegan Paul, Trench & Trubner, 1922), pp. 287–8. Compare also J. M. E. McTaggart: 'For if a whole is a combination it is built up of parts which could exist without being combined in that way, while the combination could not exist without them.' *Some Dogmas of Religion* (London: Edward Arnold, 1906), p. 108.

4 If, by any unhappy chance, there are still philosophers who think that the 'therefore's' above *are* in order, I would commend to them, as essential reading, Chapters One and Two of Plantinga's *The Nature of Necessity* (Oxford: The Clarendon Press, 1974).

5 See Alvin Plantinga, 'On Mereological Essentialism', *Review of Metaphysics*, XXVII (1975), 468–76. His paper is a discussion of my 'Parts as Essential to Their Wholes', *Review of Metaphysics*, XXVI (1973), 581–603.

6 I assume that a corollary of principle c would be this: 'For every *x* and *y*, if *x* is possibly part of *y*, then *x* is part of *y*.' There could hardly be ground for supposing that, although our world is one such that things have to have the parts they do have here, other worlds may be such that things *don't* have to have the parts they do have there. The corollary, then, would seem to tell us that my car couldn't have had any part other than precisely the parts it does have.

7 One could consider saying: 'The parts a thing had when it first came

into being were *then* essential to it'; or 'Every whole is such that it has some parts that are essential to it'. Variants of the latter thesis are discussed by Josiah R. W. Strandberg in *Some Metaphysical Questions about Parts and Wholes*; PhD thesis, Brown University, 1975.

8 *The Organisation of Thought* (London: Williams & Norgate, 1917), pp. 158*ff*. Whitehead adds another axiom, to the effect that, if *x* is part of *y*, then there is a *z* such that *z* is part of *x*. Whitehead applies his theory of part and whole to *events*. Although Whitehead has no axiom corresponding to (A3), our principle of mereological essentialism, I believe it is accurate to say that he conceives of events in such a way that they may be said to have their parts necessarily.

9 This point was brought to my attention by Neil Gupta.

10 But this use of '*x* is an appendage of *y*' would be contrary to the ordinary use; for ordinarily one does not call one thing an 'appendage' of another unless the latter thing is larger or in some respect more interesting or more important than the former.

11 We should recall in this connection (1) the view of Lucretius, according to which there is joining and separating (assembly and disassembly) but no coming into being and passing away and (2) the view of some contemporary philosophers and logicians, according to which, for any two discrete things, *x* and *y*, there is a third thing which is made up of *x* and *y*. According to this latter view, nothing could lose a part unless the part itself ceased to be, and the part itself couldn't cease to be unless a part of it disappeared, *in nihilum*, without remainder. The second view is implied by the doctrine of Lesniewski, according to which, for every non-empty class *a* of individuals, there exists exactly one individual *x* such that *x* is the *sum* of all the members of *a* – i.e. an individual *x* such that every member of *a* is a part of *x* and every part of *x* has a part in common with some member of *a*. See Alfred Tarski, *Logic, Semantics, Metamathematics* (Oxford: The Clarendon Press, 1956), pp. 24–9; compare the theories in Henry S. Leonard and Nelson Goodman: 'The Calculus of Individuals and Its Uses', *Journal of Symbolic Logic*, v (1940), pp. 45–55; and Nelson Goodman, *The Structure of Appearance*, second edition (Indianapolis: Bobbs-Merrill, 1966). If this view of sums were true, there would be an individual thing composed of my left foot and the carburettor of my neighbour's car. Axiom (A4), proposed above, provides for the possibility of their being non-empty classes of individuals that have no sums.

12 *Generation and Corruption*, 321a. St Thomas, in his exposition of Aristotle, puts the problem more explicitly: 'He says therefore first that, since a thing grows by the addition of something, the question still remains as to what it is that is increased: whether only that to which something is added, but not what is added, or whether both are increased.' *Exposition of Aristotle's Treatise on Generation and Corruption*, Book I, trans. R. F. Larcher and Pierre Conway (Columbus Springs, Ohio.: College of St Mary of the Springs, 1964), Paragraph 102.

13 D. P. Henry, *Medieval Logic and Metaphysics* (London: Hutchinson University Library, 1972), p. 120.

NOTES TO APPENDIX C

1 My thought on these questions has been influenced by discussions with Michael Corrado, Fred Feldman, Richard Feldman, Edmund L. Gettier,

Herbert Heidelberger, Michael Hooker, Gareth Matthews, Mark Pastin, Ernest Sosa and Robert Swartz.

2 This is the conception of *de dicto* belief that is presupposed in the writings of Bolzano, Frege, Husserl, Johnson and others referred to in Section 2 of Chapter IV. For its relevance to contemporary problems about reference and translation, compare Stephen Leeds, 'How to Think about Reference', *Journal of Philosophy*, LXX (1973), pp. 485–503.

3 Compare the discussions of this question in W. V. Quine, 'Quantifiers and Propositional Attitudes', *Journal of Philosophy*, LIII (1956), 177–87; W. V. Quine, *Word and Object* (Cambridge, Mass.: The Massachusetts Institute of Technology, 1960), Chapter IV; and Robert Sleigh, Quantifying into Epistemic Contexts', *Nous*, I (1967), 23–31.

4 For a defence of this latitudinarian account of *de re* belief, compare: Ernest Sosa, 'Propositional Attitudes De Dicto and De Re', *Journal of Philosophy*, LXVII (1970), 883–96, and 'Rejoinder to Hintikka', *Journal of Philosophy*, LXVIII (1971), 498–501; and Mark Pastin, 'About De Re Belief', *Philosophy and Phenomenological Research*, XXXIV (1974), 569–75. Hintikka holds that a man s can have a belief, with respect to a certain thing *x*, only if s knows, with respect to *x*, that *x* is identical with *x*; but he does not attempt to reduce the latter locution to a *de dicto* locution. Compare: J. Hintikka, *Knowledge and Belief* (Ithaca, N.Y.: Cornell University Press, 1962), Chapter 6, and 'On Attributions of "Self Knowledge" ', *Journal of Philosophy*, LXVII (1970), 73–87; and Dagfinn Follesdal, 'Knowledge, Identity, and Existence', *Theoria*, 33 (1967), 1–27.

5 Wilfrid Sellars makes essential use of the concept of an individual concept in analysing belief; see 'Some Problems about Belief', in D. Davidson and J. Hintikka, eds, *Words and Objections: Essays on the Work of W. V. Quine* (Dordrecht: D. Reidel, 1969), pp. 186–205. But Sellars's account is quite different from that proposed here. Following Frege, he assumes that singular terms within intentional contexts refer to their senses rather than to their ordinary designata; thus 'Jones believes that the tallest man is wise' refers to a relation between Jones and the concept expressed by 'the tallest man' (i.e. to the property of being the tallest man). But to *what* relation between Jones and the individual concept? Sellars concedes it is not that of believing the individual concept to be wise. Evidently the best that can be done is to say that it is a relation very much *like* that of believing the individual concept to be wise. Thus Alonzo Church, defending an analogous account of 'Schliemann sought the site of Troy', said: 'The relation holding between Schliemann and the concept of the site of Troy is not quite that of having sought, or at least it is misleading to call it that – in view of the way in which the verb *to seek* is commonly used in English.' *Introduction to Mathematical Logic*, Vol. I (Princeton: Princeton University Press, 1956), 8n.

6 Compare Quine's discussion of Ortcut and the man seen at the beach in 'Quantifiers and Propositional Attitudes', referred to above.

7 This point is discussed in detail in Appendix D.

8 The definition of '*h* is known by s' that will be proposed in Appendix D would not allow us to say that the correspondent knew that the President is a Republican. I believe that the analyses of knowledge to be found in the following writings would have a similar result: Ernest Sosa, 'The Analysis of "Knowledge that P" ', *Analysis*, XXV (1964), 1–8; Keith Lehrer and Thomas Paxon, 'Knowledge: Undefeated Justified

True Belief', *Journal of Philosophy*, LXVI (1969), 225–37; Gilbert Harman, 'Knowledge, Inference, and Explanation', *American Philosophical Quarterly*, V (1968), 164–73; Peter D. Klein, 'A Proposed Definition of Propositional Knowledge', *Journal of Philosophy*, LVIII (1971), 471–82; R. Hilpinen, 'Knowledge and Justification', *Ajatus*, XXXIII (1971), 8–39; Marshal Swain, 'Knowledge, Causality, and Justification', *Journal of Philosophy*, LXIX (1972), 291–300; Bredo C. Johnsen, 'Knowledge', *Philosophical Studies*, XXV (1974), 273–382; Keith Lehrer, *Knowledge* (Oxford: The Clarendon Press, 1974), and Ernest Sosa, 'How Do You Know?', *American Philosophical Quarterly*, XI (1974), 113–22.

9 An alternative to this account of *de re* belief is suggested by David Kaplan, in his important paper 'Quantifying In', in *Words and Objections: Essays on the Work of W. V. Quine*, eds. D. Davidson and J. Hintikka (Dordrecht: D. Reidel, 1969), pp. 206–42. I believe it is accurate to say that an exact formulation of this alternative would require a minimum philosophical vocabulary that is considerably more extensive than the one we have permitted ourselves here.

10 See Aristotle's *De Sophisticis Elenchis*, 179b 3

11 Compare Petrus Hispanus, *Summulae Logicales*, ed. I. M. Bochenski (Turin, 1947), 7.41; Franz Brentano, *Kategorienlehre* (Leipzig, 1933), p. 165. Brentano cites this version of the problem: 'Do you know who the person with the mask is?' 'No.' 'Then you don't know who your father is, for the person with the mask is your father.' An ancient version of this puzzle was called 'the Veiled' or 'the Elektra' by Lucian in 'Sale of Lives'. An English translation may be found in Emily James Smith, *Selections from Lucian* (New York: Harper, 1892); see esp. pp. 75–6.

12 This concept was defined as follows, in D.I.5 *of* Chapter I:

G is an *individual essence* (or *haecceity*) =Df G is a property which is such that, for every *x*, *x* has G if and only if *x* is necessarily such that it has G, and it is impossible that there is a *y* other than *x* such that *y* has G.

13 A clear example of this mistake may be found in the first edition of my book, *Theory of Knowledge* (Englewood Cliffs, N.J.: Prentice-Hall, 1966). I there wrote: 'A belief is *true* provided, first, that it is a belief or assertion with respect to a certain state of affairs that that state of affairs exists, and provided, secondly, that that state of affairs exists.' (p. 103) Compare Frege: 'Judging, we may say, is acknowledging the truth of something [*ist etwas als wahr anerkennen*]; what is acknowledged to be true can only be a thought. The original kernel now seems to have cracked in two; one part of it lies in the word "thought" and the other in the word "true" '. The passage is from 'Negation', in Frege's *Philosophical Writings*, ed. Black and Geach, p. 126n. Compare, finally, what I have said about truth in Chapter IV, Section 4.

NOTES TO APPENDIX D

1 I have discussed the concept of requirement in detail in 'Practical Reason and the Logic of Requirement', in Stephan Körner, ed., *Practical Reason* (Oxford: Basil Blackwell, 1974), pp. 40–53. I there define the concepts of overriding, of *prima facie* duty, and of absolute duty in terms of the concept of requirement.

2   The six axioms above were used in 'A System of Epistemic Logic', by Roderick M. Chisholm and Robert Keim, *Ratio*, xv (1973), 99–115. The *Ratio* paper also contained a seventh axiom that could be put by saying 'withholding a proposition is the same thing as withholding its negation'. But given the general principle about negation referred to above, the seventh axiom is not needed. Axioms 5 and 6 were suggested by Keim. Versions of the first four axioms may be found in: *Theory of Knowledge*, p. 22n; Roderick M. Chisholm, 'The Principles of Epistemic Appraisal', in *Current Philosophical Issues: Essays in Honor of Curt John Ducasse*, ed. F. C. Dommeyer (Springfield. Ill.: 1966), pp. 87–104, and 'On a Principle of Epistemic Preferability', *Philosophy and Phenomenological Research*, xxx (1969); and Roderick M. Chisholm and Ernest Sosa, 'On the Logic of "Intrinsically Better"', *American Philosophical Quarterly*, iii (1966), 244–9.

3   The epistemic definitions here set forth will suggest others. Thus a proposition may be said to be *unacceptable* if and only if it is not acceptable; a proposition is *gratuitous* if and only if accepting it is not preferable to withholding it; and a proposition is *counterbalanced* if and only if there is no presumption in its favour and no presumption in favour of its negation.

4   If the reader wonders whether the set of definitions to be offered here is circular, he should note that, although the *de re* epistemic concepts are defined in terms of *de dicto* knowledge, the concept of *de dicto* knowledge is defined in terms of *de dicto* epistemic concepts.

5   G. W. Leibniz, *New Essays Concerning Human Understanding*, Book iv, Chapter 9. Compare Franz Brentano, *The True and the Evident* (London: Routledge & Kegan Paul, 1966), English edition ed. Roderick M. Chisholm, esp. pp. 123–32.

6   Two propositions may be said to be 'strictly equivalent' if each entails the other, in the sense of 'entails' defined in D.IV.2.

7   The definiens of D.D.11 could also be read as 'e is a basis of h being evident for s'. We could define, in an analogous way, 'e is a basis of h being beyond reasonable doubt for s', 'e is a basis of h having some presumption in its favour for s', and similarly for our other epistemic categories.

8   These points are spelled out in more detail in the second edition of my book, *Theory of Knowledge* (Englewood Cliffs, N.J.: Prentice-Hall, 1976).

9   The probability or confirmation relations that hold eternally among propositions could be explicated in the above manner. Thus 'e is a basis s has for saying s has some presumption in its favour' could be defined by replacing the last occurrence of 'evident', in the definiens of D.D.11, by 'such as to have some presumption in its favour'. Then 'e tends to make h such as to have some presumption in its favour' (or 'e confirms h') could be defined as: 'Necessarily, for every s, any basis s has for e is a basis s has for saying h has some presumption in its favour.' The conception of probability set forth in John Maynard Keynes, *A Treatise on Probability* (London: Macmillan, 1952) could readily be supplemented to the present account of our epistemic concepts.

10 Given the conception of propositions set forth in Chapter IV, Section 4, 'true' in the formulation of the second condition may be replaced by 'occurs' or 'obtains'.

11 *Analysis*, xxv (1963), 121–3. The paper is reprinted in Michael D. Roth and Leon Galis, eds, *Knowing: Essays in the Analysis of Knowledge* (New York: Random House, 1970). The latter work includes a number of attempts by other philosophers to deal with the problem posed by Gettier's paper. Compare the works referred to in footnote 8 of Appendix c, p. 223.

12 Further details on these points may be found in the second edition of *Theory of Knowledge*, referred to above.

INDEX